UNIVERSITY OF WINCHESTER

D0533557

European Muslims, Civility and Public Life

WITHDRAWN FROM
THE LIBRARY

UNIVERSITY OF
WINCHESTER

KA 0371978 2

ALSO AVAILABLE FROM CONTINUUM

Mirror For Our Times, Paul Weller
Muslim Youth, edited by Fauzia Ahmad and Mohammad Siddique Seddon
Time for a Change, Paul Weller
Young, British and Muslim, Philip Lewis

European Muslims, Civility and Public Life

Perspectives On and From
the Gülen Movement

*Edited by Paul Weller
and Ihsan Yilmaz*

continuum

UNIVERSITY OF WINCHESTER

03719782 | 305. 6
WEL

Continuum International Publishing Group

The Tower Building	80 Maiden Lane
11 York Road	Suite 704
London	New York
SE1 7NX	NY 10038

www.continuumbooks.com

© Paul Weller, Ihsan Yilmaz and Contributors 2012

All rights reserved. No part of this publication may be reproduced or transmitted in any form or by any means, electronic or mechanical, including photocopying, recording, or any information storage or retrieval system, without prior permission in writing from the publishers.

Paul Weller, Ihsan Yilmaz and Contributors have asserted their right under the Copyright, Designs and Patents Act, 1988, to be identified as authors of this work.

British Library Cataloguing-in-Publication Data
A catalogue record for this book is available from the British Library.

ISBN: HB: 978-1-4411-2048-9
PB: 978-1-4411-0207-2

Library of Congress Cataloging-in-Publication Data
European Muslims, civility and public life perspectives on and from the Gülen movement / edited by Paul Weller and Ihsan Yilmaz.
p. cm.
Includes bibliographical references and index.
ISBN 978-1-4411-2048-9 (hardcover) -- ISBN 978-1-4411-0207-2 (pbk.) 1. Muslims--Europe. 2. Gülen, Fethullah. 3. Muslims--Ethnic identity. 4. Islamic education--Europe. 5. Islam and politics--Turkey. I. Weller, Paul, 1956- II. Yilmaz, Ihsan. III. Title.
D1056.2.M87E975 2011
305.6'97094--dc23
2011028605

Typeset by Fakenham Prepress Solutions, Fakenham, Norfolk NR21 8NN
Printed and bound in India

This book is dedicated to Margaret Preisler-Weller, wife of Paul Weller and mother of David, Lisa and Katrina who, in July 2010 after a terminal illness of almost a year, died in Christian faith, hope and love but also at whose hospital bed and funeral service Muslim friends offered Islamic recitations, prayers and reflections.

CONTENTS

Part II: Civility, co-existence and integration

Part III: European contexts

EDITOR AND CONTRIBUTOR BIOGRAPHIES

Editor biographies

Paul Weller is Professor of Inter-Religious Relations at the University of Derby, United Kingdom, and Head of Research and Commercial Development in its Faculty of Education, Health and Sciences; Visiting Fellow in the Oxford Centre for Christianity and Culture at Regent's Park College, University of Oxford; and a Trustee of the Multi-Faith Centre at the University of Derby. He holds a Master of Arts in Theology from the University of Oxford; a Master of Philosophy in Social and Pastoral Theology from the University of Manchester; a Doctor of Philosophy in Religious Studies from the University of Leeds; and a Doctor of Letters from the University of Derby. He is author of (2005a) *Time for a Change: Reconfiguring Religion, State and Society*, London: T & T Clark; (2008) *Religious Diversity in the UK: Contours and Issues*, London: Continuum; (2009) *A Mirror for our Times: 'The Rushdie Affair' and the Future of Multiculturalism*, London: Continuum; and (2006c) of 'Fethullah Gülen, Religions, Globalisation and Dialogue', in R. Hunt and Y. Aslandoğan (eds), *Muslim Citizens of the Globalized World: Contributions of the Gülen Movement*, The Light Inc. and IID Press, Somerset, NJ, pp. 75–88.

He is a member of Advisory Council of the Dialogue Society in London and acts as an expert consultant to the development of the European Gold-Prize winning training programme on Religious Diversity and Anti-Discrimination within the Belieforama community of practice. Until its disbandment by the United Kingdom's present coalition government, he was a member of the Expert Panel on Faith, advising the Secretary of State for Communities, other Ministers and civil servants in the Department for Communities and Local Government. He is currently Principal Investigator of a research project (2010–12) on 'Religion and Belief, Discrimination and Equality in England and Wales: Theory, Policy and Practice' funded within the 'Religion and Society' programme that is sponsored by the UK Arts and Humanities and the Economic and Social Research Councils.

Ihsan Yilmaz is Associate Professor of Political Science at Fatih University, Istanbul, as well as the Director of the PhD Programme in Political Science and International Relations at the Institute of Social Sciences of Fatih University. He received his BA in Political Science and International Relations from the Bosporus University in 1994, and completed his PhD at the Faculty of Law and Social Sciences, SOAS, University of London in 1999. He then worked at the University of Oxford as a Fellow between 1999 and 2001, and taught Turkish government and politics, legal sociology, comparative law and Islamic law at SOAS, University of London between 2001 and 2008. He was also the Deputy Chair of the Centre for Ethnic Minority Studies at SOAS (2003–8) and the director of the London Centre for Social Studies (2003–8).

He is the author of *Muslim Laws, Politics and Society in Modern Nation States: Dynamic Legal Pluralisms in England, Turkey and Pakistan* (2005a), and co-editor (with John L. Esposito) of *Islam and Peacebuilding: Gülen Movement Initiatives* (2010). He is the editor-in-chief of both the *European Journal of Economic and Political Studies* (EJEPS) and the *Turkish Journal of Politics* (TJP). He has published his work in international scholarly journals including: *British Journal of Middle Eastern Studies*, *Middle East Journal*, *Journal of Ethnic and Migration Studies*, *Muslim World*, *International Journal of Turkish Studies*, *Journal for Islamic Studies*, *Journal of Muslim Minority Affairs*, *Journal of Caucasian and Central Asian Studies*, *Journal of Economic and Social Research*, *International Law and Politics Journal*, *European Journal of Economic and Political Studies*, *Turkish Journal of Politics* and *Insight Turkey*.

Dr Yilmaz is frequently interviewed by nationwide TV channels on Turkish politics and also Islamic movements; he is a regular participant of the Abant Platform and a regular columnist of *Today's Zaman* (an English language daily newspaper published in Turkey). His current research interests are Turkish government and politics; political parties; Islamism in Turkey-Central Asia-the Middle East; faith-based movements; society-law-politics-religion relations; and diaspora studies. Email: ihsanyilmaz@yahoo.com, iyilmaz@fatih.edu.tr

Other contributor biographies

Yusuf Alan completed his Bachelor and Master's programme in English translation and interpretation at the Hacettepe University in Ankara, Turkey. He is Knowledge Manager at Dialogue Academie in Rotterdam. His publications include: (2001) *Aktif Dusunme ve Yenilenme* (Active Thinking and Self-Renewal), Rotterdam: Libertas Media; (2003) *Sözün Gücü* (The Power of Discourse), Rotterdam: Libertas Media; (2003, together with Gürkan Çelik), *Hizmetkar Liderlik* (Servant-Leadership).

Y. Alp Aslandoğan PhD is an adjunct faculty member at Prairie View A & M University, USA. He is also editor of *The Fountain* magazine and Vice President of the Institute of Interfaith Dialog, in charge of academic programmes. Together with Robert Hunt he co-edited (2006) *Muslim Citizens of the Globalized World, Contributions of the Gülen Movement*, Light Inc and IID Press, NJ. In this he has a paper entitled 'Educational Philosophy of Gülen in Thought and in Practice'. His current publication projects include a book on spiritual time management, and an illustrated Qur'an commentary in English.

Gürkan Çelik completed his PhD at Tilburg University, the Netherlands, entitled (2010) *The Gülen Movement: Building Social Cohesion through Dialogue and Education*. He received his Bachelor and Master's degree in Policy and Organization Studies from the same university. He has written articles for learned journals, and is (co-)author of several publications, including (2010) *Fethullah Gülen & de Vrijwilligersbeweging* (The Volunteers Movement); (2007) 'Gülen's approach to dialogue and peace' in *The International Journal of Diversity in Organizations, Communities and Nations*; (2007) 'Fethullah Gülen as a servant leader' in *International Journal of Servant-Leadership*; and (2005) *Voorlopers in de Vrede* (Forerunners for Peace).

Bekir Cinar holds a PhD from the University of Hull, UK, entitled *Terrorism, Countering Terrorism, and the Security Services in Liberal Democratic Countries*. During his doctoral studies, he continued to undertake volunteer activities in many parts of the UK. He is expert in many issues including security and terrorism. He is a lecturer and teaches in Warsaw and Tirana on Politics, International Relations, Terrorism and Research Methods on social science.

Emre Demir is a PhD candidate in political sociology at the École des Hautes Études en Sciences Sociales (EHESS) in Paris, France. He wrote an MA thesis entitled *Les Identities Neo-Communautaires Dans la Communauté Turque en Allemagne et en France* (Neo-Communitarian Identities in the Turkish Community in Germany and France) at the Institut de Sciences Politiques (IEP) Strasbourg. He is interested in Turkish faith-based social movements, political Islam in Turkey, the organization of Turkish Islam in France and Germany, Islam in Europe and religious minorities in France.

Shanthikumar Hettiarachchi (PhD on majority–minority ethnic and religious conflict from Melbourne College of Divinity, University of Melbourne, Australia) is Senior Trainer, Lecturer and Consultant in the Bureau of the Commissioner General for Rehabilitation (BCGR), Sri Lanka. He currently works on the rehabilitation and de-radicalization processes initiated for the reintegration of ex-combatant population in the post-war situation in

Sri Lanka. He is the founder Co-ordinator of the Luton Council of Faiths (LCOF) Bedfordshire, and was instrumental in developing inter-faith infrastructure and promoting inter-community relations and cohesion both in Luton and Leicester in the UK (1997–2010). His primary research interests are in diaspora communities and their religious affiliations specifically in the UK, Europe and Australia; their social adjustment processes; radicalization of religious faith; and land, history and notions of chosen-ness as political tools to define identity. He has published widely on related topics.

Asaf Hussain is an academic from the University of Leicester. He teaches modules on Islamic civilization. He has been writing and publishing books on Islamic fundamentalism since the early 1980s, and in the course of his research visited many fundamentalist groups in the Middle East and South Asia. Currently he is engaged in writing three studies: 'Islamic civilization', 'Islamic fundamentalism in Britain' and 'Islamic fundamentalism in Pakistan'.

Wanda Krause is Assistant Professor and co-ordinator of the Gulf Studies Programme, Qatar University, United Arab Emirates. She holds a doctorate from the University of Exeter, UK, on Middle East Politics. Her interests include Gulf politics, civil society development, Islamism, gender politics, modes of governance and state-society relations. She has several refereed articles on politics in the Middle East, and in particular the Arab Gulf. Her recent books are: (2008) *Women in Civil Society: The State, Islamism, and Networks in the UAE*, New York: Palgrave-Macmillan; and (2011) *Women Activists in the Middle East: Islamic and Secular Organizations in Egypt*, London: I.B. Tauris. Her current research includes a book project on 'Spiritual Activism'.

Jonathan Lacey completed a Bachelors Degree in Social Sciences at University College Cork (UCC) before being awarded an MPhil in Ethnic and Racial Studies from Trinity College Dublin (TCD). He is currently a PhD candidate in the Department of Sociology in TCD. Jonathan's research interests include issues relating to ethnic and racial studies, with a particular focus on religion, migration, social movements and global networks. Jonathan worked as a teaching assistant in the Department of Sociology from 2006 to 2011 and was employed as a research assistant to one of Intel's senior ethnographic researchers, focusing on Independent Living for Older People.

Araks Pashayan is an Associate Professor in Yerevan State University, Armenia, teaching a course on modern Islamic movements in Arab and Muslim countries; and is senior researcher on Arab countries with the Institute of Oriental Studies, NAS Armenia. She specializes in political Islam, having undertaken her doctorate on the *Organization of the Islamic*

Conference (1969–2002). She is the author of several learned articles and of the monograph *Organization of the Islamic Conference: The Objectives, Activity, Position towards the Karabakh Conflict* (Yerevan, 2003).

Tineke Peppinck was born in 1980 in The Hague, the Netherlands. After attending high school at the Haagland College, she was educated in the teaching of contemporary foreign languages (OALT, Opleiding tot Leraar Allochtone Levende Talen) at the Hogeschool Brabant in Breda. In 2001 she began a university education in Turkish at the Department of Languages and Cultures of the Middle East at the University of Leiden. Along with this, since September 2004 she has been a Turkish teacher at the Volksuniversiteit Amsterdam. In August 2007 she finished her Turkish studies with her thesis entitled *The Vision of Fethullah Gülen on Renewal as an Alternative to Modernization, and its Reflection on the Dutch Context*. Her interest in this subject came from her desire to deepen the way that Christians think about the activities of Turkish Muslims in the Netherlands.

M Fatih Tetik holds an MSc in Politics from University of London, and an MA from Ankara University, Turkey. He is currently carrying out doctoral research in sociology on 'The Reconstruction of the Turkish Diasporic Identity'. His research interests include the Turkish minorities in Western Europe, and religion and Turkish identity in Diaspora.

Erkan Toguslu is Dr Assistant in Anthropology at University KU Leuven. He received his MA and PhD in sociology from École des Hautes Études en Sciences Sociales (EHESS) in Paris. He continues his research on European Muslims and European Islam.

Steve Wright is a Reader in the School of Applied Global Ethics and an Associate Director of the Praxis Centre, Leeds Metropolitan University. His PhD – *New Police Technologies and Sub-State Conflict Control* – was from Lancaster University. For almost 30 years, Dr Wright has lectured extensively across five continents on the social implications of new internal security tactics and technologies. His most recent work covers new border control technologies and the climate change crisis. Concerned that the US 'War on Terror' may be masking new and unsustainable global security agendas, his ambition is to evolve human security programmes based on mutual respect which put the well-being of people first.

UNIVERSITY OF WINCHESTER
LIBRARY

UNIVERSITY OF MICHIGAN

ACKNOWLEDGEMENTS

Specific permissions and acknowledgements

The origins of this volume go back to two conferences organized by the Dialogue Society in collaboration with a range of other organizations. The first was a conference held at the House of Lords, the School of Oriental and African Studies and the London School of Economics, in London, 25–27 October 2007, under the title of 'The Muslim World in Transition: Contributions of the Gülen Movement'. This was supported by the University of Birmingham, the Irish School of Ecumenics, Leeds Metropolitan University, London Middle East Institute, Middle East Institute, and the School of Oriental and African Studies and London School of Economics of the University of London.

Papers prepared for that conference were published in a pre-conference volume edited by Ihsan Yilmaz, Eileen Barker, Henri Barkey, Alan Godlas, Muhammad Abdul Haleem, George Harris, Asaf Hussain, Johnston McMaster, Thomas Michel, Simon Robinson, Zeki Saritoprak, David Thomas, Colin Turner, Paul Weller, Ian Williams and Tim Winter (2007), *The Muslim World in Transition: Contributions of the Gülen Movement* (Conference proceedings of a conference of the same name, held at the House of Lords, the School of Oriental and African Studies and the London School of Economics, London, 25–27 October 2007).

The second conference was organized by the Dialoog Academie, Rotterdam, in collaboration with Leeds Metropolitan University, and took place at Erasmus University, Rotterdam, on 22–23 November 2007 on the theme of 'Peaceful Co-Existence: Fethullah Gülen's initiatives in the contemporary world'. Papers prepared for that conference were published in a pre-conference volume edited by Ihsan Yilmaz, Khalid Abou El Fadl, Jean-Michel Cros, Eric Geoffrey, Andreas Kinneging, Johnston McMaster, Thomas Michel, Paolo Naso, Ton Notten, Klaus Otte, Emilio Platti, Simon Robinson, Karel Steenbrink, David Thomas, Pim Valkenberg, Paul Weller and Anton Wessels (2007), *Peaceful Co-Existence: Fethullah Gülen's Initiatives in the Contemporary World* (Conference proceedings of an international conference of the same name, held at Erasmus University, Rotterdam, 22–23 November 2007), London: Leeds Metropolitan University Press.

The papers in this volume were selected according to the current volume's theme from among those presented at these two conferences. In connection with this, original copyright in these papers was vested with the Dialogue Society, London, and the Dialoog Academie, Rotterdam, respectively, by whom permission was given to Leeds Metropolitan University Press to publish the pre-conference volumes under their copyright. The conference and copyright origins of these papers are therefore acknowledged, as is the permission of the Dialogue Society and the Dialoog Academic as primary copyright holders, for the authors and editors to draw upon their originally published pre-conference texts.

At the same time, the papers as published in chapters in the present volume – while having continuity in parts of their text with their published pre-conference content – have all been re-written to the focus and length requirements of the present volume. Given the passage of time between original presentation of papers at these conferences in 2007 and the present volume's publication date of 2012, the papers as they appear here have also incorporated necessary updates of content with regard to more recent developments and relevant published materials.

Permission to quote at more length across the chapters of the book as a whole than is normally covered by full acknowledgement and referencing under 'fair dealing' provisions for the purposes of criticism and review, is acknowledged from The Light, for quotations from a key book containing the thought and teaching of Fethullah Gülen, namely Fethullah Gülen (2004), *Towards A Global Civilisation of Love and Tolerance*, New Jersey: The Light; as also from *The Fountain* for quotations from A. Ünal and A. Williams (eds) (2000) *Advocate of Dialogue*, Fethullah Gülen, Fairfax, Virginia: The Fountain.

General acknowledgements

The authors and editors also wish to acknowledge the many other authors and editors of books, and the authors of journal, magazine and newspaper articles listed in the bibliography from whose work ourselves and the authors of the chapters have either quoted within the generally recognized provisions for 'fair dealing ... for the purposes of criticism or review', or to whose work has been referred. Every attempt has been made to identify any copyright material appearing in this book that may go beyond the generally recognized permissions for 'fair dealing ... for the purposes of criticism or review'.

If, in error, we have failed specifically to identify and/or acknowledge such, or have by mistake inaccurately or not fully represented or referenced any material originally written by anyone than ourselves or the authors of the chapters, then we offer our sincere apologies. If any such copyright holders were to bring the matter to our attention, we are committed to rectifying any such failure in any future editions of this book that may be published.

A final word of thanks

In closing these acknowledgements, the editors would like to end with some personal thanks to Kirsty Schaper (the original Commissioning Editor for Religious Studies at the Continuum International Publishing Group for commissioning the volume) and to Tom Crick (formerly Editorial Assistant: Humanities also at Continuum) for his help and support in the range of practical issues that need attention between the initial conception and the final phase of editing the book. The editors would also like to thank Lalle Pursglove, who became Continuum's Commissioning Editor for Religious Studies towards the end of the editorial process and Rachel Eisenhauer, Editorial Assistant, for their support in its completion. Thanks are also due to Kim Storry and colleagues at Fakenham Prepress Solutions for their preparation of the text for publication.

The book took longer to edit and publish than was originally planned largely due to the terminal illness and death of Paul Weller's wife, Margaret Preisler-Weller, to whom this volume is dedicated. However, both of the editors would wish to express their thanks for what they acknowledge as the continued patient support of their families throughout all their work on this volume.

FETHULLAH GÜLEN, THE MOVEMENT AND THIS BOOK: AN INTRODUCTORY OVERVIEW

PAUL WELLER AND IHSAN YILMAZ

European context

There has been a longstanding presence of Muslims in Europe – especially in the Balkan countries, but also in less widely known locations for smaller groups of longstanding Muslim presence, such as the Muslims of Tartar origin who settled in the territories of what in the sixteenth to seventeenth centuries became the Polish–Lithuanian Commonwealth. But in the late twentieth and early twenty-first centuries Muslim minorities in Europe have emerged more clearly into the centre of European public life and debate due to effects arising from a mixture of decolonization, labour migration, asylum from conflict, and the pursuit of higher standards of living. Thus today, 1 million or more Muslims live in each of France, England, Germany and the Netherlands, and they are also present in the rest of Europe. As a result, there are now approximately 13 million Muslims in Western Europe (Yükleyen, 2009: 292).

This edited collection deals with the challenges and opportunities faced by Muslims and the wider society in Europe following the Madrid train bombings of 2004 and the London Transport attacks of 2005. In the wake of the 'social policy shock' (Weller, 2008: 195) brought on by these events, the 'multiculturalist' policy consensus that had shaped several Western countries' public policy understanding for several decades became subject to increasing criticism. Shared values and social cohesion were emphasized and the promotion of 'moderate Islam' and 'moderate Muslims' was advocated. However, as Paul Weller argues in the first chapter of this volume, legitimizing simplistic distinctions between 'good' (understood as 'liberal' or 'modernist') and 'bad' or 'suspect' (understood as 'traditionalist', 'radical' or 'fundamentalist') Muslims and forms of Islam does not ultimately help in combating terror or in building a properly inclusive society.

In fact, such reactions run the risk of eliding the condemnation of acts of terror conducted on religious grounds into the criminalization, or at least social marginalization, of religious conservatism and/or radicalism. Therefore even from a pragmatic perspective, in order to combat the attraction of young Muslims to understandings that see the world in highly dichotomized ways and to contribute to the growth of civility in our multi-ethnic, multicultural and multi-religious European societies, the perspectives and actions of radicalized young Muslims need robust challenge from Islamic resources that draw upon the deep wells of Qur'an and Sunnah; are informed by the rich history of multicultural Islamic civilization; and yet are also fully engaged with the contemporary global realities of modernity.

Fethullah Gülen: challenging terror and promoting civility

It is within this context for Muslims in Europe and for the wider European societies of which Muslims are a part that the contributors to this volume explore the challenges to the concept and practice of civility in European public life and discuss the contributions that can be made in this regard by the thought and practice of the global movement inspired by the Turkish Muslim scholar Fethullah Gülen who, on Islamic grounds, condemns terrorism in the name of religion.

Fethullah Gülen is a Turkish Islamic scholar, thinker, preacher, writer and poet who has attempted to 'synthesize tradition and modernity, religion and science' (Koyuncu-Lorasdaği, 2010: 221). He is not an academic or theorist in the modern sense of these terms. Rather, he is more a scholar in the classical Islamic sense, but importantly, one who seeks actively and critically to engage with this world by teaching and presenting his *Weltanschauung* and by inspiring a movement that seeks to put this inspiration into concrete practice. In this, the importance of Gülen's contribution is that it is not only one of condemnation and critique of terror undertaken in the name of Islam. Rather, being rooted in a confident Ottoman Muslim civilizational heritage, it also offers constructive impulses. Emerging from the context of the modern history of the Turkish Republic, Gülen's contribution is one that has developed and matured through engagement with both ideological 'secularism' and political 'Islamism'. Therefore, as well as being shaped by a deep understanding of Islamic tradition, it is also informed by a realistic understanding of the dynamics of the contemporary world.

Emergence and development of the movement inspired by Fethullah Gülen

The movement began in Turkey at the end of the 1960s 'through Gülen's teachings at the Kestanepazarı Qur'anic School in Izmir, where he worked as a state imam' (Koyuncu-Lorasdaği, 2010: 225). It then further developed, particularly through schools that were founded in the Turkic republics of the former Soviet Union and then in the Balkans. As Ebaugh (2010: v) summarizes it, during the 1960s, 1970s and 1980s, Gülen preached to large crowds in mosques and public places throughout Turkey and published periodicals, articles and books espousing his ideas.

Gradually, many Turks from all walks of life responded to his ideas of education, modernization, positive relationships with the West and inter-faith dialogue by establishing dormitories, university preparatory courses and schools. With the fall of the Soviet Union, his ideas and service projects spread to the former Turkic–Soviet countries and ultimately to Western Europe where large numbers of Turkish immigrants reside as well as to North America, Asia, Africa, Australia and to Middle Eastern countries. The schools have flourished because they preserve 'a modern, secular curriculum, while engaging rather than threatening the state' (Clement 2011: 76).

By the 2000s, the movement's loose educational network was operating in many countries across all the continents and as Koyuncu-Lorasdaği (2010: 226) says, '[T]he reputation and success of these schools can be explained by the high-quality education they provide and top-notch students selected on the basis of their success.' Today, the Gülen-inspired movement has more than 1,000 schools in 130 countries. In Europe, the movement 'has established tutoring centres and dormitories to support the education of the second and third-generation immigrants, and it targets the emerging middle class among Turkish immigrants to finance its activities through fundraising dinners' (Yükleyen and Yurdakul, 2011: 75).

The movement inspired by Gülen is a civic movement rooted in Islam and committed to educating youth, fostering inter-faith and inter-cultural dialogue, assisting the needy in society and contributing to global peace (Ebaugh 2010: v). The movement schools endeavour 'to lay the foundations for a more humane, tolerant citizenry of the world where people are expected to cultivate their own faith perspectives and also promote the well being of others' (Kurtz, 2005: 380). The religious discourse of Gülen has become global and adapted to local circumstances. At the same time, since there is no central and hierarchical bureaucratic organization, the actual size of the movement participants and sympathizers is not exactly known. But it is certainly the largest civil society movement in Turkey.

Gülen himself regards the movement as a cultural activity whose essence is based on the altruistic and sacrificial voluntary co-operation of many people who may not know each other, have no organic or official ties or, in some cases, not even any mutual acquaintance, but who all share similar ideals of serving humanity. Gülen has come up with 'a concrete socio-economic and cultural analysis of the current spatio-temporal context and based on this analysis offers concrete solutions to tackle Muslims' enemies rather than insisting on abstract rhetoric' (Esposito and Yilmaz, 2010: xxviii).

In Gülen's worldview, there are three major enemies of not only Muslims, but also humanity as a whole: ignorance, poverty and disunity. According to Gülen, the major problem in today's world 'is lack of knowledge which includes the production and control of knowledge, as well as acquiring existing knowledge. Producing, maintaining and disseminating knowledge can only be achieved through quality education, not by politics or force' (Ebaugh 2010: 34). Gülen 'sees education as requisite for social, economic and political modernization and advocates that individuals will respect democratic law and human rights only if they receive a sound education' and that social justice and peace 'are achieved by intellectually enlightened people with strong moral values and a sense of altruism' (Ebaugh, 2010: 34).

Gülen encouraged business people who were sympathetic to his cause to spend their money as seed-capital to establish schools in several different countries. One of the five fundamental pillars of Islam is *zakat* (charity) and wealthy Muslims have to donate 2.5 per cent of their wealth every year. Traditionally, Muslims have donated their *zakat* to poor families or to establish mosques and Qur'anic literary schools. Gülen reinterpreted this tradition and advocated convincingly the view that spending *zakat* for establishing secular educational institutions and for giving scholarships to students that study in secular schools and universities is also an act of worship. He himself has donated 90 per cent of his earnings from the more-than 60 best-selling books he has written to scholarship funds for the institutions inspired by him or for humanitarian aid (Yucel, 2010: 8).

Gülen argues that the universe is also a book of God similar to the Qur'an. Morever, the Qur'an repeats in many verses that studying this book of God (universe) is also a kind of worship. In his view, 'science and faith are not only compatible but complementary. He sees a faith-based worldview as providing a comprehensive and sound narrative that can support and give meaning to secular learning' and 'he advocates educating the young generation in Islamic knowledge through informal publications, sermons and within the family rather than through formal curricula in schools' (Ebaugh, 2010: 35).

Gülen does not see the world in political terms and does not draw imaginary boundaries. As skilfully expressed by Klas Grinell (2010: 67) Gülen is a 'border transgressor'. Gülen's frequently used term *dar al-hizmet* (country of service) reflects his border transgressing vision (Yilmaz, 2003: 234). Indeed, among those inspired by his teaching, *Hizmet* (service) is often the name given to their activities and to the movement. By employing

ijtihad, he bases this border transgressing understanding on Islamic jurisprudence *(fiqh)*. He does not divide the world by employing the mutually
exclusive concepts of *dar al-harb* (abode of war) and *dar-al Islam* (abode
of Islam, peace) that were developed in medieval Islam and have been used
by modern 'Islamists' to justify an ideologically divided view of the world.
Rather, he sees the world as a whole that needs to be served continually by
utilizing the concept *dar al-hizmet* – the abode of service to humans, and
thereby also to God (Yilmaz, 2007: 35). Gülen stresses that wherever a
Muslim is, even outside a Muslim polity, he or she has to obey the law of
the land, to respect others' rights and to be just, and has to disregard discussions of *dar al-harb* and *dar al-Islam*.

Starting from the early 1990s, well before the 9/11 attacks in New York,
Gülen 'was intent on promoting dialogue and tolerance among all strata
of the society in Turkey and elsewhere' (Gözaydın, 2009: 1224). Gülen
pioneered the establishment of the Journalists and Writers Foundation in
1994. He was perhaps the first Muslim scholar publicly to invite leaders of
other faith groups in Turkey to dinners and was definitely the first Turkish
Muslim scholar to visit the Pope in Vatican in 1998. His dialogue, tolerance
and peaceful coexistence discourse has been promoted by institutions
abroad, such as the Dialogue Society established in London in 1999 and
the Rumi Forum established in Washington, DC in 1999. There are now
hundreds of inter-faith and inter-cultural dialogue associations and charities
all over the world founded by the movement's Muslim and non-Muslim
volunteers, engaging in inter-faith and inter-cultural dialogue with people
of different faiths, backgrounds and cultures (Gözaydın, 2009: 1224).

The approach of this book, its authors and editors

The authors of the chapters in this book represent a mix of established
scholars in related relevant areas of work and emerging scholars who have
become engaged in this specific field of study that has begun to develop over
the past few years in relation to Gülen and the movement. As the title of
the book itself already suggests, the chapters include perspectives both 'on'
and 'from' the movement. This is in the sense that some of the writers, while
writing here in their academic capacity, are also 'insiders' to the movement,
while others are 'outsiders'. But in seeking to understand and evaluate the
phenomenon with which the book is concerned, all the writers also discuss
other 'insider' and 'outsider' perspectives, including from those who are
enthusiastic 'supporters' of the movement; those who aspire to be neutral
'observers'; and those who are 'critics'.

Nevertheless, while approaching their individual chapters in different
ways and with different evaluative nuances, the authors in this book all

share an overall assessment that Gülen's teaching as well as much of the practice of the movement inspired by it provide positive impulses for the wider European society as well as offering to Muslims in Europe the possibility of a contextualized renewal of Islam that is fully engaged with modernity while being at the same time fully rooted in the teachings of the Qur'an and the Sunnah of the Prophet.

Contents of the book

The book consists of four parts. Part one is on 'Perspectives from Gülen on Muslim identity and public life'; Part two is titled 'Civility, co-existence and integration'; Part three is 'European contexts'; and Part four is on 'Challenging terrorism'.

Part one comprises three chapters. *Chapter 1*, by Paul Weller, takes as its starting-point the growing debate on the relationship between religion and public life in Europe that is informed by the continuing evolution of the European Union (EU) by incorporation of new member states and the extension of its competence into ever-wider areas of social policy; the increasing cultural and religious diversity of its populations; the debates over the accession of Turkey into the EU; and the emergent questioning of the previously held European models of 'multiculturalism' through to models of 'laïcité'.

Since the Madrid train bombings on 11 March 2004 and the London Transport attacks on 7 July 2005, many of these debates have focused on the position of Islam and Muslims. Because of these events, the debates have often been constructed in terms of a conflict between ideologically 'Islamist' and ideologically 'secularist' positions, as if these were the only alternatives. However, this chapter argues that there are other – more constructive – ways forward that promote equity for religious minorities, inclusivity on the part of the state and participation in civic society.

In exploring these alternatives, the chapter brings perspectives from the teaching of the Turkish Muslim scholar, Fethullah Gülen, into critical inter-action with seven theses on religion and public life that have been developed by the chapter's author over more than a quarter of a century of practical and academic engagement with issues of religious diversity and public life. Through interaction with these theses, key aspects of Gülen's thought and teaching are explored through the notion of what Ihsan Yilmaz (2002) articulates in terms of the possibility of a commitment to *dar ul-hizmet*, in which an Islamic contribution is made to public life, but as one contribution to civil society set alongside others.

Chapter 2, by Gürkan Celik and Yusuf Alan, applies seven textual linguistic principles (cohesion, coherence, intentionality, acceptability, informativity, situationality and intertextuality) to Gülen's teaching and movement. In doing so it examines if, and if so to what extent, modern ideals and Muslim identity are in harmony or are in contradiction with each other. In this context, Celik and Alan define 'text' as a communicative occurrence that meets seven standards of textuality. Here, Fethullah Gülen is, metaphorically, considered as the 'writer' of the text; his teaching and the movement inspired by him are the 'text'; and the 'readers' are the participants of the transnational movement, and the whole of humanity. These seven linguistic standards are modelled on the social sciences as a new theoretical and methodological approach for exploring and analysing social movements and phenomena.

Chapter 3 (the final chapter in Part one) is by Shanthikumar Hettiarachchi and investigates the emergent Islam in Europe with reference to the varied cultures, traditions, customs and places of origin of European Muslims. It focuses on the encounter between the Turkish inflection of Islam and the diaspora derived from it and the South Asian Muslim presence and argues that this presents a defining and historic opportunity to carve out a new European Islamic identity. The chapter suggests that this encounter can benefit greatly from Fethullah Gülen's insights, teaching and relentless campaign for an inclusive society where love and compassion, justice and honesty, knowledge and critical thinking are promoted, and where cruelty and fanaticism, dogmatism and ignorance are eradicated.

Part two, 'Civility, co-existence and integration', also comprises three chapters. In *Chapter 4*, Wanda Krause questions aspects of the received knowledge developed about Islamic-based activism and its role in relation to civil society. As spearheaded by Huntington's earlier writings (1993: 22–49; 1996), the view has gained popularity that Islamic politics will inevitably contribute to an impending 'clash of civilizations'. Such theorization overlooks and marginalizes Islamically inspired movements that contribute to inter-faith dialogue, East–West relations, and the vibrancy of civil societies in countries around the world. As such, within a civil society theoretical framework, the chapter addresses the knowledge developed about Islamically inspired forms of activism and examines the Gülen movement as a key actor in civil society.

Within the dominant theorization that promotes an imminent 'clash of civilization', Islamically inspired forms of organization are often presented as deficient in, or even as antithetical to, the principles of 'civility'. The danger is that they therefore become simply excluded from normative definitions of civil society and as a result both their actual and potentially positive role in civil society is diminished. Thus this chapter argues for expanding the very concepts through which we view and come to judge civility and citizenship. A full illumination of the role of shared values in building civil society is facilitated by expanding the concepts by which we measure and exclude crucial components. Recognizing the value systems behind Islamic forms of organization helps to develop better tools for deciphering shared values among various parts of civil society. Focusing on the Gülen movement, through an investigation of its beliefs, values and practices, the chapter illustrates not only its international contribution in terms of expanding civil societies, but also how it is positioned as a leading example for contemporary challenges.

In *Chapter 5*, by Erkan Toguslu, Fethullah Gülen and Tariq Ramadan are highlighted as two major personalities whose ideas and views are admired and valued by the Muslim community in Europe. Both thinkers are calling for a better understanding of civilizational and religious pluralism, a moderate way of practising Islam, and the co-existence of different ethnic and religious affiliations. This chapter analyses the influence of their ideas among the younger generation, their education and dialogue initiatives, and the circulation of cassette recordings of their lectures that have opened up a space in which ideas about human civic responsibility, democracy, citizenship, pluralism, dialogue and tolerance can take root.

Chapter 6, the final chapter in Part two, has been written by Araks Pashayan and looks at the integration of Muslims in Europe. At the beginning of the twenty-first century, humankind faces a number of tendencies related to the resurgence of radical trends in major religions: the increasing role of religion in the universal civilization, and cultural, ideological and religious diversity on global and local levels. In particular, the troubled integration of Muslims into European societies is evidence of a perceived incompatibility between Christian and Islamic traditions.

There are two main tendencies within the Muslim communities of Europe. The first one is related to what is often referred to as 'radicalization'. Fethullah Gülen mentions four reasons why Muslims often have problems with dialogue: the first, he says, is that many Muslims, including those who are educated, believe that the West seeks to undermine Islam. The second tendency is related to a newly established identity. There are circles that tend to retain their Muslim identity, and as a distinctive feature they choose their religious identity, which is more determining and powerful element within the European/Christian civilization.

This chapter argues that it is not Christian and Islamic civilizations that clash in Europe but post-Christian secular/liberal values and Muslim traditional values. In this case, the only alternative to sectarianism, isolation and radical relativism is inter-faith and inter-cultural dialogue. As both an Islamic scholar and a peace activist Fethullah Gülen argues that to oppose and resent the West will never benefit Islam or Muslims. As a dialogical method he commends forgetting the arguments of the past and concentrating on common points. Gülen stresses tolerance as an extremely important virtue that should always be promoted and argues that Christianity and Judaism have much in common with Islam. He insists that the world is becoming more global and both sides feel the need for a give-and-take relationship. The Gülen movement aims to promote creative and positive relations between the West and East.

In Part three, 'European Contexts', there are four chapters. *Chapter 7*, by Tineke Peppinck, examines how Fethullah Gülen's vision is elaborated in relation to renewal and modernization. This includes discussion of the historical context for this vision and what effect this has had within the Dutch context.

From all of this she highlights that, since the nineteenth century, Turks have always wanted to be on the same level with the Western world. Modernization was seen as a necessity to remove the risk of Turkey being exploited by so-called 'more civilized' nations. As a result of reforms under-taken in the Turkish top-down modernization, the role of religion (Islam) in the public domain was marginalized.

In his vision, Fethullah Gülen challenges this interpretation of moderni-zation. Rather, he argues that, in fact, it is the reducing role of historical and religious values that leads to a weakening of the Turkish nation, because in this way Turkey loses its identity and becomes subjugated by materialism. Gülen advocates that the renewal of the nation can be achieved through what he calls a 'golden generation' of young people who have found their identity as a 'new man' in their history or belief, but at the same time are developed and so form a leading group in modern science and being of service to humanity. In this way they can fulfil an exemplar function for the rest of the society, and unite these around shared values, so that these will also form and show a strong unity and example to the rest of the world.

Peppinck points out that in many ways Gülen's solution resembles the goals of Kemalism, but the content is completely different: create a new generation of people who are free. Not free from the influence of religion to be able to think freely, but free through the notion that they are servants of God, who only have to obey his commands and need not bow before other kinds of power. Free because they are aware of the fact that the core of belief is to strive to God's approval, so they can free themselves from the worldly desires. Free to do scientific research in an honest way, because in this they are not manipulated by their own interests, so they can use science for the good of the whole humanity. With a broader look into science, a holistic view, because as well as the book of the religion, the book of the universe is consulted during scientific research, one can obtain deeper insight. Active, not because of chasing luxury, but because one strives for the approval of God, which is obtained through loving all creatures because of the creator himself, so one can become conscious of one's own responsibilities towards fellow men, society and the world.

In the Dutch context it seems that the Gülen movement participants are striving to bring people of different backgrounds into dialogue and to facilitate them in working together on shared goals. In this regard the development and participation of the Turkish community to pioneer the development of the Dutch youth into 'world citizens', who are tolerant towards other beliefs and culture, is emphasized. The means that are used here are completely in line with the vision of Fethullah Gülen and the Gülen movement's role models. The movement is socially very active as a mission for serving humanity regardless of ethnicity, religion and culture, in the hope that this will positively reflect on the Dutch society. Some of those in the movement in the Netherlands have even expressed their expectation that, in this way, the Netherlands might itself, as a diverse but peaceful society, become a role model for other countries within Europe.

Chapter 8, by Emre Demir, looks at the organizational and discursive strategies of the Gülen movement in France and Germany and the movement's place within Turkish Islam in Europe, with a primary focus on its educational activities. The chapter describes the characteristics of organizational activity among Turkish Muslims in Europe. It then analyses two mainstream religious-communitarian movements and the contrasting settlement strategies of the "neo-communitarian" Gülen movement. Despite the large Turkish population in Western Europe, the movement has been active there for only ten years or so – relatively late compared to other Islamic organizations.

The associational organization of Turkish Islam in Europe is based on two main axes: the construction/sponsoring of mosques, and Qur'anic schools. By contrast, the Gülen movement's participants in Europe, insisting on 'the great importance of secular education', do not found or sponsor mosques and Qur'anic schools. Their principal focus is to address the problems of the immigrant youth population in Europe, with the initial goal of reintegration of Turkish students into the educational system of the host societies. As a neo-communitarian religious grouping, the movement strives for a larger share of the 'market' (i.e. more participants from among the Turkish diaspora) by offering a fresh religious discourse and new organizational strategies, much as they have done in Turkey. Accordingly, a reinvigorated and reorganized community is taking shape in Western Europe.

In *Chapter 9,* Fatih Tetik starts from a recognition that the two World Wars and ensuing political events created a brave new world for Muslims in which three great empires of the sixteenth century were carved up into 42 nation-states. This separation led to one-third of the Muslim population living as minorities in non-Muslim countries. The number of minorities has noticeably been augmented after Muslims voluntarily migrated to the Western world as well as to Australia and New Zealand in expectation of a new and better life.

Although European countries experience social-political problems with their minorities, in the light of declining birth rates and an aging population, Europe has little real alternative but to continue with 'minority impor-tation' in order to sustain the economic growth of the continent. Therefore, in spite of not being welcomed by significant sections of the Western European public, it seems as if immigration will be an irreversible aspect of the continent.

Because of this, if an effective method cannot be implemented to facil-itate the integration process, then a serious problem, if not a social crisis, is impending within European society. Considering this historical account, this chapter endeavours to analyse the potential contributions of the Gülen movement to the integration process of Turkish community in Europe in the medium-run and the feasibility of this process with reference to existing constraints within these communities.

The chapter proposes Gülen and the movement inspired by him as a possible solution to the integration problems of the Muslim communities due to the nature of the principles adopted by the movement and the likelihood of those principles being implemented. That is to say, in the Muslim world there have been certain Islamic scholars prior to or contemporary with Gülen who have formulated certain ideas related to inter-faith dialogue and/or integration. What makes Gülen significant is the presence of a movement or people that are at least sympathetic to his ideas and put them into operation. His ideas do not remain in the world of ideas but become the charter or action plan that is pursued by the members of the movement. Because of this, while for the other scholars a more gradual personal, communal and then organisational acceptance and realisation of these notions needs to take place before societal recognition occurs, Gülen's ideas can move more easily and rapidly into wider social acceptance.

The final chapter in this part of the book, *Chapter 10*, is by Jonathan Lacey. In it, he recounts how, when the Good Friday Agreement was signed in Northern Ireland in 1998, it adopted a model of consociational democracy in the way that it institutionalized 'parity of esteem' for the two dominant groups in Northern Ireland. It thereby largely ignored the minority ethnic groups also living in the region. However, there are now 20,000 people from minority ethnic backgrounds living in Northern Ireland, including roughly 300 Turkish people. This chapter analyses how the Gülen-inspired Northern-Ireland Tolerance, Educational and Cultural Association (NI-TECA) engages with various actors in mainstream society through dialogue activities. It makes the case that NI-TECA's dialogue activities are strategic in the sense that their main aim is to challenge the pejorative representation of Islam dominant in Western societies, and to promote Fethullah Gülen's ideas. In doing so, the chapter draws on concepts developed in social movement theory, namely identity deployment and framing, in order to capture the strategic nature of these dialogic engagements.

Part four of this book comprises four chapters. The first of these, *Chapter 11* (by Paul Weller) begins by highlighting the way in which the 7/7 (7 July 2005) attack on London Transport by Muslims brought up in the UK shocked the government, many Muslims and the wider civil society. Subsequently, the UK's 'multiculturalist' policy consensus has been subject to intensive questioning. Politicians and some parts of civil society have challenged a perceived 'separatism' among Muslims; emphasized a need for shared values and social cohesion; and advocated the promotion of 'moderate Islam' and 'moderate Muslims'. This chapter argues that, in legitimizing simplistic distinctions between 'good' (understood as 'liberal' or 'modernist') and 'bad' or 'suspect' (understood as 'traditionalist', 'radical' or 'fundamentalist') Muslims and forms of Islam, there is a risk of eliding the condemnation of crimes of terror against humanity conducted on religious grounds into the criminalization, or at least social marginalization, of religious conservatism and/or radicalism. This approach, it is argued, is more likely to undermine the development of inclusive approaches to the common good.

It is also argued that what is needed instead are authentically Islamic approaches that can offer both a resource and a challenge to government, Muslims and the wider civil society, and that such resource and challenge can be found in themes from Fethullah Gülen's teaching who, on Islamic grounds, condemns terrorism in the name of religion. At the same time, being rooted in a confident Ottoman Muslim civilizational heritage and having engaged with both ideological 'secularism' and political 'Islamism' within the Turkish Republic, Gülen offers a critique of the political instrumentalization of Islam while arguing for an active Muslim engagement with the wider (religious and secular) society based on a distinctive Islamic vision characterized by a robustness and civility that could make a positive contribution in the present UK context.

In *Chapter 12,* Y. Alp Aslandoğan and Bekir Cinar analyse Gülen's multifaceted response to the phenomenon of violence against civilians such as terrorism and suicide attacks. In particular, the chapter examines Gülen's humanistic and theological rejection of terrorism. It also provides an overview of how these views and the various educational projects of the Gülen movement contribute towards eradicating the root causes of terrorism. Gülen declares that acts of violence against innocent civilians including women and children are inhumane. He uses clear statements in categorically condemning killing of innocent civilians. As a Sunni-Muslim scholar, Gülen has strong theological objections to violence against civilians carried out under the guise of religious rhetoric. In categorically objecting to these acts, Gülen meticulously justifies his position based on traditional Islamic sources, Islamic history and pre-modern juristic views.

Gülen highlights the principles of Islamic jurisprudence that deem the declaration of war by individuals or entities other than the state, to be illegal. Hence, self-declared wars of individuals or groups under the banner of Islam cannot be regarded as legitimate. He offers explanations for misinterpreted verses and prophetic sayings that are abused by those who justify acts of violence. In addition, Gülen argues that Muslims have positive obligations towards the state in which they live – such as obeying the laws of the state. Gülen offers practical approaches to rooting the problem of unjustified antagonism, hate-mongering and violent conflicts. The underlying dynamics of this approach are education, mutual understanding, respect, opportunity and hope. The movement has educational institutions that foster inter-faith and inter-cultural dialogue, mutual understanding and respect. All of these offer hope for upward mobility, such as that established by participants in the Gülen movement. Gülen's emphasis on Islamic spirituality provides an example that is significant for Muslim communities.

Steve Wright's chapter (*Chapter 13*) argues that we are living in dangerous times. In a context in which he argues that the polarization between Islam and the West can be anticipated as the official line becomes increasingly focused on achieving military solutions to what are essentially political and cultural issues, Wright discusses the potential role of non-violent approaches. In connection with this, Wright enquires how far Gülen's teachings on non-violence could contribute to peaceful transformation on the ground? He asks if Gülen's approach is a static and passive one boundaried by dogma, or whether we witnessing an innovative, active and self-aware spirit of transformation which can lead to a new way of defining Islam in action?

Wright's chapter attempts to explore these questions through a comparison with Western writers such as Johan Galtung and Paul Smoker who have deconstructed positive and negative peace and recognized that structural violence is as important as direct violence, both of which need to be eliminated to establish new cultures of peace. In a similar way to that in which Gene Sharp's work (Sharp, 1973: 2005) was utilized to support non-violent peaceful revolutions in Romania, Serbia and Ukraine, is Gülen's teaching capable of being translated via techniques that can turn a non-violent belief into change and social justice? Or are Fethullah Gülen's teachings most useful for spiritual salvation in the hereafter and inappropriate or insufficiently integrated for effective practical action in his world?

Wright notes that Gülen's approach is to work within an Islamic framework and apply the principles of the Qur'an to create positive change based on mutual respect. How does this differ from more Western approaches that share similar outcomes? It is important to hear something of past voices that share the vision of peace through peace and their similar experiences in what is sometimes referred to as 'speaking truth to power'. A key question is the extent to which these different approaches converge or diverge and the extent to which learning can be mutual. This goal is particularly pertinent in a time of terror when extant counter-insurgency models incorporating organized violence against innocents can easily provoke responses that are then used to justify even more violent repression. A crucial issue is whether or not Fethullah Gülen's teachings on non-violence can inspire a new non-violent praxis towards peaceful social change?

The concluding chapter of the book (Chapter 14) is by Asaf Hussain and Ihsan Yilmaz. Here they highlight that Western policies are generally focused on fighting terrorist groups rather than terrorist ideologies and their root causes. By contrast, Hussain and Yilmaz try to identify those root causes and the means of minimizing the potential dangers of the terrorist ideologies. A common misunderstanding is that Islam is prone to violence and extremism, if not itself the cause of terrorism. This misconception is based on ignorance of the many Muslim groups and faith-based movements that work towards peace and better relations in the world because of Islam, not despite it.

The Gülen movement is highlighted as one of the most successful and famous of those faith-based movements. It is argued that policy makers need to become familiar with such movements, their motivations, methods and arguments. The extremist/ terrorist ideology must be rebutted: however, of the many interpretations of Islam circulating in the world the most extremist and pro-violence ones dominate the public sphere, mainly the media, and therefore the attention of younger Muslims. Media and policy makers have not paid enough attention to the mainstream interpretations of Islam embraced by the majority – the interpretations of mainstream Muslim thinkers like Fethullah Gülen. The teachings and principles of thinkers like Fethullah Gülen and the movement's activities and projects can help to inform and shape state policies in ways that can positively contribute to overcoming the actual and potential threat of terrorism.

The book ends with a conclusion by the editors, Paul Weller and Ihsan Yilmaz, entitled 'Fethullah Gülen and the Hizmet: towards an evaluation' that, as its title suggests, attempts a preliminary evaluation, highlighting a number of issues arising from the contributors' chapters and identifying a number of key questions for the future: for European Muslims; for the wider European societies of which European Muslims are a part; and for the movement and activities that are inspired by Fethullah Gülen.

PART I

Perspectives from Gülen on Muslim identity and public life

1

Dialogical and transformative resources: perspectives from Fethullah Gülen on religion and public life

PAUL WELLER

European context for religion(s), state(s) and society relations

In the Europe of today there are considerable tensions and challenges to peaceful co-existence in terms of the relationship between Muslims and others in a secular context. With the continuing evolution of the European Union (EU) by incorporation of new member states; the increasing ethnic and religious diversity of its populations (Davie, 2000); the debate over the accession of Turkey into the EU (Bilici, 2006); and the questioning of previously developed European models for the relationship between religion(s), state(s) and society (Robbers, 1996), the issues in the relationship between religion(s), state and society are ones with which all states and societies in the EU and in the wider Europe are having, once again, to wrestle (Madeley and Enyedi, 2003).

While tensions and even violent conflict involving religions continued to exist in parts of Europe (for example, in the religiously related dimensions of the national conflict in the North of Ireland), for the majority of Europeans these were seen largely as things of the past. The overall perspective of the majority was one that – perhaps somewhat complacently – had come to see religion as primarily something for the private sphere.

Although labour migration and refugee movements of peoples changed the composition of European societies in the years following the Second World War, there was initially very little reflection on the implications of this diversity in relation to religion, with ethnicity and culture receiving much more emphasis. But the controversy that developed around Salman Rushdie's (1988) book, *The Satanic Verses* contained in microcosm many of the themes, issues and debates that have since come to form such a large part of public, religious and political debate and consciousness and, in relation to which, with hindsight, one can see that the controversy was an early 'lightning rod' (Weller, 2008). However, although there were firebombings of some bookshops stocking the book, threats against those supporting Salman Rushdie, the killing of an *imam* in Belgium, and threats to a number of Muslim organizations and places of worship, the conflicts that ensued were, at least in Europe, primarily located in the cultural, social and political domains.

More recently, many of the original issues involved in *The Satanic Verses* controversy were reprised in the so-called 'Cartoons Controversy' that developed around the images published in the 30 September 2005 edition of the Danish daily newspaper *Jyllands-Posten*, and which gave rise to similar widespread media, public and street-level debate (see Lægard, 2007). However, while the *The Satanic Verses* controversy entailed (following the *fatwa*, or 'legal opinion', pronounced by the Iranian religious leader, the Ayatollah Khomeini) the threat of violence targeted towards Salman Rushdie and those directly associated with the publication of his book, the 'Cartoons Controversy' took place in the context of a more general association of Islam and violence in Europe. This association was itself a contributory factor in the controversy since the *Jyllands-Posten*'s cartoons were deemed so offensive by many Muslims because they depicted the Prophet Muhammad as having a bomb under his turban, with the *Shahadah* – or basic Muslim declaration of faith – being written on the bomb.

What had happened in between was the seismic global impact of the events of 9/11 in the USA (National Commission on Terrorist Attacks Upon the United States, 2004), followed in Europe by the 3/11 (2003) Madrid train bombings; the 2 November 2004 van Gogh murder; and the 7/7 (2005) London transport attacks. In other words, in between *The Satanic Verses* controversy and the 'Cartoons Controversy', the violence associated with the emerging cultural conflicts had become very explicit, and also in the heart of Europe itself (Guelke, 2006; Abbas, 2007). Because of these events, debate sharpened about the possibilities for peaceful co-existence of Muslims and non-Muslims in a secular and European environment.

Old models and their alternatives

As a result of all of this, the opening years of the twenty-first century saw an accelerating growth in questioning of the previous European models for the management of religious and cultural diversity – including those of 'multi-culturalism' in the UK (see Modood, 2007); *verzuiling* (or 'pillarisation') in the Netherlands (see Post, 1989); and 'laïcité' in France (see Nielsen, 1995). Unfortunately, the debates that have emerged around this have often been constructed in terms of a conflict between ideologically 'secularist' and ideologically 'Islamist' positions, as if these were the only alternatives.

It is, however, the contention of this paper that there are other ways in which these debates can be approached. On the basis of both academic reflection upon, and practical engagement with, issues arising from religious plurality over the past quarter of a century, the author of this paper has elsewhere argued (see Weller, 2005a) that these alternatives are not the only options and that there are other, more constructive ways forward.

These perspectives were distilled into seven theses, propositions or principles on religion and public life in the UK and Europe which have been developed by the author over the past decade since they were first formulated, and so have appeared in slightly variant published forms (see Weller, 2002a; 2002b; 2002c; 2005a; and 2005b). But in exploring these and other approaches it is important that this is done in active dialogue with Muslims and their thinking on these matters. This is because it is unlikely that any positive way forward can be identified, and much less implemented, unless European Muslims can contribute to its creation as active social participants rather than merely passive recipients. And a key Muslim contribution to this dialogue comes from the teaching of the Turkish Muslim, Fethullah Gülen, and the work of the movement inspired by his teaching.

Theses on religion(s), state and society: a conversation with Gülen

This chapter therefore focuses on key themes in Gülen's teaching by bringing them into critical interaction with the theses on the relationships between religion(s), state and society that have previously been developed by the present author. They are quoted in this paper in the form in which they are published and discussed in P. Weller (2005a) *Time for a Change: Reconfiguring Religion, State and Society.*

In a way these theses are the equivalent of newspaper headlines. There is much that could be said about them by way of qualification. As proposi-tions they do not claim to be either a detailed survey or the last word. They paint on a broad canvas, standing back a little from the detailed histories and variations that exist within the European context. Thus they are intended to provoke reaction, not as systematic statements, but as succinct formulations that others can react to in affirmation or disagreement, and in the process uncovering the presuppositions that underlie particular positions on the relationships between religion(s), state and society.

'The importance of not marginalizing religions from public life'

> States which assign religions to the private sphere will impoverish themselves by marginalising important social resources and might unwittingly be encouraging of those reactive, backward- and inward-looking expressions of religious life that are popularly characterised as 'fundamentalisms' (Weller, 2005a: 197).

In relation to use of the term 'fundamentalism' (which in the thesis is deliberately framed by inverted commas to indicate that the term can legitimately be used only in the context of more carefully defined meanings), Gülen does not accept the kind of uncritical use of the term that has become commonplace among the media and among the commentators of the 'chattering classes' when referring to a whole range of different religious phenomena beyond those of liberal religion.

Thus Gülen (2004e: 35) points out that the term has become 'another fashionable term with which to smear ... those who did nothing more than express their religious feelings' and 'have been branded as reactionaries, fanatics, and fundamentalists'. In other words, concerns about conflictual and violent religion can all too easily result in a simplistic secular misunderstanding in which, as Gülen goes on to put it, 'Unfortunately some people do not distinguish between being truly religious and blind fanaticism', and fail to differentiate between different strands of more conservative religious expression. But given that there are forms of religion that do tend towards the undermining of civility and co-existence, the irony is that some understandings of the 'secular' – such as those that argue for keeping religions out of public life – can, in fact, precisely lead to the further entrenchment and development of these forms of religion.

While the 'secular' is often said to be foundational of contemporary European models for the relationship between religions, states and societies, its meaning is not self-evident or uncontested (see Weller, 2006b; and 2007b). As explained by Hakan Yavuz and John Esposito (2003a: xvii), 'In many developing countries, secularism has become a theology of progress and development' and that 'normative fault lines of modernity are nowhere else as clear as in Turkey', which is the context from which Gülen and the community that has emerged around his teaching derive.

In the twentieth century, Turkey's story is one that has been dominated by the ideology of Mustafa Kemal Ataturk (1881–1938), the founder of the modern Turkish state who abolished the Muslim Caliphate in 1924. Yavuz and Esposito argue that in Kemalist ideology modernity and democracy require secularism. Indeed, the version of secularism that has been dominant in Turkey is what Yavuz and Esposito (2003a: xvi) call a 'radical Jacobin laïcism' in which secularism is treated 'as above and outside politics' and in which, therefore, 'secularism draws the boundaries of public reasoning'.

Notwithstanding the developments that have followed the Turkish electoral victories of Recep Tayyip Erdogan, the leader of the Justice and Development Party (Adalet ve Kalkinma Partisi, or AKP), ongoing conflicts related to this historical inheritance are, as yet, to be fully resolved. Forged in this crucible, Gülen's teaching offers a critique of a socially exclusive secularism. Thus of the Turkish Republic, Gülen (in Ünal and Williams, 2000: 148) warned that:

> The republic is obligated to protect its citizens' religious faith, feelings, and thoughts. If its leaders do not do so, but rather hold people in contempt because of their religious feelings and thoughts, violate their rights, and smear their good names, in reality they are holding the republic in contempt and violating all that it represents.

At the same time, in contrast to those Muslims who advocate a defensive holding back from the public sphere, Gülen's teaching – as also expressed in the educational, media, and other social institutions created by the movement inspired by it – encourages Muslims actively to engage with the wider (religious and secular) society. Simultaneously, it also critiques those forms of involvement in which religion is politically instrumentalized and instead argues for an engagement that is based on a distinctive Islamic vision characterized by robustness and civility (see also Chapter 11 by Weller in this collection).

Thus, in ways that speak both to ideological 'secularists' and political 'Islamists' Gülen distinguishes between an understanding of the 'secular' that is concerned with the participation of citizens of all religions and none in the public life of a society, and an ideological form of 'secular*ism*' that promotes positivist philosophical positions and their philosophical and political consequences.

'The need to recognize the specificity of religions'

Religious traditions and communities offer important alternative perspectives to the predominant values and power structures of states and societies.

Religions are a reminder of the importance of the things that cannot be seen, touched, smelled, tasted and heard, for a more balanced perspective on those things that can be experienced in these ways (Weller, 2005a: 197).

There is a fundamental sense in which religions cannot allow nation, state or political ideology to claim ultimate value. In the perspective of religious traditions, this usurps the loyalty which should only be offered to the unconditioned. Religions thus offer important institutionalized reminders that the nation and the state are not the only significant realities; that they do not represent the only form of authority; and that the authority they do have is not absolute. As Gülen (in Ünal and Williams, 2000: 149) summarizes it in his own words,

Power's dominance is transitory, while that of truth and justice is eternal. Even if these do not exist today, they will be victorious in the very near future. For this reason, sincere politicians should align themselves and their policies with truth and justice.

This does not mean civil belonging and loyalty is unimportant. But it does mean they must be understood in the context of more ultimate values. In his reflections on European attempts made to build societies in the absence of spiritual values, Gülen (2004e: 194) explains it as follows:

Enlightenment movements that began in the eighteenth century saw human beings as consisting of the mind only. Following that, positivist and materialist movements saw humans as solely material or corporeal entities. As a result, spiritual crises have followed one after another. It is no exaggeration to say that these crises and the absence of spiritual satisfaction were the major factors behind the conflict of interests that enveloped the last two centuries and that reached its apex in the two world wars.

At the same time, Gülen (2004e: 194) recognizes that the historical record of religions has not always been in line with that to which they seek to point, noting: 'Claims are made today that religion is divisive and opens the way for the killing of others.' Simultaneously, Gülen points out that criticism of the role of religions by those who are secular can be informed by as much lack of self-criticism as can be found among the religious. As Gülen (2004e: 196–7) explains it, religion did not lead to what he calls the 'merciless exploitation' that was found in 'the wars and revolutions of the twentieth century that killed hundreds of millions of people and left behind even more homeless, widows, orphans, and wounded'.

Gülen argues that the root of this suffering was to be found in '[s]cientific materialism, a view of life and the world that had severed itself from religion'. He furthermore reflects that, 'Each of us is a body writhing in a network of needs; but this is not all, we also possess a mind that has more subtle and vital needs than the body' and that, 'Moreover, each person is a creature made up of feelings that cannot be satisfied by the mind, and a creature of spirit; it is through the spirit that we acquire our essential human identity' (Gülen, 2004e: 196–7).

'The imperative for religious engagement with the wider community'

> Religious communities and traditions should beware of what can be seductive calls from within their traditions to form 'religious unity fronts' against what is characterised as 'the secular state' and what is perceived as the amorality and fragmentation of modern and post-modern society (Weller, 2005a: 197).

Gülen's approach to the distinctive contribution that religion can offer contrasts with an idealization that (by analogy with the history of communism in Europe) can be blind to the failings of 'really existing Islam'. At the same time, it is also to be distinguished from a modernist political 'Islamism', which could be seen as a kind of 'Trotskyite Islam' that is dedicated to a permanent revolution against not only the 'secular', but also all existing forms of governance developed among 'really existing' Muslims, and which seeks the future establishment of an ideal global Muslim Khalifate.

In societies where there is clear evidence of at least some degree of hostility towards Muslims and Islam (see Allen and Nielsen, 2002), a significant section of the 'really existing' Muslim community with migrant origins can tend towards a defensive cultural and intellectual insularity by reference to the secular. Such Muslim reactions and groups are concerned primarily with trying to preserve Islam – sometimes understood in a way that is all too uncritically elided with specific minority cultural traditions – in what can be perceived as a sea of alien cultural, religious, intellectual and legal influences. In relation to this kind of response among Muslims, Gülen (2004c: 3) notes that, 'Islam has become a way of living, a culture; it is not being followed as a faith.'

Other Muslims have a more ideological project in relation to the secular which is concerned with what, for example, the 'Islamist' group Hizb ut-Tahrir calls the 'carrying' or 'passing on' of 'the concepts' (see Husain, 2007). This they seek to inculcate among Muslims in contradiction to what is seen as a *kafir* secular system. Thus they campaign against this system using the slogan 'democracy is hypocrisy', on the basis that it is *haram*, or forbidden, to participate in something that is rooted in secular principles that are, by them, deemed to be contrary to the fundamental principles of Islam.

With regard to 'Islamism', the contradictions that can emerge are well illustrated in Ed Husain's autobiographical book, *The Islamist: Why I Joined*

Radical Islam in Britain, What I Saw Inside and Why I Left (2007). Of his personal experience, Husain (2007: 148) says, 'My life was consumed by fury, inner confusion, a desire to dominate everything, and my abject failure to be a good Muslim. I had started out on this journey "wanting more Islam" and ended up losing its essence.' By contrast, while teaching that that religions have something distinctive to offer, Gülen stresses that only those who are self-critical can make an effective contribution. Therefore, instead of the spiritually bankrupt 'Islamism' vividly portrayed by Husain, Gülen (in Ünal and Williams, 2000: 9) argues that:

> Those who want to reform the world must first reform themselves. In order to bring others to the path of traveling to a better world, they must purify their inner worlds of hatred, rancor, and jealousy, and adorn their outer worlds with all kinds of virtues.

And because of this, rather than anathematizing the secular world, Gülen's practical actions have been geared towards overcoming the divide between the 'religious' and the 'secular' that can otherwise so easily be exploited by the ideological zealots of both traditions.

What this means can be seen especially in the work of the Journalists and Writers Foundation, founded in 1994, and the seminars held by the so-called Abant Platform, one of the aims of which is 'dialogue and reconciliation in the light of knowledge and experience'. The Platform's first three meetings (1998–2000) – all held in Abant, Turkey – were on the themes, respectively, of 'Islam and Secularism'; 'Religion, State and Society'; and 'Pluralism and Social Reconciliation'. Two meetings have also been held in Europe. One of these was on 'Culture, Identity and Religion in the Process of Turkey's EU Membership', held in Brussels, Belgium, in 2004. The other was on the 'Republic, Multiculturalism and Europe', held in Paris, France, in 2006. The last two of these meetings were also followed up outside Europe, but with a Turkey–France emphasis in the Platform's 2007 meeting in Istanbul, Turkey, on 'Turkey–French Conversations II'.

The principles of the Platform can be seen as embodied in the commitment to it of some of its key participants. Thus, its former chair was Professor Mehmet Aydin who, from 2002–7 was Minister of State for Religious Affairs in the AKP (Justice and Development Party) government. But also, since 2006, Professor Dr Mete Tuncay of Bilgi University has been Academic Co-ordinator. Professor Tuncay refers to himself as 'a person who believes in agnosticism in religion' and as one those 'who accept the notion of living in justice and freedom without referring to metaphysics'. Tuncay points out that, 'In Turkey, there has been a dispute among those who acknowledge religion and those who believed that religion and religious thought was the cause and the sign of ignorance and underdevelopment for at least two hundred years' and so '[w]e have to comprehend and implement secularism in an appropriate manner'. This he defines in the following way: 'The bottom line is to attain a capacity of living together with a common sense of citizenship without changing each other' (http://en.fgulen.com/content/view/1778/18/).

As Gülen (in Ünal and Williams, 2000:167) summarizes it, 'Secularism should not be an obstacle to religious devoutness, nor should devoutness constitute a danger to secularism.'

'The need for a reality check'

> National and political self-understandings that exclude people of other than the majority religious traditions, either by design or by default are, historically speaking, fundamentally distorted. Politically and religiously such self-understandings are dangerous and need to be challenged. (Weller, 2005a: 197).

Gülen's thought has sometimes been seen as related to a strain of Turkish nationalism that posits a close relationship between the Turkish nation, the religion of Islam, and the glorious past of the Ottoman Empire. Thus Bekim Agai (2003: 63) argues that Gülen's notion of a 'Turkish Muslim identity' (*Türkiye Müslümanliği*) was, until the late 1980s, 'to a large extent based on a nationalistic, Islamic chauvinism' which included such ideas as 'Europe wanting to destroy Turkey by Christianizing it' and 'enemies within Turkey wanting to destroy the Islamic identity of the Turks'. But in a 2000 interview with Hakan Yavuz (in Yavuz, 2003a: 45), Gülen acknowledged: 'We all change, don't we? … By visiting the States and many other European countries, I realized the virtues and the role of religion in these societies. Islam flourishes in Europe and America much better than in many Muslim countries.' At the same time Gülen (2004e: 42) is not apologetic about the achievements of Ottoman Muslim civilization. In particular, he highlights the religiously informed realism of the Ottoman rulers in dealing with the cultural and religious diversity of their Empire:

> [O]ur glorious ancestors captured the hearts of people by means of tolerance and became the protectors of the general peace. The longest period of peace in the Balkans and the Middle East, which have always been volatile areas, was realized with the enduring tolerance of our ancestors. From the moment that tolerance and those great representatives left history, this region became void of peace and contentment.

Simultaneously, while noting and praising the close relationship between the Turkish nation, the Ottoman Empire and the religion of Islam, Gülen (in Ünal and Williams, 2000: 166) makes the telling observation that:

> Politicizing religion would be more dangerous for religion than for the regime, for such people want to make politics a means for all their ends.

Religion would grow dark within them, and they would say: 'We are the representatives of religion.' This is a dangerous matter. Religion is the name of the relationship between humanity and God, which everyone can respect.

In the European inheritance, in many Orthodox, Catholic and Protestant forms, very close relationships have existed between religion and the state. As the modern notion of the 'nation state' developed, there also emerged what the Church of England Bishop and critic of established forms of religion, Colin Buchanan (1994), has called religion as a 'nationalised monopoly'. The forms of these 'nationalised monopolies' varied throughout Europe (Robbers, 1996) but in each case they reflect the outcome of struggles for power and influence between different versions of Christianity as well as the espousal by rulers and politicians of these various forms of religion for diverse motives. These 'institutionalised monopolies' of religion have been responsible for centuries of discrimination on the basis of religion, extending from the more 'passive' effects of disadvantage experienced by those with less 'social space' and access to the instruments of state power, through to the active persecution of religious minorities.

The tensions between these new forms of relationship and the old socio-religious order resulted in the savage and bloody religious bigotry of the European Wars of Religion. The moral reaction to the suffering and destruction of these years led to a growing religious indifference, scepticism, and the desire to confine religion to the private sphere. Eventually, this reaction also led to the development of the notion of the secular state. For much of the second half of the twentieth century, in the central and eastern parts of the continent that had communist governments, this reactive historical inheritance was further reinforced by the state-enforced separation of religion and state, informed and under girded by the promotion of state-sponsored atheism, more less vigorously pursued according to specific national contexts (see Beeson, 1974).

In contrast to much of this and also to 'Islamist' attempts to form either nation state-based (for example, Iran under the mullahs or Afghanistan under the Taliban) or more global forms of theocratic systems (of the kind that Hizb ut-Tahrir and others are seeking to establish), Gülen (2004c: 3) argues that, 'In my opinion, an Islamic world does not really exist. There are places where Muslims live. They are more Muslims in some places and fewer in other.'

'The need to recognize the transnational dimensions of religions'

Religious communities and traditions need to pre-empt the dangers involved in becoming proxy sites for imported conflicts involving their co-religionists in other parts of the world. But because they are themselves part of wider global communities of faith, religions have the potential for positively contributing to a better understanding of role of the states and societies of their own countries within a globalising world (Weller, 2005a: 198).

The salience of this thesis is much clearer in the European context after the Madrid and London bombings than it was when it was first articulated in the mid-1990s. In relation to this globalized transnational network of ethnic and religious communities, Gülen (2004e: 230) has observed:

Modern means of communication and transportation have transformed the world into a large, global village. So, those who expect that any radical changes in a country will be determined by that country alone and remain limited to it, are unaware of current realities. This time is a period of interactive relations. Nations and people are more in need of and dependent on each other, which causes closeness in mutual relations.

In an increasingly 'glocalized' world in which all religions are increasingly becoming 'diaspora' religions, the transnational connections of religions can offer channels of insight into varied cultural contexts and/or become conduits through which conflicts are transported from one part of the world to another. This, of course, is not only a by-product of scientific and technological developments, but also a result of the history of colonialism and imperialism – words and concepts which are in many ways out of fashion in the polite Western society of today, but which do describe historical realities of immense significance and import for contemporary life. As Gülen (2004e: 239) has observed in realistically evaluating the current global context:

Islamic societies entered the twentieth century as a world of the oppressed, the wronged, and the colonized; the first half of the century was occupied with wars of liberation and independence, wars that carried over from the nineteenth century. In all these wars, Islam assumed the role of an important factor uniting people and spurring them to action. As these wars were waged against what were seen as invaders, Islam, national independence and liberation came to mean the same thing.

And it is against such a background that, despite the routine denials of, for example, the UK government that terror actions should be discussed in relation to the impact of foreign policy and wars in Afghanistan and Iraq, there can be little doubt that for radicalized young people of Muslim background in Europe such a connection exists. This was clearly expressed by Shehzad Tanweer, one the young 7/7 bombers in London who, in a taped message broadcast on the Aljazeera satellite TV station on the first anniversary of the bombing, concluded with the warning that there would not be peace in Western countries until there was also peace in the Muslim lands that were experiencing violence and injustice.

In the face of such perceptions of the world that are held much more widely among Muslims far beyond the small numbers who carry out acts of terror, the US and UK governments have argued that military intervention in Afghanistan and Iraq and the 'War on Terror' is necessary for ultimately enabling the possibility of peaceful co-existence. In contrast with this, however, Gülen (2004c: 5) argues that: '[T]he only way to prevent this kind of deeds is that Muslims living the countries seeming to be Islamic – and I stated earlier that I do not perceive an Islamic world, there are only countries in which Muslims live – will solve their own problems.'

'The importance of religious inclusivity'

> Religious establishments as well as other traditions and social arrangements that provide particular forms of religion with privileged access to social and political institutions need to be re-evaluated. There is a growing need to imagine and to construct new structural forms for the relationship between religion(s), state(s) and society(ies) that can more adequately express an inclusive social and political self-understanding than those which currently privilege majority religious traditions (Weller, 2005a: 198).

In recent years there has been considerable debate among both Muslims and others around the relationship between Islam and democracy (Esposito and Yilmaz, 2010). Radical secular liberals, traditional 'Islamists' and modern 'Islamists' have all shared agreement that there is a fundamental incompatibility between the two. But secular liberals insist that Muslims have to 'reform' and to 'modernize' Islam in order for Islam and democracy to be compatible in a way that, from the perspective of the 'Islamists', would be tantamount to 'selling-out' authentic Islam.

Traditional 'Islamists' have generally been ready to use electoral politics as a means towards the more ultimate end of using the modern instrument of the state to introduce a polity based on the application of the Shar'iah. Others, such as the Wahabis of Saudi Arabia assert their traditions as the authentic form of Islam, while the dominant clerical groupings among the Shi'a in Iran claim that the revolution that was ushered in by the Ayatollah Khomeini has created a real Islamic state. In contrast with these views, Gülen (in Ünal and Williams, 2000: 151) points out that while 'Supposedly there are Islamic regimes in Iran and Saudi Arabia', in fact 'they are state-determined and limited to sectarian approval'. Gülen's perspective is different and starts from the position that:

> Islam is a religion. It can't be called anything else. When the West defeated the Islamic world in military and technology, salvation was sought in

politicizing Islam or transforming it into a political system ... Islam as a religion is based on enlightening the mind and brightening the heart. Thus faith and worship come first. The fruit of faith and worship is morality.

In contrast with the regimes in majority Muslim countries that adopt the mantle of Islam, many modern 'Islamists' seek to bring about an Islamic polity that is not national in scope, but global and that is understood to be a recreated global Muslim Khalifate. As Husain explains it, in such a vision, existing majority Muslim countries are 'imperial creations and deserved no recognition' (2007: 142), while the duty of Muslims living in any historical state is, 'to prepare the *ummah* for the caliph, to swear allegiance to the future Islamic state' (Husain, 2007: 135).

In such an approach, in words originally coined by the Egyptian Muslim Brotherhood, *al-Islam huwa al-hall*, or 'Islam is the solution'. This is a phrase which has widespread resonance among ordinary Muslims but which, in the thinking and action of 'Islamists' of both the more traditional and more modern kinds, has usually been reinterpreted to refer to the establishment of an Islamic state as the answer to the fragmentation, tensions, conflicts of the contemporary world.

Again, Gülen's vision is one that differs from this. Based not only on political realism but even more so on Islamic scholarship and Qur'anic interpretation, Gülen argues strongly against entertaining the illusion that difference will be left behind. Rather, he maintains that the 'different beliefs, races, customs and traditions will continue to cohabit in this village' and that wanting anything else is 'nothing more than wishing for the impossible'. As a result, he argues that the future peace of the world lies in 'respecting all these differences, considering these differences to be part of our nature and in ensuring that people appreciate these differences'. Without such dialogue Gülen believes that 'it is unavoidable that the world will devour itself in a web of conflicts, disputes, fights, and the bloodiest of wars, thus preparing the way for its own end' (2004e: 249–50).

Therefore, Gülen accepts neither the attempt to recreate an imagined historical unity, nor one to bring this about in the future. At the same time, he does advocate a future-oriented vision of Islam, but of a different kind and with equal relevance to Muslims in both majority and minority contexts. Thus in a 2000 interview Gülen summarized his position as being that, 'Islam does not need the state to survive, but rather needs educated and financially rich communities to flourish. In a way, not the state but rather community is needed under a full democratic system' (in Yavuz, 2003a: 45).

'The imperative of inter-religious dialogue'

Inter-religious dialogue is an imperative for the religious communities and for the states and societies of which they are a part. There is a need to continue the task of developing appropriate inter-faith structures at all levels within states and societies and in appropriate transnational and international structures (Weller, 2005a: 198).

Modern 'Islamists' have little or no time for dialogue – certainly not as a principled activity. As Husain (2007: 142) explains, 'Muslims who advocated inter-faith dialogue and co-existence we condemned as having a "defeated mind".' By contrast, the core of Fethullah Gülen's (in Ünal and Williams, 2000: 241–56) commitment to such dialogue is set out in his article on 'The necessity of interfaith dialogue: a Muslim perspective'. This, it is important to note, was published prior to 9/11. His commitment to dialogue is therefore not reactive to religiously inspired terror. It is also not merely pragmatic in the face of social and political reality. Rather, it is rooted in his vision of Islam and the contemporary world. Perhaps the most comprehensive collection of his thinking about dialogue was developed in his book, *Towards a Global Civilization of Love and Tolerance* which included his reflections for the millennium that set out his conviction about the importance of dialogue in the following way:

> I believe and hope that the world of the new millennium will be a happier, more just and more compassionate place, contrary to the fears of some people. Islam, Christianity and Judaism all come from the same root, have almost the same essentials and are nourished from the same source. Although they have lived as rival religions for centuries, the common points between them and their shared responsibility to build a happy world for all of the creatures of God, make interfaith dialogue among them necessary. This dialogue has now expanded to include the religions of Asia and other areas. The results have been positive. As mentioned above, this dialogue will develop as a necessary process, and the followers of all religion will find ways to become closer and assist each other (Gülen, 2004e: 231).

Conclusion

At this historical juncture in Europe, there is a need for positive resources that can be drawn upon by Muslims, Christians and other members of civil society, to contribute to a transformation in the relationships between religion(s), state and society that will allow peaceful co-existence to become embedded in the present and to flourish for the future.

That the historic relationships in Europe between religion(s), state and society are shot through with ambiguity is clear for all to see. And that the presence of Islam and Muslims presents a challenge to previous models is also clear. Within this ferment, it is important for Muslims to engage with, and to try to understand, the particular histories that gave rise to the current sets of arrangements (see, for example, Weller, 2005a, 2005b, 2006b, 2007a) in different European countries. It is also important for the wider society to try to gain a better and more refined understanding about the inherited traditions of the Islamic world that have a bearing upon contemporary Muslim understandings of these questions – from classical forms of Islam found in Muslim Empires of the past, through the newer perspectives of traditional 'Islamists' and of more modernist 'Islamists', to the kind of ideas expressed by Fethullah Gülen.

In parts of the world where Islam has had particularly strong influence, such as the Middle East, the image of a 'mosaic' of religions and culture rather than a 'melting pot' has historically been invoked as one that offers the most appropriate pattern for structuring these complex and challenging relationships. The classical expression of this was the 'millet system' that developed in the Ottoman Empire and has often been held up by Muslims as an example of the Islamic accommodation of the plurality of beliefs. In reality this was historically far from perfect, with Christians and Jews often being treated as inferior members of the Islamic empires (see Ma'oz, 1978). But in due course reforms granted Christians and Jews official equality within the political community, although those who insisted on their legal rights of emancipation were often bitterly opposed.

It is also the case that, within the Islamic Empires, those of traditions other than the majority Sunnis, such as the Shi'as, Ismailis, 'Alawis and Druzes, have often had an even more difficult position since they were viewed as being unorthodox or, at best, heterodox. They were therefore sometimes seen as more of a threat to the unity of the *ummah* than people of religious traditions and communities distinct from the household of Islam.

Nevertheless, relative to the history of the Holy Roman Empire and the Papacy, or the later Protestant-influenced approach of *cujus regio, ejus religio*, the traditional 'mosaic' approach was relatively successful within the boundaries of the predominantly Muslim societies in which it operated. Hence, for many Muslims in Europe today, it continues to have an appeal as a possible model that, with appropriate modifications, could now be applied for accommodating of a variety of religious beliefs and practices in public life.

Within contemporary Europe there are, in fact, some adaptations of this classic 'treaty-based' approach, such as the *Acuerdo de Cooperacíon del Estado Español con las Comisíon islamica de España* (in English, the *Co-operation Agreement of the Spanish State with the Islamic Commission of Spain*) that, in 1992, was ratified by the Spanish Parliament. This is an agreement between the Spanish state and its Islamic communities (see Antes, 1994: 49–50) and is parallel to other treaties of a similar kind established with both Protestant Christian and Jewish communities. This guarantees a range of rights for Muslims such as civil recognition of religious marriages and the declaration of mosques as inviolable. As Peter Antes (1994: 50) commented, 'The treaty is the most comprehensive recognition of Muslim rights signed in Europe so far.' However, the weakness of the 'treaty' model is that it admits of little movement or change. It is therefore questionable how adequate it is in the context of the globalized population movements and the highly mixed societies of the contemporary world.

There are no easy solutions here. But the following points about the 'secular' within the contemporary Christian, secular and religiously plural landscape of Europe may be helpful to bear in mind. First, that in the totality of a global historical perspective it is perhaps worth remembering that it is the 'secular' that must be considered to be a new experiment in social organization and integration. Second, that the reactive origins of the 'secular' can be found in the European inheritance of the Inquisition, the 'nationalised monopolies of religion' and the impact of the seventeenth-century Wars of Religion, as well as the responses to these found in economic liberalism, revolutionary Republicanism, and the emergence of socialism and Marxism. Third, that the European roots of the 'secular' can make it problematic for societies whose other experience of imports from Europe has been of colonial and imperial takeover. Fourth, that there remains a need to discern how the 'secular' can relate especially to the Muslim civilizational heritage. And finally, that acknowledgement of the need explicitly to consider the 'secular' can result in formerly 'common sense' formulations of problems and issues being turned on their head, making it possible to see them from new and previously unrecognized perspectives.

The Christian theologian Robin Gill once argued that, while reductionist sociological theory sought to explain away religion in terms of social and economic determinates, because religious teaching is itself a social factor, and religious bodies are social actors, it is possible that theological variables can become social determinates (Gill, 1975). Bearing this in mind, it is the argument of this chapter that the thinking of Gülen and the practical initiatives of the community that has been inspired by his teaching offer resources that engage with the secular; are ready for dialogue with Christians; are confident of what Islam can offer: and yet also acknowledge the current reality of the situation for Muslims and Islam in Europe rather than promoting only an idealized vision of the past or the future.

While reflecting in a mature way about the achievements of Islamic and Ottoman civilization they do not idealize past Islamic states; support current theocratic claims of 'really existing Islam'; or support a radical Trotskyite type 'Islamism' that aims to establish a future global Khalifate. Because of this, the 'theological variables' of Gülen's teaching and of the movement inspired by his teaching have the potential to become positively transformative 'social determinates' towards the embedding and development of co-existence in European societies.

For the Muslims of Europe, the transformative resources offered by Gülen's teaching recognize the need for Muslims, by the way in which they articulate and seek to live out Islam, to overcome the association between Islam, Muslims and terror that, post-9/11 and 7/7, has become widespread in European societies. Taken in the round, Gülen's key approaches offer the possibility for Muslims not to live according to a traditional distinction between *dar al-Islam* (the land of Islam, or peace) and *dar al-harb* (the land of war, or conflict) which, in the hands of 'Islamists', have become corrupted politicized concepts that tend to accentuate division and promote conflictual understandings that undermine the possibility for peaceful co-existence. Rather, the vision that is promoted by Gülen is to live according to the newly articulated concept of *dar al-hizmet* (country of service).

Such rethinking is not an example of the kind of calls for superficial 'modernization' of Islam heard so often today among the secular liberal elites of Europe. Rather, as Yilmaz (2003: 208–37) explains it, what Gülen's teaching stimulates is an '*ijtihad* and *tajdid* by conduct'. It is thus the deployment of an appropriate *ijtahad* or interpretation that is directed towards Islamically faithful engagement with the realities of current historical and geographical and socio-political contexts. And such *ijtihad* is both based upon, and directed towards, a *tajdid* or 'renewal' of Islam and of Muslims in which Muslims are once again called to live according to the authentic spirit Islam, whether doing so in majority Muslim societies or as minorities.

For the wider society, the challenge is to appreciate the great depth and breadth of resources that exist in the rich history of Islamic civilization; the particular contribution that the Anatolian heritage can make through the full membership of Turkey in the European Union; and also the spiritual insights and alternative perspectives offered by Islam itself.

For both Muslims and European societies and states, neither phantasmagoric and prejudicial enemy *images*, nor *real threats* to co-existence, can ultimately be overcome by security measures, however important such measures may be for immediate safety. Rather, whatever are the enemy *images* and even the enemy *realities*, Muslims and others have no choice but to live alongside one another in Europe. The only question is about the *way* in which Muslims and others are currently living in European societies will do so in the future. In responding to that last question, resources from Fethullah Gülen and the movement inspired by his teaching offer important and transformative resources for religion in public life, and for the co-existence of people of diverse religions and philosophical beliefs.

2

Modern ideals and Muslim identity: harmony or contradiction? A text linguistic analysis of the Gülen teaching and movement

GÜRKAN ÇELIK AND YUSUF ALAN

Introduction

The world has undergone drastic changes over the last few decades. An increasing number of people struggle to balance different, often opposing, identities in light of increasing social mobility including migration. This inter-cultural contact, both real and virtual, has not necessarily made the world more harmonious. In this postmodern age, in which the grand narratives of religion, culture and political ideologies are melting together in transcultural spaces, an increasing numbers of Muslims across the globe are offering a model for society that is pluralist, participatory and is marked by socio-economic prosperity. The Gülen movement is particularly concerned with the need for peaceful coexistence between Muslims and non-Muslims at a local as well as international level.

This chapter primarily examines how, and to what extent, Gülen's teaching and the movement inspired by him are contributing to the dynamic and peaceful co-existence of Muslims and non-Muslims. First, in order to explore and analyse this concept of co-existence, seven textual linguistic principles (cohesion, coherence, intentionality, acceptability, informativity, situationality and intertextuality) are applied to Gülen's teaching and movement (Çelik, 2010; Alan, 2005; Beaugrande and Dressler, 1981; Demir, 2004; Tas, 2004; and Van Dijk, 1998). Second, these linguistic standards are modelled within the social sciences as a new theoretical and methodological approach for exploring and analysing social movements and phenomena. The originality of this study can be found in its attempt to establish correlations between a movement and a text, including the processes of cognition, production and reproduction of knowledge and its dissemination and transition in the Muslim world, and in multicultural, secular societies and liberal democracies. In this chapter, Fethullah Gülen is, metaphorically, considered as the 'writer'; his teaching and the movement are the 'text'; and the 'readers' are the participants of the transnational Gülen movement and the whole of humanity. This study's practical relevance lies in the fact that it facilitates an understanding of how the Gülen movement has been formed and accomplished, both nationally and internationally.

According to its participants, the movement uses dialogue and education as ways to build peace, by developing social cohesion and mending the social cleavages dividing Muslims and non-Muslims (Çelik, 2011). The movement has invested heavily in the development of dialogue centres, as well as media outlets and schools that form 'islands of peace' (*sulh adacıkları*) on the earth, as Gülen called them. Notable examples of the movement's schools are deliberately located in areas where ethnic and religious conflicts are escalating, places such as Albania, Afghanistan, Bosnia, Kosovo, Macedonia, the Philippines, Banda Ache, Georgia, Darfur, Kenya, Northern Iraq, Southeastern Turkey, Central Asia and the Caucasus (Ateş, Karakaş and Ortaylı, 2005).

Methodological considerations

In our study, we have used linguistic principles to understand the Gülen movement. Our study is an empirical inquiry that investigates the Gülen movement as a social phenomenon within its real-life context. This investigation includes qualitative evidence, relies on multiple sources of evidence and benefits from the prior development of theoretical propositions of text linguistic analysis. It is a paradigmatic case which may be defined as an exemplar or prototype (Stake, 1995; Yin, 2002), and shows that the basic mechanisms, actors, motifs or background practices of the Gülen movement are studied in terms of 'exemplars' or 'paradigms'.

In addition to a systematic review of the relevant writings and speeches on and by Fethullah Gülen, a number of qualitative interviews were used. Further, we conducted internet, ethnographic and participant observation research. The authors attended major cultural and religious events like Ramadan Iftar Dinners in the Netherlands and abroad, gatherings, conversation groups and meetings of participants. We used an ethnographic research approach in order to understand a community by looking at the activities in which the movement's participants engage. This approach also emphasizes language activities as a community-instantiating force. Language practices are a 'microcosm of the communities in which they are used' (Lave and Wenger, 1991: 22).

Nine semi-structured interviews were conducted face-to-face or via electronic mail. Interviewees were selected from a group of Gülen movement experts and some participants who know Gülen personally and are well acquainted also with relevant ideas and initiatives. It is of particular interest to investigate what these respondents think about Gülen's teaching, how they interpret his discourse and actions, and how Gülen inspires and influences individuals in the movement that is associated with him. Interview questions were designed using the seven text linguistic principles. Directed data analysis was used to analyse the data collected from the qualitative interviews and participant observations, while our themes and sub-themes served as an initial framework for content analysis.

By applying seven metaphorical textual linguistic principles (standards of textuality) to Gülen's teaching and to the movement as an empirical case, we examine whether modern ideals (for example, democracy, equality, justice, human rights, and freedom of thought and expression) and Muslim identity can harmonize or are contradictory. In this chapter, text is defined as a communicative occurrence that meets seven standards of textuality (Beaugrande and Dressler, 1981; Van Dijk, 1998). After briefly outlining each standard of textuality, we apply questions regarding the correlation of these standards to Gülen's teaching and to the movement.

Cohesion

Cohesion is the first textual linguistic principle: 'When a text is analysed in terms of cohesion, the continuity has an important role at a grammatical level. The continuity can be supported by sub-items which help to form and give meaning to a text' (Demir, 2004). Cohesion refers to the grammatical unity of a text in which different components exist. Here the importance lies in the surface components, which depend on each other according to grammatical forms and conventions (Tas, 2004).

The question this chapter will answer is: what are the elements of social cohesion in Gülen's teaching and movement in relation to the surface structure? The surface structure in a text is composed of tangible words, clauses and sentences. These explicit factors are interlinked through references, parallelisms or paraphrases. In the context of a social movement, the tacit factors are participants, institutions, publications and activities. These elements in the Gülen movement are loosely connected with each other. There are no organized links among the related institutions. Each institution is independent and can survive even if all the rest become 'extinct'.

Cohesion within this loosely structured network is realized through reading and watching common media sources (e.g. *Zaman*, *Samanyolu* TV, *Mehtap* TV, *Sızıntı* magazine, works published by Gülen); sharing knowledge (correspondence, seminars, conferences); visiting successful organizations (national and international); and applying best practice (such as the science fairs of the educational centres in Turkey and Europe). According to respondents, the social cohesion of the movement is also expressed in social networks of people who are inspired by Gülen's vision and who, supported by business people, make efforts in the fields of education, media and dialogue.

Dialogue, peace, tolerance, compassion and forgiveness are the key elements of social cohesion in Gülen's teaching and in the movement. His inter-cultural and inter-faith dialogue approach calls for social cohesion; a respect for education; and an end to ignorance and dissension. His call for dialogue is bipartite. First, people should learn about the other's cultural identity, religious beliefs and spiritual values; and second, this knowledge should be used to learn more about their own moral and cultural values. One of the most important points in Gülen's texts and speeches is the toleration of differences in order to live together. The significant factors in his teaching are collective consciousness, shared vision, social responsibility, tolerance, respect and spiritual depth (Gülen, 2005d).

Coherence

Coherence is the second textual linguistic principle and refers to the continuity of sense in a text. Cohesion deals with the surface structure whereas coherence refers to the deep structure in terms of experiences or thoughts (Carrell, 1982: 479). In this section, we will give an answer to the following question: what are the elements of social coherence in the Gülen teaching and movement with regard to its deep structure?

The deep structure of a text is related to intangible concepts such as reputation, trust, and social capital. 'Culture and tradition are not limited to the tangible. Styles of life, customs, aesthetic sensibilities, and ideas are intangible, invisible aspects of culture and tradition' (Kurokawa, 1987: 238). The continuity of sense is the foundation of coherence. The Gülen movement has a particular shared vision: to serve humanity for the sake of God. *Hizmet* (service) is a key concept that binds participants and institutions. Gülen frequently uses the concept of *dar al-hizmet* (Yilmaz, 2003: 234). It means, if one's intention is to serve Islam by presenting a good example, then one can stay wherever one desires (Yilmaz, 2003: 234). In the countries where sympathizers reside, they utilize this concept and either establish inter-faith organizations, associations and societies, or are in close contact with 'People of the Book' (Yilmaz, 2003: 235). Without the concept of *Hizmet,* which is utterly represented by the personality of Gülen, the movement might keep its cohesion but would probably lose its coherence. Being the servants of One God, and the *ummah* (community) of one Prophet, reading one Book (the Qur'an) and turning to one *qiblah* (direction of prayer) are the most significant spiritual ties among the participants.

'Anatolian Muslimness' as represented by the Gülen movement can be a coherent resource for processes of dialogue and mutual understanding between Muslims and non-Muslims. For instance, the Turkish Cultural Centre, which is initiated by the Gülen movement and which is located in New York City, organizes Annual Ramadan Friendship Dinners. The dinners are dedicated to mutual understanding, dialogue, and tolerance among peoples of different cultures and faiths. This can be seen as a concrete example of this process occurring.

We observe no contradiction in Gülen's texts, speeches and actions. There is a social coherence between the local and the global. This means that participants in the movement experience no serious dichotomy between the local and the global, and have an holistic perspective. Common values unite people. Thus, common concepts such as compassion, love, tolerance, and dialogue are internalized through conversations and common media, as well a knowledge sharing.

One of the significant elements of social coherence in the movement is consultation, which means reaching consensus among local participants and resolving common issues and possible problems. Gülen (2005d: 43–58) teaches that mutual consultation is the first condition for the success of a decision made on any issue related to society. Before they take one step, they should talk about all the probable consequences. They call their activities 'serving' and they see themselves as servants. Servanthood is a central theme in Gülen's teaching (Gülen, 2007a; 2007b; 2007c). A continuous need for a deep spirituality in the movement is also a remarkable aspect of the social coherence. The participants in the movement believe that everything they have is a gift of God. Their activities are just a prayer of thanks for those gifts. They believe that social development is only possible when individuals are developed in heart and mind. Love is stronger than hate. For this goal they spend their time and money even if they are without sufficient means themselves.

This deep structure could also be understood as the backbone of the Gülen movement, an explanation of the degree of dedication and commitment found in its voluntary activities. The very basic questions facing humanity have yet to be answered and neither philosophy nor any other field of hard science has been truly successful in answering fundamental questions such as: who am I? What is my purpose on this planet? Is there an afterlife where the soul and body will be rewarded or punished for deeds done on earth? Focusing on the surface structure of the Gülen movement only portrays an earth-bound set of explanations, however the real engine of activity in the movement comes from these questions and provides the most satisfying answers. These activities gave birth to a new understanding of education in which spirituality and the spirit of scientific enquiry can be brought together and shows that religion and science are not mutually exclusive and can be complementary.

Intentionality

The writer of a book produces a text to achieve his/her purposes. The writer's intentions are ephemeral, but they leave a mark or trace on the text. When the writer's intentions were active, they helped to shape the text. They were critical factors at the early stages of the text production process when the overall plan and ideational sequence were formulated. At the time of writing, the sender wanted to do something, to achieve certain results which had been projected. This desire to have 'effect', to achieve something with the text, shapes the profile of the text (Neubert and Shreve, 1992: 71). With regard to intentionality, we will focus on the following questions: what is Gülen's intention? What is the ultimate ideal behind Gülen's teaching and movement? How does the movement avoid irrelevant messages and/or actions regarding his intentions and vision?

Gülen's ultimate declared intention is to be accepted, loved and honoured by God. He frequently states that there is no attractive goal beyond this one (cf. Gülen, 2007a; 2007b; 2007c). In order to reach this goal he endeavours to serve humanity, encourages everyone to solve world problems such as ignorance, poverty and disunity, respects the rights of God, the rights of human beings, the rights of creatures, and the rights of his own soul, promotes what is good, right and beautiful, and discourages what is bad, wrong and awful.

According to Gülen, belief necessitates a climate of freedom, peace and stability to flourish and breathe. In justification of this point, Gülen states that the Qur'an, in reference to the *Hudaybiyah Pact* (Treaty) – signed between the Muslims and Meccan polytheists agreeing to a period of peace after the Battle of Trench in 627 CE – considers peace as victory for the believers; a believer must always seek to establish peace and stability. Furthermore, a constructive form of activism requires the dismantling of discord, disunity and division.

The respondents agreed that Gülen is of the firm opinion that the existing social tensions and ideological rifts in Turkey and abroad need to be overcome and this can only be achieved through dialogue, tolerance and understanding. Therefore, the initial objective behind worldwide dialogue initiatives has been to calm public tension, normalize relations and create a sense of mutual trust and tolerance. In addition to the afore-mentioned arguments, the Gülen movement experts and the movement participants whom we interviewed pointed out that his intention and ultimate ideal bears primarily on his faith and concerns basic theological foundations:

> Gülen's ultimate aim is to have the consent of God. His teaching is premised on the belief that there is no aim or reward beyond the approval and love of God. The easiest way to acquire this is obeying the rules explained by the Prophet Muhammad, and imitating the Prophet's way of life.

The intention of the movement is to produce a humane world by educating new generations and contributing to world peace. All the movement's activities are done for the sake of such a peaceful world and an harmonious co-existence. This peace and harmony can be realized through the cultivation of eternal happiness based on attaining the consent and love of God. Every activity or message should be considered as God's will. In his teaching, Gülen (2004e: 52–3) frequently emphasizes this ultimate goal of attaining the approval of God.

The movement's intention has always been questioned and thus questions concerning its mindset (Harrington, 2011) and convictions are responded to in various ways by a range of people include leading journalists, academics, TV personalities, politicians, and Turkish and foreign state authorities (Ateş, Karakaş and Ortaylı, 2005; Ünal and Williams, 2000). In this context, some groups have accused Gülen of attempting to 'take over state control, bring 'darkness' and introduce sharia using force and violence' (see Harrington, 2011). In relation to this, a number of respondents pointed out that Gülen never made choices for 'himself' but has lived and thought how to live for others (altruism). If there is an ultimate goal that limits itself to this world, that would be none other than truly to understand the religion of Islam in its entirety, which enlightens the contested minds and souls of today's Muslims, while engaging with other groups.

In Gülen's intention and vision, common interests are regarded as more important than personal ones. Self-criticism and self-control make the movement's participants proactive. They are not busy with the circle of interest, but are focused on the circle of influence. Moreover, the respondents argue that co-operation and collaboration both in his native Turkey and abroad bring new opportunities for common projects and dialogue. Those activities supporting the national and international interests are accepted in various societies.

Acceptability

Readers of a text receive that text for various purposes. Reading a text means expecting something from it. Consequently, for the matching of readers' expectations with what is meant in the text, there must be a coherent and cohesive set of components forming it. In this sense, the type of the text and readers' intention as well as the producer's intention must build a whole body. This is, to some extent, dependent on such factors as text type, cultural setting and the desirability of goals. For example, if the topic is about sports yet the body of the text focuses on some subject matter other than sports, then it cannot be acceptable for a reader who wants to read something about a branch of sport (Tas, 2004). Using this fourth textual linguistic principle, the following questions will be answered: who are the 'readers' of Gülen's teaching and movement and what do they expect? Do the intentions of Gülen and his movement's situation build a whole body of material? Are there any unacceptable messages and/or actions?

The readers are both the insiders, the participants of the movement from all segments of society, and the whole of humanity. More precisely, the readers of Gülen's teaching are students, academics, businessmen, alumni of universities, the whole society, and the secular segment in Turkey, Africa, Asia, Australia, America and Europe. Naturally, the insiders expect to be inspired and motivated by Gülen's preaching, taking his example as a guide for their life and activities. Academics and other highly educated people are able to reproduce an image reflecting the nature and characteristics of Gülen's preaching and his movement. Academics thus have the important role of bringing his ideas and teaching to the readers of the movement.

Gülen's approach to dialogue and peaceful coexistence has been criticized from several points of view (see Çelik and Valkenberg, 2007). Radical Islamic groups and ultra-nationalistic circles in Turkey have opposed Gülen's dialogue with members of other religions, arguing that this will lead to the assimilation of Muslim identity, and that Muslim distinctiveness must not be compromised, including by not giving precedence to matters and grounds of common concern and belief. Many adherents of the Kemalist state ideology in Turkey also see the Gülen movement as a threat to the secular and laicized nature of the modern Republic of Turkey and its political and societal institutions (Saritoprak and Griffith, 2005: 336; Yilmaz, 2005b: 38–411). On the other hand, those in favour of celebrating pluralism and cultural diversity have also criticized Gülen for placing far too much emphasis in meeting on common ground issues (Çelik, 2010: 124).

Some respondents argue that his common ground approach is not targeted at those in favour of engagement and dialogue but at those who are not. By emphasizing matters of common belief and interest, Gülen is attempting to persuade people that human beings have sufficient commonality to build a peaceful future. On the contrary, some others stress that Gülen's efforts and underlying philosophy regarding dialogue and tolerance may be seen as a political strategy to avoid the convulsive debate on laicism which was introduced by Atatürk in Turkey in order to create a secular political culture (Agai, 2003: 51). However, several respondents see Gülen as a role model who discusses secularism by constantly bringing the importance of dialogue and tolerance to the fore.

Informativity

Informativity is the fifth textual linguistic principle and is concerned with how expected/unexpected or known/unknown the occurrences are in the text. This is a critically important standard for an effective text. It can be understood in relation to first order informativity, second order informativity, and third order informativity. The first requires ordinary trivial knowledge such as articles, prepositions, etc. It is not about the content; therefore, it receives little attention. The second, which is concerned with normal standards, is content-related. The third is a much more attention-demanding occurrence which is caused by discontinuity and discrepancies (Tas, 2004; Neubert and Shreve, 1992: 98). The questions are thus: what makes the Gülen teaching and movement unique? How do they manage the balance between the known/unknown for their 'readers'?

According to some respondents, the uniqueness of the Gülen movement can be seen as twofold. It provides, on one hand, a new perception of spirituality and science, and on the other hand, a very high degree of commitment, loyalty and sincerity with no intentions of seeking worldly flattery. Following the enlightenment, 'religion' has been criticized for not providing satisfying answers for the modern world and dismissing scientific endeavours. The movement seeks the 'best fit' between modernity and spirituality. According to Gülen, the Qur'an is an eternal translation of the great book of the universe: 'The Universe is the universe of Allah, the Qur'an is the speech of Allah and humans are the servants of God. God is the one to establish the interrelation between these three' (1997: 25).

He has stated that a committed Muslim should not only read the book of Islam, but must also 'read' the book of the universe, since the universe is also a verse, an art work of the Creator. Only then can the true harmony between universe and religion emerge. The metaphor used for this is that of a bird needing two wings to fly, hence the universe and spirituality are these two wings. Gülen's teaching is not intended just for some intellectual goals, but for spiritual richness. To respondents, his compassion, sincerity and altruism are seen as being unique. Participants in the movement are generally evaluated as practicing what they preach. With the support of the movement, people soar intellectually, socially and spiritually. The positive developments manifest themselves very quickly. Further, the discourse of 'individual and society' and 'local and global' makes the movement an interesting phenomenon.

The respondents indicate that Gülen gives importance to timing. He does not prioritize the matters that the sympathizers of his movement are not ready for, where the global conjuncture is not suitable. Thus some potential new developments (for example some new projects concerning art and aesthetics) are delayed within the movement and the well-known enterprises of education, the media and dialogue are prioritized. Everyone can get something from a text depending on his own position. The openness of the movement and its readiness for change reduce the difference between the known and the unknown. The movement is not closed. It interacts with different societies and, as a result, develops new discourses according to changing circumstances. In this regard, the participants' attitudes towards modernity and globalization are contingent.

In order to understand the balance between the known and unknown within the Gülen movement, one must seek to understand the concept of 'destiny' and the way it is portrayed within Islam. What is unknown for humankind is an 'absolute knowledge' for the world beyond – for which a sincere patience is required. However, once again, this patience is an 'active patience' as Gülen (2009) describes it. In simple words, the knowledge comes to those who seek it. In his teaching, Gülen also takes known elements (for example, current problems, scientific results) and couples these with a deeper spiritual and religious content, which perhaps was less known (unknown).

Situationality

A text also must be relevant to a situation of occurrence. This is related to the context and the situation of the reader. Here we can conclude that different people in different situations can take away different meanings from the same text. But what is important here is that in order to make sense, the text must present knowledge with a minimum use of words (maximum economy). Otherwise, it may even not be received at all (Tas, 2004). In this section we will answer the following questions related to situationality: what is the context for the Gülen teaching and movement? How they decide what to do for a specific situation?

As a leading faith-inspired movement with an educational and inter-faith agenda, the Gülen movement aims to promote positive inter-group relations and attitudes between the Muslim world and the Western world and to articulate a constructive position on issues such as democracy, multiculturalism, globalization, and inter-cultural dialogue in the context of modernity (Çelik and Valkenberg, 2007; Yilmaz et al., 2007a; Yilmaz et al., 2007b; Hunt and Aslandoğan, 2006). Turkish Muslims in particular, and the global community in general, are the contexts of the movement. The acclimatization of the teaching to the specific cultural environment in each country is realized through sympathizers living in the country concerned. It is a movement in which social cohesion and commitment, an ethical sense of responsibility, a free and critical mentality and a global view of aesthetics and culture are prerequisites. In sum, Islam, the Prophet Muhammad, the contemporary world, and the history of humankind, provide the context for Gülen's teaching.

The sympathizers exchange ideas and benchmark and apply best practices. The decision-making processes are democratic. The opinions of senior participants are carefully considered and taken account of. Respondents maintain that those who have expertise, merit and talent direct the activities. Finally, the context of the Gülen movement does not really show great discrepancies in different parts of the world. This is due to the participants in the movement referring to the same sources and methods of interpretation. This is also due to the fact that Gülen himself minimizes his role within the movement and repeatedly underlines the achievements of the movement and how any future successes to come cannot be limited to a few key figures within the movement.

Intertextuality

Intertextuality concerns the factors which make the utilization of one text dependent upon knowledge of one or more previously encountered texts (Beaugrande and Dressler, 1981: 10). From this perspective we will search for answers to the following questions: what are the relations of the Gülen teaching and movement with other communities? How do they produce knowledge and action regarding the current situation of the 'readers'? What are their references?

The respondents stress that 'positive action' (*müspet hareket*) is a foremost and guiding principle of the movement. Participants naturally eulogize their movement and formulate a positive attitude in all areas, but they do not disrespect or disregard others by claiming that theirs is the only philanthropic and constructive group. They seek to realize social relations and to move away from all attitudes and behaviours that might lead to fighting, conflict or disturbance of peace and order (cf. Ergene, 2008: 18, 47, 185).

In his life, Gülen emphasizes an apolitical, proactive and constructive type of activism. Participants are open to co-operation and collaboration. They dislike criticizing and insulting other groups even if they have different priorities. Gülen considers dialogue necessary in order to increase mutual understanding. To this end, several respondents noted that, in 1994, in Turkey he helped to establish the Journalists and Writers Foundation which organizes activities to promote dialogue and tolerance among all strata of society and the activities of which have been welcomed by people from almost all walks of life.

Other Gülen-inspired organizations include the Abant Platform, the Intercultural Dialogue Platform and the Dialogue Eurasia Platform, where Turkish intellectuals meet with political and religious leaders from various backgrounds. Gülen has visited and received prominent religious leaders, not only from Turkey, but from all over the world. Pope John Paul II at the Vatican and the late John O'Connor, Archbishop of New York are among many leading representatives of world religions with whom Gülen has met to discuss dialogue and take related initiatives. In Turkey, he has meetings with the Vatican's Ambassador, the Patriarchs of the Orthodox and Armenian communities, the Chief Rabbi of the Jewish community and many other leading figures.

These meetings exemplified his sincere commitment to dialogue between people of faith. Separation between 'self' and the 'other' cannot be observed in the Gülen movement. Instead of ignoring them, the movement prefers to accept 'others' in their own position and try to find common denominators. As an interviewee put it:

> The movement, in their relations with other communities, reflects the need for dialogue and common values that all communities should dedicate themselves to protect. The movement produces its knowledge based on teachings of the Prophet and the Qur'an itself. In specific cases, Gülen also refers to the Bible and other religious books as well as historical memories that most of the people are aware of.

Gülen's appreciation of Western philosophies, history, literature and science is evident from the references he draws from these disciplines and the interpretations that he makes of contemporary issues. In an interview with Can (1997: 33–4), Gülen lists Kant, Descartes, Sir James Jeans, Shakespeare, Balzac, Victor Hugo, Tolstoy, Dostoyevsky and Pushkin as some of the Western intellectuals whose works he has read. It can be concluded from his memoirs that, during his military service in 1961, Gülen studied Kant, Rousseau, Voltaire, Schiller and the works of existentialist philosophers such as Camus, Sartre and Marcuse (see Çelik, 2010; Erdoğan, 1997).

Finally, however, the primary references of movement participants are religious. The secondary ones are related to local and universal values (for example, peace, freedom, social progress, equal rights, human dignity). In sum, the Qur'an, the Prophet Muhammad, the universe, science and their consciences are the main references and sources but they very frequently also refer to Gülen's texts, speeches and actions.

Conclusion

In a sociological and a methodological sense this chapter uses the linguistic analysis of a social phenomenon by applying seven metaphorical principles of textuality to Gülen's teaching and the movement. This metaphorical approach to exploring and analysing a movement or an activity provides useful pointers and encourages 'outside-the-box' thinking. Indeed, the theoretical perspective and methodological approach of this chapter can be used to examine other social movements emerging in other countries.

The application of the seven textual linguistic principles (cohesion, coherence, intentionality, acceptability, informativity, situationality and intertextuality) to Gülen's teaching and the movement is helpful in exploring and describing its impacts and implementations in different contexts. Our analysis underscores Kuru's (2005) observation that the Gülen movement demonstrates the contextual change and diversity in the Muslim world as it relates to modernity, liberalism and democracy. The Gülen movement represents a new expression of Islam, and instigates the art of living together with difference in modern democracies.

Despite the suspicions with which the movement has met since its inception in the 1960s, its participants still have constructive attitudes and activities. The participants in the movement see modern ideals and Muslim identity as compatible and complementary instead of contradictory. Thus, the Gülen movement is illustrative of the fact that a majority of the Muslim population in the world does not perceive a contradiction between modern ideals and their attachment to Muslim identity. The sociological result of this dialectic is a global-Islamic synthesis, a new identity uniting a Muslim mentality with modernity into one subject position, a merging of Islamic values and Western ideals. The concepts of dialogue, love, forgiveness and tolerance are important values in Gülen's teaching and are key to the movement's praxis.

Finally, we suggest that the Gülen movement could be better understood by further work that analyses both the attitudes of its supporters and adversaries, especially the psychological and ideological mechanisms behind structures underlying their arguments. Why do they support the Gülen movement or oppose it? Such a study from two diametrically opposite points of view can provide useful information – not only about the movement's path and pattern, but it will also help us to understand its contributions to, and critiques of, approaches to harmony or conflict.

Acknowledgement

We thank Dr Kate Kirk for her valuable comments and her customary keen editorial insights on earlier drafts of this work.

3

Turkish Muslims and Islamic Turkey: perspectives for a new European Islamic identity?

SHANTHIKUMAR HETTIARACHCHI

Introduction

It is a fact that societies have evolved in human history both in positive and negative ways. There are significant references for the development of society when humans first found fire, then the wheel and most recently the silicon or microchip with which humanity has revolutionized its thought and behaviour, progress and creativity. However, the negative historical data bring back the horrors of just the last century from the Holocaust to the Balkan conflict and the Rwandan genocides, to the ongoing epicentres of conflict in the Middle East, Kashmir, Afghanistan, Iraq (and, until recently, Sri Lanka) to name just a few. These polarities of creativity and dishonour glued to violence continue to mystify communities, demanding new routes for forming social and community practice for adapting to the rapidly changing world. Fethullah Gülen's contribution to the formation of community and society based on dialogue and tolerance, self-sacrifice and altruism, avoidance of political and ideological conflict, taking action in a positive and harmonious way and taking responsibility has had a formidable influence on individuals and groups (Hermansen, 2007).

Over the past three decades Fethullah Gülen has evoked a thought-changing movement both within Turkey and several other parts of the world and has potential to redefine what it means rationally to be Islamic and European at the same time. The Gülen movement both in Turkey and in the diaspora has Islamic, patriotic, liberal and modern characteristics. Its ability to reconcile traditional Islamic values with modern life and science has won a large, receptive audience. The group has even brought together divergent ideas and people, including the poor and the rich, the educated and the illiterate, Turks and Kurds, as well as Muslims and non-Muslims. The movement could thus be a model for the future of Islamic political and social activism and has created an archetypal canopy where ideas, thoughts devoid of political ideology, cultural roots, traditions and varying expressions of Islam without historical baggage, can seek harmony in a practical way for all who wish to subscribe to a way of life that is both deeply Qur'anic and positively modern.

The current predominant European Islamic voice is arguably South Asian with the strong British Muslim presence, even though other European Muslim voices have been present within the Union. However, the South Asian Muslim voice would be positively challenged in its encounter with a different cultural manifestation of Islam with Turkish roots as Turkey plans to enter the European Union even though there is political resistance within the member states. This encounter is fundamental to the life of twenty-first century Europe in its expansion both as a demographic unit and an economic power even though there are stark cultural, political, ethnic and epistemological differences embedded within it.

Europe of yesterday looking to the future

Today's Europe is associated with a geographical area, stretching from the Atlantic Ocean in the West to the Ural Mountains in the East, to the Black sea, the Hellespont and the Aegean sea in the South east and from the Arctic Ocean in the North to the Mediterranean Sea in the South. Europe's Eastern borders continue to 'move'. For many centuries the River Don remained the border, until in the eighteenth century when it was pushed back to the Ural mountains. However, there is no specific reason why a certain border may remain as the defining factor for the East-West geopolitical demarcation. In his classic book, *Orientalism*, Edward Said (1995) contentiously moved from an East–West debate to an Orient–Occident polarity, each defining itself with its socio-political and religio-cultural dynamics. He observed that:

[M]en make their own history, that what they can know is what they have made, and extend it to geography: as both geographical and cultural entities – to say nothing of historical entities – such locales, regions, geographical sectors as 'Orient and Occident' are man-made. Therefore as much as the 'West' itself, the 'Orient' is an idea that has a history and a tradition of thought, imagery and vocabulary that have given it a reality and presence in and for the West. The two geographical entities thus support and to an extent reflect each other (Said, 1995: 4–5).

Turkey is yet another classic case as the main part of Turkey lies to the east of the Aegean sea, and so geographically belongs to Asia (in Western history it was often known as 'Asia Minor'). Its Western part, across the sea and around the city of Istanbul, is considered European and represents the remnant of the former Ottoman empire that for several centuries encompassed a large part of South East Europe. Karel Blei (2002: 4) says: '[T]he words Europe and Asia probably derive from Semitic or Phoenician words: Europe from *ereb* (sunset, evening) Asia from *acu* (sunrise or morning). Asia and Europe belong together, as morning and evening, as Orient and Occident.'

European plurality and hybridity

From its very genesis, Europe has been a land mass of highly complex geo-political, religio-cultural, socio-economic and ethno-tribal composites. Tribes and nations that settled in Europe brought with them their own cultures, languages and religions. Europe today is a conglomeration of ever-changing patterns and behaviours of people, customs and rituals. It is a nation of nations, culture of cultures that over centuries has developed not so much as a geographical entity but as a cultural entity characterized by values it has formed itself to uphold. If there is an overarching recognizable element that makes this mosaic tenable over several centuries, then arguably the Greco–Roman culture is described as the basic determinant of European civilization, with Christianity being the medium through which this Greco–Roman culture was preserved and sustained.

It could be argued that Europe came into being out of Athens, Rome and Jerusalem. Athens representing arts, science and Greek culture, and other forms of life: Rome representing the state, law and justice systems; and Jerusalem, the Jewish and Christian religious traditions. Christianity became a synergy of the faith of historical Israel with the spirit of Greece mingled with Roman military endeavours and its zest for expansion. The new Europe will now need to respond to the growing and formidable Islamic presence within Europe side by side with the Jewish and Christian paradigm and its centuries old influence on every aspect of life in Europe from art to politics and economics to social welfare.

Europe's difference is fundamental to its very being. It has a capacity for the hybridization of its peoples, cultures, tribes, languages, customs and rituals which is natural to its identity as a land mass filled or invested with skills and innovative behaviours. It is only as this unique civilizational reconstruction that Europe can be understood and grasped in all its divergent facets. It is sociologically accepted (Bhabha, 1994; Young, 1995) that difference is a direct result of hybridity, which is a natural process of societal growth and expansion. Intermixing of groups is still a taboo in certain societies, while unconsciously those very societies have undergone serious processes of hybridization, despite socio-cultural and even political pressures that seek to restrict this.

This process, too, is natural to Europe because its previous sociopolitical engineering projects that sought to establish purity of ethnicity and nationhood have historically failed. Europe's ethnic, national or tribal claims for a sense of chosen-ness or purity may be found in individual nation states or in national debates across the borders. However, such claims are becoming more redundant as present priorities have been shifted from political nationalism, nuances of statehood or national pride to a new sense of being European. This sense of direction has been enhanced by the processes of globalization and the unprecedented migration patterns that Europe has been experiencing since the primary migrations in the aftermath of the Second World War.

Turkey and modernity

Istanbul is a growing European city. The secular influence of a metropolitan city is evident even though there are hundreds of minarets to be sighted from a boat ride in the Bosphorus as if to signify that there is the possibility within Islam to open up a new critical chapter to modernity and its historical passion for science and advancement. It seems that difference and hybridity is conspicuous not just in Istanbul, but also in other smaller medium-size cities like Konya, Izmir, Kayseri and Ephesus in Cappadocia. Turkey and its 'Muslim population' symbolize an acute evidence of hybridity from Istanbul to Ephesus, with a history of vibrant Christian presence and its folk expression and the expression of Islam in Konya with the 'veneration' of the tomb of Mevlana Rumi to the similar manifestation through the monumental statue of Rumi in the heart of Izmir. Both Konya and Izmir, which are now Muslim places of pilgrimage, depict a symbiosis of Islam throbbing to give its new expression in a modern secular state, even though there are conspicuous democratic deficits in governance and structures which include the military institutions of the present political architecture of Turkey.

This internal hybridization is what 'Turkish Muslims' are expressing, and my reading of Turkey particularly in the latter year of the last decade, is that it is Islamic, but in a Turkish idiom. These are clear signs of a people in a hybridized disposition despite what their religious and political norms require them to become. This hybridity is a deeply sociological factor and it is a natural part of how a people act and react after years of submission to authority, hegemony and lack of contact with other communities. Even though Turkey has a majority Muslim population that is seemingly homogenous, its behaviour and customs indicate that it is no exception to the changing and challenging forms of life which it either adopts by choice or has to embrace, with or without consent, since the defining criteria are beyond its control.

In his extensive writing Gülen does not name this process as hybridization but he passionately identifies hybridity and difference in his own unique way: '[I]t is a condition for the development of nations that the individuals of which they consist should have the same aim. It is not possible for a community, although it shows activity, to develop and make progress while some of its members say "black" and others say "white" for the same thing' (Gulen, 1996: 44). The future of Europe alongside South Asian Muslims, 'Turkish Muslims' and other Muslims could create such a symbolic and actual difference, which Gülen reiterates can positively contribute to the well-being of Islam itself and in its theological and fundamental ethico-spiritual openness to science and technology, philosophy and politics, culture and art, family and society. Invariably, then it would be possible for the Muslims of new Europe conspicuously to counteract the un-Islamic portrayal of Islam and its misrepresentation through 'martyrdom-paradise' concepts by means of suicide-terror tactics. It is a challenge for the Muslims themselves as an engaged faith community that needs to take a lead in rectifying its present image as painted by the media.

South Asian Islam in Europe:
a 'home away from home'

Considering the theological expositions that undergird the notion of *ummah*, in many ways it can seem awkward to associate Islam and its heritage with ethno-nationality or any other contemporary divisions. However, it has also become impossible to define Islam or its traditional heritage without modern socio-cultural tools and mechanisms for fully understanding it and its progressive developments. If one component is undermined the other looses its meaning and integrity. Hence, this section purposefully deploys an analysis of the regionalism of Islam even though it takes on board the broader understanding of the theological sense of *ummah*

It is in this sense that South Asian Islam is distinctly significant to Europe more specifically since the Second World War. Between the fall of the Ottoman Empire and the influx of French-speaking North African and the South Asian Muslims into the heart of Europe, there was a conspicuous absence of Islamic presence and activism in Europe, as if the continuing Muslim population in Europe had surrendered to the socio-political and religio-cultural voices then spearheading the European priorities in the context of the global changes. What I wish to argue here is the thesis of the internal tussle between the lofty concept of *ummah* that is integral to the theological axioms of *tawhid* and *risalah* and the diversity of the regionalism of Islamic ways of life. This regionalism is further manifested within the South Asian Muslim community which is predominantly settled in the United Kingdom which is also part of the Union.

The South Asian manifestation of Islam in Europe is distinct for several reasons. First is its originally immigrant nature and associated adaptation and settlement process. Second is its expressive (but at times over-assertive) regionalism with historical and cultural nuances. Third is the practice of Islam and its way of life with South Asian roots in the heart of a world of difference in Europe. Fourth, it is clear that some Muslim communities have migrated from being a majority and are now having to live both as an ethnic and a religious minority. South Asian Muslims were, or perhaps still are, at a crossroads with a view to carving out a 'home away from home'. This is a collective psychosocial trauma which requires a healing process and an acculturation mechanism at least for the first generation of immigrants becoming nostalgic about the 'home' they left and the struggle they have gone through to carve out 'a home' here in Europe.

These are not simple challenges for any community to undergo, socially, culturally and religiously. It is in this context that I argue that there is a strong possibility of a critical but enriching mutually beneficial encounter between the South Asian idiom of Islam and the Turkish manifestation of Islam as Turkey begins to interact more with the EU, in a movement away from 'a self-imposed isolation' from the geopolitical and religio-cultural activities of the world to the West of Istanbul.

South Asian Muslims have now to recognize that the nearly seventy million Muslim population, which is concentrated in one single country will invariably impact upon the better known Islamic way of life in Western Europe since Second World War. The 'Islamic Turkey' has a new responsibility to encounter this sister Muslim community or communities that have settled in to embrace the life of Western Europe for more than a half century. There would hardly be any no-go areas for these two culturally different, regionally distinct Muslim populations (Turkish and South Asian) if they were all to be part of the EU. It is possible that the celebrated mystical strand of the Sufi tradition within Islam could be one great bridge builder between these two worlds of Islam as both Turks and South Asians have had access to the Sufi tradition and their revered spiritual masters across all schools of thought within Islam.

Rediscovering and redeeming Islam in Europe

The Islamic presence in Europe was a constant historical factor since 717 CE, when the Arab armies under the command of Tariq ibn Ziyad crossed the Mediterranean and invaded Europe. Many fierce battles and conflicts have been a regular feature to assert living space and political claims. However, Islam's 'golden age', on a par with Spanish Jewry and its intellectual and spiritual growth, marks religious freedom and co-existence within the continent. However, some argue that an appropriate explanation might be that it was, rather, a period of a mixture of co-existence and rivalry between religious groups. There is a perceived fear and designated danger associated with Islam and Muslims since 9/11 being in enmity with 'the West'. Historical rivalries between and among the Abrahamic traditions and the vilification of both the Prophet of Islam and the religion's Bedouin origins have been rejuvenated in political rhetoric and slander which have supported the gross generalising of the Huntington thesis of the clash of civilizations (Huntington, 1996) igniting bitter memories of past wars and untold sufferings inflicted on one another.

Some sections of the European Muslim community are torn apart culturally in a situation of '*in-between-ness*'. It is a politico-cultural uncertainty either to belong in Europe or to continue to live like an alien, an immigrant with a 'myth of return' but without any idea where to return. It is my view that both South Asian Muslims and the Turkish Muslims live in this *politico-cultural uncertainty*. South Asian Muslims are perplexed about the complexity of the integration processes in the adopted land without compromising their core beliefs and attached values, even though individual Muslims may have uncritically embraced certain aspects of European life and even values. Turkish Muslims are torn between their historical Islam and the demands of the politically assertive secular state and the promotion of its values. These two issues are at the heart of the European Muslims struggle to live and express themselves both as Europeans and Muslims. It is in this context that Islam in Europe requires a rediscovery of its historical credentials as a religious faith glued to a system of law, governance and social care. It is Muslims who need to engage alongside their allies in this soul-searching self-discovery about Islamic selfhood in Europe.

Gülen's thought is key to this self-discovery as he does not portray Islam as a political project to be implemented. For him, Islam is a repository of discourses and encounters that are spiritually charged and ethically motivating to build, strengthen and fortify a society with justice and compassion. As set out in interview with Fethullah Gülen (2005a), his practical proposition is distinct and redeems Islam and Muslims from an historically inbuilt sense of undue protectionism, as a burden and a feeling of guilt bestowed on them by their previous generations.

The future of Europe is a complex reality. Islam and its current manifestations challenge all institutions to seek avenues to understand it as Europe's second most influential faith, alive and active in Europe albeit in very diverse ways. Two positions seem to apply. While Islam, from its inception, has been well rooted in an inspirational and formative way, there are some operational waves led by groups of Muslims within contemporary history, which seem to have (mis)used Islam in un-Islamic ways, bringing destruction, suspicion, political rivalry and shame on Islam through the use of terror tactics.

This challenge from within Islam must be critically appraised not only as a sloganized political assault on the West as the sole *enemy* of Islam, but also in relation to how such acts have evoked a deconstruction of Islam, Islamic theology, practice and invoked interpretations of Islam to suit politically motivated groups in creating an ideology to drive their objectives. Although there has been mutual dislike and misunderstanding and years of intellectual neglect of Islam and its ethos by academia, the Muslim communities in Europe who have adopted it as their home now must rediscover ways and means to portray Islam's way of life as a positive contribution to the life and progress of Europe. The most recent and deeply scandalous wave of Islam which is misrepresented through religiously motivated acts of terror must be redeemed. The Europe of tomorrow can no longer be a battlefield, as it is now among the world's most diverse societies with extensive human resourcefulness, competence, heritage and wealth that can be shared with the rest of the world.

Gülen's faith-based movement contains vital ethico-social parameters that can set out a new discourse between Islam and globalizing communities in which science and technology are integral to its meaning and survival and where Muslims are invited play their part as citizens. Gülen offers tolerance positively towards secularists and non-believers in Turkey. This position is not just about promoting multi-culturalism but is part of a continuous campaign for an inclusive society as distinct from a baseless religious rivalry leading to conflict and instability which is, for him, the root cause of institutional decay and the failed states of the present day. Gülen revisits the fundamentals of Islam and offers an ethical basis for governance and justice, economics and trade, international relations and political maturity. These socio-anthropological ingredients are fundamental to an integrated functionality of a society.

Is there anything rediscovered in Turkish Muslims or Islamic Turkey with this duality of the secular state and its throbbing religiosity beneath the surface? If Islam is to be *rediscovered* and *redeemed* in Europe then the Turkish model through the thought processes of Gülen and the faith-based movement inspired by his teaching needs to be taken seriously as a fine example of a way forward to the debate on European Islamic identity.

Self-search: a path to the rediscovery of identity

Rediscovering self-identity is the roadmap for a progressive path of understanding, in which the *self* is a unique participant and not an absolute icon of power, prestige and hegemony. The construction of the *other* is healthy as long as the *other* remains a criterion for the *self* to be reminded that the *self* has meaning and usefulness in interaction with the active existence of the *other*. The construction of the prominence of the *self* has been a key to the dominance of the *self* over the *other*, creating a 'purity theory', absolutizing truth claims, exclusive ethnic roots and territoriality.

Europe is no exception to these dynamics, even within liberal democratic dispensations. The notion of the *self* and the *other* is fundamental to the rediscovery of both European Islam and Europe itself as a political unit, without which Europe will remain within a 'fortress Europe' mindset. In order to portray itself as a politically and economically productive element, the rediscovery of self is therefore significant for Islam especially within the context of current global events. Diverse European institutions and European Islam can mutually benefit from each other's strengths and could together even challenge unfair trade-politics and the unchecked agendas of financial institutions with their profit-based designs for world development and global governance. Such would be the calibre of cooperation and mutuality that new European communities would be able to muster for a Europe with a soul, wiser and more generous.

Islam as a faith tradition must also be redeemed from its self-imposed and apathetic sense of aloofness, which it sometimes portrays without a healthy critique from modernity in this age of globalization. It also needs to shun disparaging levels of a victim syndrome. There are three apparent issues for European Muslims. First, how best Muslims may disassociate themselves from the gross misrepresentation of Islam, which is a religion of peace although it is often being used to redress grievances through recourse to violent means. Second, how best the South Asian, North African and Arab Muslims in Europe may be able to relate to their fellow Turkish Muslims, living in a secular state and who have links to the Western apparatus of governance and style of living. Third, it is a fact that Muslims of South Asia who have now settled in Europe (whether they have migrated from India, Pakistan, Bangladesh, East and North Africa or the Arab world) have come from societies where they have been either a majority or a minority. And it is important to understand that their pre-migration majority-minority social consciousness has largely contributed to the adaptation mechanisms of these early immigrants, and determined the processes of their behaviour and other cultural patterns distinct to each group.

An example would be the Kashmiri-Pakistanis who were the majority and whose population is largely concentrated in northern cities in the UK with another concentrated population in Luton (Bedfordshire), UK. They hail from the two districts of Mirpur and Kotly (the Pakistani part of Kashmir, also designated by some as *Azad* or 'free' Kashmir). They migrated as the dominant group and suddenly found themselves as a minority which required a massive psychosocial adjustment apart from being socially and culturally relocated even though by choice. By contrast, the East African Indians who migrated during and after the Idi Amin regime already lived and had adjusted as a minority within their African situation. Their re-migration to different parts of Europe, more particularly to the UK, seems to have undertaken their adaptation process with less baggage of a majority-minority consciousness.

Ihsan Yilmaz (2005: 385) observes that, 'Turkey is one of the very first Muslim countries that encountered the modern West and attempted to respond to the challenges posed by the Western power and civilisation.' Was or was it not the Republicans that paved the way to understand he cultural Muslims of Turkish society? If they did attempt it, then would someone argue that Islam was undermined or whether Islam rediscovered a 'Turkish flavour'? A good example is that Qur'an was translated into vernacular Turkish instead of its use in traditional Arabic. Was Turkey then an exception as an Islamic model? It is obvious that a secularization process might have been accelerated by staunch Republicanism for a state to function in its vision for governance, distancing itself from both Islam and Sharia in their ultra-interpretation and forms of understanding. Until very recently, when it was challenged by the Gülen movement's international dialogue activities, 'official Islam' in Turkey was cold and numbed to dialogue (for detail see Yilmaz: 2005). At the same time, from Istanbul to Konya, Ephesus, Izmir and Kayseri, there is a mixture of intense folk religious practices, perhaps institutionalized in some cohesive way via Sufi expression. Or, might it be the modern Turkish state with its secular project that is capable of changing the way in which Muslims engage with Islam? Or is it the collective religiosity of the masses that might be the key to humanizing the secular state, enabling it to hear the different voices of the collective?

Religiosity and transition

Islam in Europe is the second largest faith tradition, and the proposal that it should rediscover Islam may sound as if it has lost its identity as a faith in Europe. Currently it appears to be embroiled in a state of flux, transition and change. This creates an obvious opportunity to seek wisdom and spiritual maturity. It is in this sense that Islam as a European institution now needs to plunge into a fuller engagement through not being so competitive and reactive, but rather constructively to contribute to the expanding socio-political, religio-cultural, economic and business life of Europe. Theological

Islam contains sufficient material within itself not only to comment on these strata of life but also generously and critically to share its value-based principles not just for Muslims but for the well-being of all.

Even though Europe claims that its foundations are built on Jewish–Christian patterns of thinking, in practice it is currently, by and large, a post-Christian society. Stuart Murray describes it as a 'culture that emerges as the Christian faith loses coherence within a society that has been definitively shaped by the Christian story and as the institutions that have been developed to express Christian convictions decline in influence' (Murray, 2004: 20). It also struggles to carve out its own 'European-ness' and identity with a rapid expansion of the membership of the EU and its ever-growing radical migratory patterns that the current European governments have mismanaged most of the time both at policy level and in practical terms. In this sense, it is not only the Muslims or other minorities that struggle to locate their identity amidst the majority but also the majority is at a crossroads in terms of its self-definition.

A time of transition is a time of threat and fear, but also an opportune time for positive change and hope. History almost demands European Muslims to seize the moment as every nation state, culture, nationality, ethnic group and religious community is at a critical juncture, each repositioning themselves within the context of a rapidly changing society. Defining a group identity and perhaps a group's very survival is now determined by the existence and the productivity of the *other*. *Self* can define itself and have meaning in relation to the *other*. Hence the majority requires a minority and vice versa, and Muslims in Europe will rediscover their potential in relation to the potentialities that they discover face to face in their fellow European religious and ethnic communities.

Gülen's social formula

Gülen's thought and perspectives on *istighrag* (immersion), which means 'absorption, diving into, becoming deeply involved in, denotes transportation by joy, oblivion of the world, the cleansing of the heart of worldly worries' (Gülen, 2006d), are that one is filled with wonder, and one travels between love and witnessing truth that finally rests in the divine command. Gülen sums up his view of immersion with *hurriya* (freedom) as being freed from selfishness and self-conceit. To follow the evil-commanding self who always pursues evils is to 'die before you die'. The real *falah* (enshrining success) of an individual or of collective pursuits is embedded in goodness and virtue (Gülen, 2006d). Gülen suggests a new social behaviour that can be found in the fundamentals of Islam, not exclusively for Muslims, but for all who pursue honourable social interaction.

In a geo-political sense, South Asian Muslims may feel that they could be dominated by Turkish Muslims. However, this need not be a fear, but could well be a source of a revival of new spirituality in the East–West encounter in the West. Gülen attempts to instil into this encounter a character-formation through processes of education at all levels of society. In this he is articulating an Islam that it is neither of the Ottomans nor the Moguls and their expression of Islam that Europe needs today. He appeals to his hearers and readers to revisit the roots of virtues and to adopt them to revitalize their relationships within their own community and with other communities on the basis that, if brought together, then religious space and its practice, intellectual acumen, social conscience, economic justice and moral principles could help to evolve a society that can honour and respect human dignity, mutuality and freedom. What he wishes for his fellow countrymen and women both in Turkey and in the European diaspora is to take up the challenge of creating a *dar al-hizmet* (abode of service to others).

South Asian Islam has taken its roots now in the European soil and the time is right to feel 'at ease and homely'. Its encounter with the Turkish Anatolian form of Islam would be of historical significance in Europe and sociologically fascinating for understanding how one religious faith can have multiple expressions within a single geo-political context.

Gülen's 'bridge-building' approach to the 'big and small' in Europe

The dynamics between 'big and small nation states' both in the post-Second World War period and during the Cold War era caused a real East–West divide with public support, alliance and allegiance in each political camp. Hence, it was rightly called the Cold War, potentially at war but never fighting, even though during almost half a century the political gurus were absolutely sure that such was imminent. However, Turkey, with its enigmatic geopolitical circumstances, has remained at least symbolically transcontinental because of its *Ottoman residue*, developing strong links with the West, while fostering relations with the East more specifically via its special affinity with the central Asian people.

Since its embrace of republicanism in 1923, Turkey has been involved in both creating and sustaining many regional and international organizations. It is a founding member of the United Nations, the Organization of the Islamic Conference, the Organisation for Economic Co-operation and Development and the Organization for Security and Co-operation in Europe, a member state of the Council of Europe since 1949, and of NATO since 1952. Since 2005, Turkey has been in accession negotiations with the EU, having been an associate member since 1963. Turkey is also a member of the G20, which brings together the 20 largest economies of the world, to name but a few. These European and international associations and Turkey's internal radicalism in the post-Ottoman political restructuring and Istanbul-elitism have all shaped a secular society achievable and workable in Turkey.

It is with this crucial entry into a world of debate, controversy, opportunity, and discourse on religion, governance and modernity that Fethullah Gülen innovatively introduces views, ideas and praxis. Gülen speaks intensely of Islamic praxis being fundamentally Qur'anic but freshly compatible beyond the medieval interpretation of certain fundamentals of Islam. Gülen unequivocally and devoutly respects and honours the primordial religiosity expressed in the Qur'an and the 'Allah-experience' unique to the Prophet of Islam. Gülen's practical proposition is that he roots his discourse within the historical tradition of Islam but introduces a fresh way to understand Islam and to adapt it to the contemporary issues of political, scientific, cultural and social paradigms which he thinks are part of the praxis of Islam. For him Islam without praxis is empty and it must speak to modern men and women as relevantly as during the time of the Prophet. It is in this sense that Gülenian thought offers a bridge-building approach to the difficult issues that Islam is facing under the current and more vociferous manifestations of Islam in the world arena.

The highly exceptional character of the movement inspired by Fethullah Gülen lies in its attempt to revitalize traditional values as part of modernizing efforts such as the Turkish state's official modernization programme. Thus far, it has had some success as it attempts to harmonize and integrate the historically diverse lands of Turkey in their socio-political affinity with central Asian people, and to reconcile hundreds of years of tradition with the demands of modernity, which is not an easy task. In brief, much as the Ottomans attempted to Islamicize Turkish nationalism and to re-create a legitimate link between the state and religion, Gülen seeks to construct a new way to understand Islam but through his own Turkish-style. At the same time, Gülen emphasizes democracy and tolerance and encourages links with the Turkic republics, opening them to modernity and its challenges. It is his proposition for people to recognize that religious faith can create change and can be comfortable in a decent engagement with politics and economics, culture and ethnicity. He reverses revolutionary methods to an evolutionary praxis evoking it from within his own known world of Islam.

Gülen aspires for his nation and people to look towards both the East and the West – to the East for Islam and its spiritual roots, civilization, and moral code of conduct; while geopolitically to the West, but informed by Islam's own praxis of inquiry; its science and the Qur'anic sense of justice. Gülen's socio-spiritual project is simple, not even as complex as that of Gandhi. Gandhi's socio-political responsibility was enormous, in that it was critical to find a solution on religio-political lines to the political mess that was being created purely on religious grounds, as his project was a united India – an abortive dream. There were no victors in the freedom project of

India. However, all can be participants in a victory if the European dream can be achieved through wise political decisions and cross-fertilization of ideas and views – not for a fortress-Europe but a Europe with porous borders, to cultivate critical inquiry and freedoms for all. It is a dream worth dreaming alongside Gülen.

The movement inspired by Fethullah Gülen seems to have no intention of evolving into a political party or seeking political power, even though his critics have suspected him of such community-based agitation within Turkey. The militarist elite continues to be suspicious of the Gülen movement, as the Ankara establishment abhors any potential religio-cultural or socio-political threat to its survival. On the contrary, Gülen continues a long-standing and profound personal affinity with the Sufi tradition of seeking to address the spiritual needs of people to build a work ethic, social and moral behaviour and to educate the masses, and has in fact provided some stability to the nation in times of turmoil.

Like many previous Sufi figures, including the unique thirteenth-century mystic Jalal ad-Din ar-Rumi (for whom Gülen has admiration and devotion), Gülen has influenced many Turks and has become a considerable spiritual force in differentiation from totalitarianism and the politicization of Islam. The Sufi expression of Islam has brought understanding and value as found in the Qur'an to pluralism and diversity in contemporary society. Gülen helps Muslim Turkey to express its Turkish Islam in an inimitable way, so that Turkish Islam can be a catalyst in devising a new understanding of a European Islam beyond the traditional definitions of being Arabic, North African or South Asian. It is the right time that these three expressions of Islam understand that there is more to the cultural expression of Islam than that which has been familiar to them.

Gülen's fresh approach opens up this intra-Islamic interaction and encounter between different expressions of Islam that have found their roots in Europe. It is appropriate that Turkish Islam – with its nation-state's approach to the secular paradigm and popular allegiance to Islam – becomes a learning arena for the multifaceted manifestations of Islam, yet struggling to relate to the secular project of Europe as it has developed since the Enlightenment to the end of and the Cold War and the 'War on Terror'. Gülen's *Islamodernity discourse* (italics mine) and community-based praxis is a challenge both to the traditional understanding of Islam and to a blind following of the project of modernity. He is radically critical of both, but wishes that both speak to each other in here-and-now situations and face up to the reality of the contemporary world by being neither apathetic nor avidly passionate.

It must be noted that the state of Turkey and Turkish society could easily be two things, as the state has been created around a well-crafted elitist framework with a highly motivated plutocracy including its long-term alliance with NATO's military machine (in which Turkey's military is the second largest – after the USA). The challenge to the Gülen movement will be determined by its ability to evolve and expand its strategic and skilful conduct to improve its relationships with the Turkish military leadership and secular elites. If these endeavours are successful, then the movement could have a major impact on both the Turkish state and Turkish society and on the changes that take place in Turkey in the coming decades where – even though he may wish personally to shun such a role – Gülen could become a more important religious figure.

Gülenian positions are palatable within a democratic framework which, for him, falls within the realm of human adjustability and social sustainability that can provide people with the space to be free and to deploy their skills for the greater good. These propositions can easily be debated and tested now in the wider European context where the *Turkish understanding of Islam* is able to rectify and provide an enlightened core of Islam that counters the 'Islamo-Jihadist' interpretation that instrumentalizes the tradition and operationalizes it into the denial of its validity as a religion of peace.

The Anatolian expression of Turkish Islam's perennial links with the Sufi tradition and Gülen's own emphasis on its roots, spirituality and the wisdom guided by a chain of erudite Sufi masters has provided a crucial alternative to the 'official state religion of Islam'. This would be an ideal point of contact for many Muslims, especially South Asian Muslims who also have had exposure to a chain of Sufi masters (more particularly those who hail from the Barelvi school of thought and practice) as well as among non-Muslims who wish to develop a global sense of citizenship in which difference is affirmed and respected. The state is not considered sacrosanct and hence cannot be hegemonic towards the people it rules, but is held accountable, is scrutinized and is placed at the service of the citizens and their freedoms.

It is in this sense that the Gülen movement is a bridge-builder in the expanding European cluster of nations, cultures and plurality. The movement allows the contemporary Muslims of Europe to revisit the fundamentals of Islam and its immense provision for justice; fiscal and economic order; the institution of family; broad-based education; and other forms of promoting civic life and governance.

Concluding remarks

The land mass of Turkey has a historical past of Hittite and Hellenic periods up to the Romans. Then Constantinople became the centre of power in the Byzantine Empire with the Christian schism of 1054 CE, later succumbing to the Ottomans, who named it Istanbul, the place of Islam, where the skyline denotes it as a city of minarets. With waves of change sweeping through this nation, it is yet again at a critical juncture of its history with its possible entry into an EU of 27 member states with (already) 494 million citizens before adding the further almost-70 million of Turkey's population.

If the state of Turkey wishes to join the EU then it is imperative that the 'Turkish flavour' Islam and its diverse affiliations, together with secular pragmatism, be added to the European Muslim polity (Ünal and Williams, 2000) which, since the Second World War, has been dominated by the South Asian and North African Muslim immigrants. This encounter with the organically heterogenic nature of Islam will inevitably produce new relationships both with Muslims and non-Muslims in the new EU where the composition of this Europe with two major religious traditions side by side simply cannot afford to return to historical rivalries and painful memories of the past.

According to Gülen the adherents of a religion like Islam, whose principles are supported by reason and science, should not be doubtful of, or find difficulty in dialoguing with, adherents of other religions. For him dialogue is not superfluous, but an imperative. Gülen believes that dialogue is among the duties of Muslims on earth, to make our world a more peaceful and safer place (Saritoprak and Griffith, 2005: 336). Islam will in every way in Europe face the challenges of modernity in all its manifestations. The fear of the *other* – whether manifested in attitudes and notions of Islamophobia or Westophobia – are both negative but real social realities apparent and alive within Europe. Giving in to these would be to accept the Huntingtonian slogan of the 'clash of civilizations' which the Gülen movement wishes to transform into a culture of dialoguing communities.

It is in this context that Fethullah Gülen's three decades of work both inside and outside Turkey will be pertinent to intellectual enlightenment; to contemporary spirituality informed by abiding compassion; to striving for peace based on justice, and will display an identity created not through tribal affinities like ethnicity, culture or perhaps even religion. Instead it should evoke a sense of being a citizen of Europe, of responsibility and care not only for one's own (the *self*), but also the *other* yet to be known, in order to own an honourable and shared future. This future then will not be a debate between *us and them*, but a future of finding a sense of direction for the whole and for everyone among the former *them and us*. This new understanding of a European citizenship in no way undermines any single faith, ethnicity, race or culture, but could become the defining yardstick in order to enhance not the superiority of *self* over the *other* but the validity of each in seeking identity, a global sense of a citizenship, sharing the world's resources, and in productively contributing to its growth and sustainability.

The encounter with 'Turkish Islam' in the Gülenian sense is able to evoke a transition in understanding the core of religion within post-Christian Europe and could awaken a new form of spiritual growth between Christianity and Islam. Gülen suggests a possible transitional encounter, which would be crucial for ending the historical rivalries between these two traditions lasting over centuries, in order to open a new chapter of renewed relations of goodwill and co-operation as part of the Abrahamic legacy of faith and practice. Cordial alliances between traditions rather than obsessive allegiances and their essentialization require, as a matter of urgency, the evolution of a new code of conduct between these two traditions.

Such futuristic dreams are possible because the present circumstances compel the religious bodies to revisit each of their core teachings, in order to return to a common ground for a shared future, where they wish to wrestle with most critical issues that all communities face today: security for people, equal opportunity, economic prosperity and justice for all.

PART II

Civility, co-existence and integration

4

Civility in Islamic activism: towards a better understanding of shared values for civil society development

WANDA KRAUSE

Introduction

Within a civil society theoretical framework, the chapter addresses the knowledge developed about Islamically inspired forms of activism and proceeds by an examination of the Gülen movement as a key component of civil society. A critical rethinking is required of the dominant theoretical understandings of civil society and views within the existing body of literature about the forms of organization that contribute to its vibrancy and expansion.

The dominant assemblage of ideas is 'a clash of civilizations' discourse spearheaded by Samuel Huntington. Huntington (1996: 47) theorized that a clash of civilizations will occur as different civilizations are more likely to fight each other. Issues have emerged because of factors such as the increased interaction among peoples of different civilizations and a global resurgence of religious identity, together with demographic and economic changes that threaten to shift the balance of power among Western and non-Western civilizations. Consequently, as Özdalga (2005: 429) points out, there has been an upsurge in the visibility of Islam. For Huntington, religion is *the* central characteristic that defines identities. Such theorization needs to be contested and its fallacies revealed in order to develop a clearer understanding of global politics and the role of faith-based movements.

Islamically based forms of organization are classically presented as deficient in 'civility' or as, in fact, antithetical to civil principles. As Özdalga points out:

> [I]n spite of the increasing awareness that Islam and Islamic movements play a decisive role in modern society, they are most often brought to the notice of the public when large and sensational events take place. The result of this sporadic and sensationalistic attention is a general lack of focus upon not only non-violent forms of Islam, but also with regard to long-term analytical perspectives (Özdalga, 2005: 430).

They become, therefore, excluded from normative definitions about civil society and their positive role in it diminished. In an ever-more pressing way, a dilemma faces theorists and leaders in terms of how best to tackle the growing security threats from both terrorism and Islamophobia. In a globalized world in which terrorism has become a challenge facing individuals and state leaders, a narrow construction of the frames of actors and institutions that have the ability to create greater civility and counter anti-civil movements and actors actually exacerbates the problems of terrorism and racism.

It is true that many forms of organization preach principles of civility and world peace, all which are necessary for attaining such ambitions globally. But, for the twenty-first century, I argue that the form of organization best suited to the major challenges of terrorism and racism must not only embrace principles of democracy and universal principles of justice and rights, but also be rooted in Islamic philosophy. The Gülen movement is based on an Islamic philosophy that embraces a 'common good', and emphasizes the universality of values, spirituality and principles of justice – in short, the welfare of society and all individuals within that society. The discourse of any movement is of crucial importance in assessing any real impact on civil society. Some of the main ideas Gülen espouses are *itjihad*, democracy, pluralism and harmony between science and religion. The 2007 RAND report, developed by numerous high-level thinkers, has concluded that the way forward to the eradication of terrorism is through embracing liberal Islamic thinkers that are still rooted in the mainstream Muslim populace. Gülen strives against terrorism by lecturing on Islam's principles and against those who seek to use Islam's name in their acts of terror.

The movement inspired by Fethullah Gülen becomes a powerful civil society force because, due to its breadth, it forms a loose entity that transcends cultures, ethnicities and even religion over several countries. In this way the movement is positioned to root itself in a variety of contexts making it an 'outward-looking', rather than an 'inward-looking' form of organization which constitutes the dominant mode of religious- and interest-based organizations. The movement, therefore, has the capacity to be more effective in its ambitions for greater world peace and individual and societal development.

Thus, the Gülen movement will be analysed in this chapter in which it is argued that it is a leading model among Islamically based associations and movements that contribute to the development of civil societies. It is an example that challenges mainstream readings. It is crucial that policy makers and theorists alike question not only the basis but the effect of the current dominant framing of civil society actors, but also expand the theoretical framework of civil society in practical terms by seeking the inclusion of model civil society movements, such as the Gülen movement, that are in a position to best address and tackle these major problems. Through an investigation of beliefs, values and practices, the chapter will argue that the Gülen movement functions as a mechanism to counter threats to civility and security. The chapter illustrates not only its crucial contribution in terms of expanding civil societies internationally, but also how – through an examination of its empowering effects and the civility components of trust, co-operation, reciprocity and tolerance – it is positioned as a leading example for dealing effectively with contemporary challenges by countering forces that threaten civil societies.

In the first section, 'Islam and the idea of civil society', the theoretical underpinnings of civil society understandings that reject religiously (and specifically Islamically) motivated action will be contested. The chapter then proceeds to an analysis conducted, respectively, through the two main indicators used for the purpose of this project as titled, 'Empowerment: the Gülen movement's role in individual and societal development' and 'Civility: terrorism and racism'. Finally, 'Conclusions' summarizes the findings and discusses future prospects and dilemmas.

Islam and the idea of civil society

The inclusion or exclusion of Islamic groups or associations as civil society institutions has been a matter of considerable disagreement. Many, such as Bernard Lewis (2002), Elie Kedourie (1994), or Albert Hourani (1961), argue that Islamic groups or associations fall outside the realm of civil society. Most research on Islamic movements has been directed to 'Islamist' groups or those who use Islamic scripts to guide their political activism. Such research is applied particularly to violent groups or movements as opposed to Islamic organizations or organizations inspired by Islamic principles.

Thus, mainstream and majority Islamic faith-based forms of association have been glossed over in much of the literature and theorization. Apart from grievous misunderstandings, much research has been influenced by an Orientalist bias. Additionally, the progressive teleology of civil society often embraces anti-religious positions and particularly in relation to those with some Islamic component. Thus, some ideologically motivated behaviours, norms and practices are seen as being incongruous in relation to the project of civil society.

Other scholars assert that religious organizations have an important function in civil society. Clark (1994: 35) shows that a danger in analyses has been the blurring between the minority of violent Islamist groups and the majority of non-violent Islamist groups, in which Islamic associations are characterized as instruments of the undemocratic and extremist Islamic groups. In fact, in her study of Turkey, Göle (1994: 221) speaks of the creation of an autonomous sphere in society due to Islamic values and the Islamicization of politics. Ghannouchi (1999: 83) argues that Islam is naturally strengthening to 'civility'.

Through the specific example of the movement inspired by Fethullah Gülen, this chapter emphasizes that Islamically inspired groups are equally relevant to the sphere in which dominant discourses are challenged and competing views are put forward. Excluding forms of collaboration and movements inspired by Islam means ignoring the fact that as well as contributing to civility, they can be one of the most effective means for responding to the needs of citizens (Schwedler, 1995: 16) and to the challenges facing many governments today.

It is also important to recognize that the 'common good' is a contested domain. As Carothers (1999: 21) explains, '[S]truggles over public interest are not between civil society on the one hand and bad guys on the other but within civil society itself.' The 'common good', although a contested domain, is however best accomplished when different groupings can experience peaceful co-existence through shared value systems. Since tensions between various ethnic, racial and religious or ideological groupings are increasing (as can be evidenced in many European capitals today, to the point that individual safety is a growing concern) there has never been a greater need to establish common principles and values among these groupings and leanings. Therefore, those civil society actors that espouse ideas and practices that strengthen intra-group unity and co-operation need to be facilitated and supported by citizens and policy makers alike, as opposed to those whose interests and aspirations result in greater tensions or hatred.

Empowerment: the Gülen movement's role in individual and societal development

Analysing the empowering effects that result from the movement's efforts captures a deeper understanding of how its mode of action enables greater well-being, health and the ability of individuals to be in better positions to take greater control over their choices. Empowerment is achieved through its educational and charitable efforts. The movement is dedicated to education in a broad sense. It is an education of the heart and soul as well as of the mind, aimed at invigorating the whole being to achieve personal competence and the ability to be a useful citizen for the benefit of others (Gülen, 2005c: 5).

Education has taken a central role in Gülen's philosophy for attaining existential rewards. Gülen explains that it is enough to be a faithful Muslim while imparting secular knowledge because 'knowledge itself becomes an Islamic value when it is imparted by teachers with Islamic values and who can show students how to employ knowledge in the right and beneficial Islamic way' (Agai, 2002: 41). What Gülen has sought to achieve from the inception of the schools inspired by his teaching is a quality of education that surpasses rivalries and stagnation. This began when he confronted the problem, first in Turkey, of secular schools having been unable to free themselves from the prejudices and conventions of modernist ideology and the *madrassas* of having shown little desire or ability to break with the past or enact change in order to integrate technology and scientific thought. Through his endeavours, an empowerment over stagnation in educational systems and philosophies and rivalry has been achieved on a global scale. In Gülen's educational philosophy, scientific learning is not divorced from the development of spirituality. As Gülen has continually emphasized, faith and science are not separate entities in individual and societal development and advancement. Piety and spirituality are part and parcel of developing the conscientious citizen. He asks people to:

> judge your worth in the Creator's sight by how much space He occupies in your heart, and your worth in people's eyes by how you treat them. Do not neglect the Truth even for a moment. And yet, 'be a human being among other human beings' (Gülen, 2005c: 61).

For Gülen, improving a community is possible by elevating the coming generations to the rank of humanity through spiritual consciousness and the consciousness of others' rights. Gülen stresses:

> Civilization lies in people's spiritual evolution and continuous self-renewal toward true humanity and personal integrity-to realizing their full potential as the 'best pattern of creation.' People must realize that civilization is not ... something to be bought from a store and worn. Rather, it is a final destination that can be reached only by following a rational way passing through time and circumstances (Gülen, 2005c: 61).

As such, for a strengthened global civil society to be achieved, one must understand that to be civilized first of all entails the building of the self. Becoming socially responsible by developing oneself, sought through 'secular' learning and spiritual consciousness, consequently effects a stronger and healthier community, which in effect contributes to the wider civilization. Gülen repeats, 'Magnificent nations produce magnificent governments. It is the generations with high spirituality, scientific advancement, financial opportunities, broad consciousness, and the individuals struggling to be "themselves" that form magnificent nations' (Gülen, 2005c: 88).

More deeply, one must look at the value systems that furnish and drive this whole process. Gülen expresses that a core component of this process involves *jihad*. He explains that *jihad* occurs on two fronts: the internal and the external, both of which are based on struggling in the path of God. His focus is on the internal struggle, which he calls 'the greater *jihad*' and defines as the effort to attain one's essence. The external struggle (the lesser *jihad*) is the process of enabling someone else to attain his or her essence. The first, he comments, 'is based on overcoming obstacles between oneself and one's essence, and the soul's reaching knowledge, and eventually divine knowledge, divine love, and spiritual bliss' (Gülen, 2011a). The second is based on removing obstacles between people and faith so they have free choice in belief and unbelief. For him, *jihad* is the purpose of our creation and our most important duty.

When one conquers one's selfish desires through internal *jihad*, one becomes more giving, sacrificial and conscious of others' rights to well-being and happiness. Establishing a true civilization, for Gülen, is assisted when one learns to seek existential reward beyond worldly riches and status. He explains, 'those who want to reform the world must first reform themselves. If they want to lead others to a better world, they must purify their inner worlds of hatred, rancor, and jealousy, and adorn their outer worlds with virtue' (Gülen, 2005c: 105).

The movement inspired by his teaching has worked towards inculcating individuals with this desire and practice, and the effects of this can be seen through the numerous charitable works that its members have developed. As such, the movement can be said to have an important effect in building civil societies as the bases of civilization, through individual empowerment and societal empowerment. Empowerment is achieved, first, when the individual develops and advances his/her own skills, education and consciousness; and second, when other individuals benefit from that person's charity, education, or guidance. True civilization is premised on the empowerment of humanity.

Civility: terrorism and racism

The movement exemplifies an institution and mode of action that is indispensable to decision-makers and policy-makers struggling with the strains of ideological cleavages, growing fear and threats of terrorist and racist action. A look at four major components of civility – tolerance, co-operation, reciprocity, trust – illustrate how the teachings and philosophy of the Gülen movement are a vehicle for the development and securing of civil societies.

Tolerance is defined as a willingness to recognize and respect the beliefs or practices of others (Word Reference Com, 2006). It is something one needs to build from the inside. Gülen asks people to 'be so tolerant that your heart becomes wide like the ocean. Become inspired with faith and love for others. Offer a hand to those in trouble, and be concerned about everyone.' He emphasizes the meaning of tolerance:

> Islam is a word derived from the root words *silm* and salamah. It means surrendering, guiding to peace and contentment, and establishing security and accord …. How unfortunate it is that Islam, which is based on this understanding and spirit, is shown by some circles to be synonymous with terrorism. This is a great historical mistake; wrapping a system based on safety and trust in a veil of terrorism just shows that the spirit of Islam remains unknown (Gülen, 2005c: 75).

In this article and many of his other works, Gülen refers to the core text of Islam, the Qur'an and the *Sunnah* – the traditions of Prophet Mohammed, and practices of the companions of the Prophet and Islamic scholars throughout history – to show how the message of peace and tolerance is repeated throughout. Again and again, he underscores how misguided those people are who hijack Islam in legitimizing the terrorization of innocents. Gülen warns of present-day manifestations of groups in Islamic history that threaten civility. He refers to the Karmatis, Kharijites and Anarchists (Gülen, 2011b) to explain the groups today that often follow a literal meaning of the Qur'an, create chaos, hatred and warfare not only between Muslims and Non-Muslims but also between Muslims.

Toleration of another person's beliefs and practices does not mean that one must like them, accept them for oneself, or even believe that they are correct. But one must accept the condition of a co-existence with people of diverse beliefs, traditions and practices, with the appreciation that others have the same right as oneself to personal beliefs and ways of behaving, given that legal parameters must be in place that will curtail behaviour that harms society. As Gülen most aptly puts it:

> No matter how charming and enchanting the atmosphere that catches the eye or fills the heart is there is no permission for us to forget the truth to which we are committed. We cannot stay alien toward each other while we are in the same camp. We do not have a monopoly of the good and the beautiful; therefore we cannot be allowed to wage a war with the passengers who are heading to the same destination but on a different path (Gülen, 2006c).

Gülen believes that through education there will be sufficient understanding and tolerance to secure respect for the rights of others. However, in securing tolerance he emphasizes the need to view science or reason as part of religious understanding. As Gülen states it:

> Humankind from time to time has denied religion in the name of science and denied science in the name of religion, arguing that the two present conflicting views. All knowledge belongs to God and religion is from God. How then can the two be in conflict? To this end, our joint efforts directed at inter-religious dialogue can do much to improve understanding and tolerance among people (Gülen, 2005c: 4).

For the movement, tolerance is achieved through a form of education that does not deny the place of religion, nor denies the place of what is known as 'secular' learning. Rather this is seen as a constructed dichotomy that bears little relevance in the true attainment of building a holistic self and society.

Co-operation is, indeed, another value for which the movement strives as can been observed in its philosophy and practice. For civility to take root and grow in any context, co-operation is important not only between groups but also within groups. The movement enables the crucial civility component of co-operation in its endeavours to establish inter-faith dialogue and an ethic of inclusivity. As Ihsan Yilmaz puts it, 'The Islamic social system seeks to form a virtuous society and thereby gain God's approval. It recognizes right, not force, as the foundation of social life. Hostility is unacceptable. Relationships must be based on belief, love, mutual respect, assistance, and understanding instead of conflict and realization of personal interest' (Yilmaz, 2003: 230).

Since non-discriminatory forms of co-operation are a key to establishing norms that support plurality, the inclusivity of individuals is recognized. Thus the movement supports educational and work opportunities for women. Many women work as educators in schools and universities, and as administrators in certain areas (Afsaruddin, 2001). With regard to religious minorities, Gülen movement schools have been established in various countries with communities of various faiths. Students of all backgrounds attend these schools because of the high quality of education that they offer.

Observers will attest to how surprised they sometimes are about the high level of educational abilities of the students and the professionalism of teaching staff (Michel, 2001: 3). As Özdalga (2005: 435) notes in her observation of the staff of the schools, they give primary loyalty to their work and students as opposed to their families. This is of particular importance to the formation of a civil society because in many (especially developing) countries, and particularly in the wider Middle East, internal loyalties supersede external loyalties, causing one major source of problems in the development of healthy civil societies. When travelling to visit some of the Gülen schools, Thomas Michel (2001: 3) attests he witnessed the:

pluralist nature of the student bodies – Christian and Muslim in Zamboanga, and Buddhist and Hindu as well in Kyrghyzstan – that what they sought to communicate were universal Islamic values such as honesty, hard work, harmony, and conscientious service rather than any confessional instruction.

He further comments, 'in the Sebat International School in Bishkek, students from U.S.A., Korea, and Turkey appeared to be studying comfortably with those coming from Afghanistan and Iran' (Michel, 2001: 3).

Reciprocity is also a major component of civility. Inclusivity, as found within the Gülen school system, establishes a basis upon which individuals can share knowledge and can further an ethic of tolerance and understanding. In this way, an ethic of giving, receiving and sacrifice are spread among those who participate in such projects, as well those who are educated through them. Norms of reciprocity help communities better to achieve their interests in a peaceful and civil manner. Reciprocity strengthens relations between the members, the organizations they work with and, consequently, communities. In short, it solidifies networks in which people can rely on one another to co-operate and struggle towards the goal of global peace.

Trust is the last component of civility that we will discuss, though no less important to the building of a civil society than tolerance, co-operation and reciprocity. Gülen emphasizes the need for trust between individuals in order to facilitate co-operation and success in any endeavour. Gülen argues for the individual to be trustworthy so as to facilitate the bonds between people. This requires individual integrity and a sense of responsibility towards others' rights and needs. This is a 'virtue related self-discipline and sensitivity' (Gülen, 2005c: 81). He furthers the centrality of the principle of trust by emphasizing its importance in the wider community: 'If a state cannot protect its secrets from its enemies, it cannot develop. If an army reveals its strategy to its antagonists, it cannot attain victory. If key workers are won over by the competitors, their employers cannot succeed' (Gülen, 2005c: 81). However, trust is broader than keeping secrets. Trust is, for example, also about entrusting another with one's possessions. This can be seen to be put into practice among members of the movement who sacrifice their time and material resources, in faith that their works and charity will be put into worthy causes by others who believe in and support Gülen's dreams and philosophy.

Conclusion

The Gülen movement takes a sizeable and important role in the development of a number of civil societies around the world. This can be seen in its educational and charitable projects. Of central importance, however, are the ambitions, philosophy and dreams to which the movement aspires and the principles upon the basis of which members are motivated and base their activism. The movement aptly demonstrates how its Islamic principles are put into practice to create a better world. Its impact can be more readily seen through a systematic analysis of its contribution in terms of empowerment strategies and modes of civil action.

The movement contributes to empowerment on a massive scale as its projects and schools have spread to over one hundred and twenty countries. The features of its empowerment strategies include, first and foremost, the integrating of the secular and spiritual to educate well-rounded, capable and responsible individuals who have acquired the desire to be a source of inspiration and help in the modern market economy and global world. As many observers have attested through visits to Gülen-inspired educational establishments, individuals thrive in often multiracial/religious and supportive environments; hence, they gain the ability to provide a solid foundation for a healthy community which Gülen views as crucial component of a healthy civilization and civilized world.

Not unconnected with this is the impact that the movement has on developing civil societies through the development of civility – a crucial component of their stability and productivity. This is observed through the Gülen movement's strong commitment to civil components of tolerance, reciprocity, trust and co-operation. Practice in this direction can be found in the participation of hundreds of thousands of individuals in the numerous establishments, the foundations, schools, and charitable projects that establish these values and spread them to the wider societies in which they operate. An important example includes Gülen's fervent commitment to inter-faith dialogue that, to various degrees, takes place through all these initiatives.

This example of a humanistic movement inspired by Islamic principles should convince scholars and policy makers of its importance to the development of civil society on a theoretical level. Equally crucial, it should be viewed as a leading example of the kinds of organization that should be promoted for the benefit of civil societies, whether in predominantly Islamic countries or in what one might commonly refer to as 'secular' countries. Forms of organization that promote empowerment and civility through Islamic teachings are crucial in a world in which civility seems to be increasingly threatened.

The challenge of the future of civil societies lies not only in the ability of such forms of faith-based movements to empower, provide an example and create better conditions for civility. We are entering a time in our history where proponents of a 'clash of civilizations' are influencing public opinion towards increased hatred and polarization with growing terrorist action and the distortion of global politics and meaning of civil society. If movements such as this one, which has popular support in the Muslim world, and which solidly espouses values of democracy, human rights and civility, as well as establish the compatibility of belief with these values are not supported, then both terrorism and Islamophobia will continue to increase.

5

European public sphere, Islam and Islamic authority: Tariq Ramadan and Fethullah Gülen

ERKAN TOGUSLU

Introduction

Even though many studies discuss the crisis of the Islamic authority, new Islamic faces and intellectuals transmit Islamic tradition to public life and build new possibilities for restoring and renewing traditional Islamic approaches for dealing with issues such as pluralism, *ijtihad*, schooling, private-public and gender relations. In using 'authority' here, the reference is to persons who speak about Islam and who are endowed with a legitimacy that comes from their talents and ability to interpret Islam. Second, authority is given by Muslim followers and political institutions to new pioneers of Islam. Because of this knowledge is produced, transmitted and accepted by young Muslims.

Constituting a connection with Islamic past and tradition, these Muslim figures revitalize Islamic knowledge. Thus this chapter will seek to understand the profile of Islamic discourses and how these new Islamic pioneers accommodate their discourse in the public sphere by examining the views of Tariq Ramadan and Fethullah Gülen.

The case of Ramadan and Gülen is interesting and this chapter will discuss these two personalities not only as figures in Islamic discourse, but behind the discursive practice, the aim is to also understand how knowledge contributes to the formation of a practical language.

One of the consequences of this transformation of Islamic discourse is the formation of Muslim identity and a construction of an Islamic *habitus* and manners via the cultural and religious dispositions that we see among young Muslims in Europe. Promoting a moderate Islamic philosophy, preaching dialogue and collaboration with different faiths and countering the violent ideology of radical extremist views is one of the characteristics of these new young Muslims.

In using 'Islamist', I mean the capture of power using religion and the ideologization of Islam. This is a political Islam whose aim to restore a regime based on religious rules and its tenets invoke Islam as the source of authority for political legitimacy. It entails a political ideology that seeks a takeover of political power. It is not the production of an official Islam under the strict control of the state in an attempt to regain religious control over the public. What is observed among the second Muslim generation in Europe is becoming a transnational phenomenon that is having an influence on the shape of Islamic knowledge. In this regard, in order to understand the Muslim presence in Europe, it may be instructive briefly to look back at post-secular theories.

First, as a consequence of the fragmented modern character of knowledge and science in post-secular societies, traditional Islamic knowledge is dissociated from its dominant context. As Benjamin argues, the fragmentary character of existence towards the sense of world renders this inadequate and impracticable under modern conditions, because past practices of accessing knowledge based on storytelling give way to informational knowledge (Benjamin, 2011). Thus, the informational disposition of the modern practice of knowledge requires modern forms of implementation that challenges traditional aspects of learning processes among Muslims. Second, in the last century, the development of pedagogical and learning technologies such as the media and the internet have played a significant role in the production and expansion of Islamic knowledge. In these ways, the traditional modes of Islamic learning are acquiring new possibilities to spread as a by-product of rising literacy and mass education which, in turn, also influence the fragmentation of Islamic knowledge (Eickelman, 1992; Mandaville, 2001).

In recent years, a modern discourse of textuality has emerged and the hermeneutical-historical approach is underlined by Islamic scholars (Roussillion, 2005; Filali-Ansari, 2003). As a result of this new discursive and methodological approach and interpretation of Islam, the pluralization of knowledge is remarked upon by scholars (Mandaville, 2007). In numerous ways one can observe a meaningful shift about the production of knowledge in that the traditional setting of Islamic knowledge is changing under the mobilization of the mass media, migration, circulation of ideas, new forms of technology and information. Mandaville argues that globalization changes the intensification and extension of the nature of Islamic authority, making it more diverse and fragmented. This shift, according to Mandaville, is observed in three dimensions that construct the Islamic authority in dealing with three kinds of pluralization: textuality, discursive method and personification.

The Islamist discourse versus moderate interpretation of Islam

Asef Bayat (2002: 23) remarks on the shift that took place after the 11 September terrorist attacks (9/11), from a discourse of the politicization of Islam to an emphasis on personal pietism and ethics. In this new period, new Islamic faces are challenging with ancient discourses that which underlies the political aspect of Islam. This pluralization of Islamic knowledge and attitude has an effect in the public sphere involving social and political debates in Europe. Islamic issues are taken as a discursive practice, and in this approach we forget to examine daily practices that give rise to new debates about the implementation of Islam. The encounter with the 'West' and the secular meaning of life forces Muslim authorities to rethink the traditional settings and corpus of the text. Textuality is harmonized by new discursive methods.

The legal practice of Islam confronts new questions arising from equality between men and women and the question of radicalization. It is difficult to say that, in such debates, Islamic authority loses its capacity for monopolization in framing an Islamic response and meaning. In recent years these questions have taken on particular importance between Muslims and 'Western' societies. They not only lead Muslims to reformulate these debates but they also affect the interaction between Islam and Europe in many spaces – in the discursive parallel arenas as described by Fraser (1992). The nature of the Muslim presence in Europe is changing and we can no longer identify European Muslims as temporary guest workers. Göle (2005) notes that interpenetration and interaction bring 'West' and 'East', Islam and Europe, closer and present new challenges.

As a result of this new phenomenon, Islam cannot be linked only with Arabs, Turks and Pakistanis. It becomes a European phenomenon. Muslims are now a permanent part of Western civilization. However, the history of relations between Europe and Islam dates from the seventh century, beginning with conquest of Spain by the Umayyads and from the East by Turkish pressure, but this presence was limited and did not touch Europe as a whole. The phenomenon of a growing Muslim presence in Europe is a new phenomenon that can be seen with a new visibility – as in the Muslim headscarf; Muslim schools; markets; and everyday life practices. In major European capital cities the presence and visibility of the Muslim population can be clearly seen. The demographic aspect is increasing and the different ethnic groups of Muslims among European societies are dealing with matters of co-existence, plurality, integration, terrorism, democracy and the maintenance of habits and manners in public life.

Islam and Muslim actors shape the post-secular European mind and history through their visibility. As can be illustrated from the recent controversy over the Swiss ban on the construction of minarets, Islamic visibility has a symbolic role in the definition of European identity by creating new debates and challenges that Europe faces today in the relationship between the state and religion, the place of sacred in the common public sphere and the collective European identity. The Muslim factor is not just considered in geographical and demographic terms. This new dimension in a multicultural Europe offers a range of opportunities containing new challenges for a new Europe.

The secularization process or the individualization of religious rituals is frequently cited as a common characteristic of Europeans. Nevertheless, the new issues relating to the place of religion – and especially of Islam in Europe – seem to highlight a dilemma between the secular and the religious in Western societies. In a secular world view, Islam is always questioned and interrogated about whether it can be adjustable and flexible to change: in other words; individualization, pluralism, democracy, human rights and gender issues are the main challenges that Muslims encounter in the Western world. How can Islam take account of, and respond to, all these issues? This is not to speak about the privatization or de-privatization of Islam, but the dissemination of an 'other' religion that transmits a new culture, life and habits which contributes to the formation of post-secular Europe. The much-debated issue of Turkish membership of the European Union is also a part of this question (Roy, 2004b).

Multiple faces of Islam, including ethnic diversities and cleavages due to socio-political and generational differences, are at the core of the institutionalization of Islam in Europe. In this process of institutionalization, governmental and non-governmental organizations search for a local version of Islam. In doing so, they seek to establish new councils responsible for the organization of Islam. Europe's Muslims are divided across several groups and do not form a monolithic whole which highlights the question of how to bring these various ethnic and religious groups together under an umbrella organization that represents the whole Muslim community. In other words, who will be the authority? Who now decides what is legitimate and illegitimate in Islam? Who listens and puts forward *fatwas* and interpretations?

Despite the lack of traditional Islamic norms and culture in Europe, the new young Muslim generation continues to follow religious traditional authorities that interpret religious texts and sources. By the fact that they are looking for a 'legitimate voice of Islam', young Muslims living in Europe continue to acquire religious feeling and practices in new circumstances and situations. As an example, Yusuf al Kardawi, a recognized expert on *fiqh* (Islamic jurisprudence) *ulama*, has his own popular website, *Islamonline*, a *fatwabank*. This is a place that responds to questions on daily manners and that gives many *fatwas* about the new situations that Muslims encounter in their daily life.

In this regard, this chapter attempts to analyse Gülen's and Ramadan's views, their typology and portraits as new pioneers of Islam in a secular context that reminds us of the range of Islamic thinkers and thinking in today's Europe. The examination of change in Islamic discourse goes back to the old 'Islamist' dichotomy between modernity, enlightenment and an Islamic past. The 'Islamists' developed a language that was concerned with how Islam could be developed as a total system responding to any kind of question about social, economic and political issues. In this discourse Islam is mainly considered as an ideology asserting a politically resurgent response to Westernization.

This chapter aims to help develop an understanding of the emergence of new personalities who are quite different in terms of their evaluation of the 'West', nationalization, *ijtihad*, and of co-existence between Muslims and non-Muslims. The first generation's views and ideas drew on inspiration from such figures as Mawlana Mawdudi, the founder of Jamaat-i-Islami and known for his Islamic political ideas (see Zebiri, 1998); and Hasan Al-Banna, an Egyptian political reformer, best known for establishing the Muslim Brotherhood (Kramer, 2010). These emphasized anti-imperialism and were against Westernization. However, this second group of Islamic intellectuals speak about co-existence between 'East' and 'West', about pluralism, democracy and human rights. Becoming familiar with these notions, Muslims in Europe who are following Gülen's and Ramadan's ideas, seek ways of accommodation in public-private life as well as about how to adjust religious principles in the social and economic fields.

New Muslim intellectual portraits

A brief examination of the educational trajectory of Gülen and Ramadan demonstrates the formation of Muslim intellectuals, Muslim authority and its transformation. It shows how religious tradition is reproduced and transformed in new contexts. The production of Islamic knowledge and authority is seen as fragmented and diluted.

Recently, in order to understand how the Islamic knowledge is renewed some scholars (Zeghal, 1996 and Zaman, 2002) have written of the re-emergence of Islamic knowledge-transmission by religious institutions.

Meanwhile, the new Muslim intellectuals who studied in secular republican models are against the central role of classical Islamic institutions (see Kepel and Richard, 1990; Roy, 2004a). Their religious life is influenced by individualism, privacy, autonomy, eclecticism and ethnicity. The problems that the young Muslim generations encounter are to do with finding an authoritative Islamic tradition that can challenge the fragmented character of their identity. The difficulty of referring publicly to an Islamic identity and shaping their moral and ethical views based on Islamic principles without withdrawing into the Muslim community, pushes young Muslims to follow new figures who 'insure' them in a 'risk society' by dealing with the insecurities introduced by modernity, pluralişm and universalism.

After a traditional Islamic education in eastern *madrassas* and a mosque school, Fethullah Gülen continued his formation at a secular school. This was followed by a period as an official preacher in the Directorate of Religious Affairs. Since the 1990s, Gülen has spoken about this when he has appeared in the public secular sphere during the inter-faith dinner organized by the Journalists and Writers Foundation which gathers people from various religious, political and ideological identities. Since 1998, following pressure from the Kemalists, he has been living in voluntary exile in the United States. On Gülen's Islamic pedigree, Özdalga notes that:

> [he] adopts a solid, conventional Hanafi/Sunni understanding of the religious traditions. So it does not seem to be the content of the religious interpretation as such, but the very existence of a new relatively strong group, filled with religious fervor and claiming a place in the public arena that annoys the establishment in Turkey radical margins who see this as a threat to their ideology (Özdalga, 2005: 441).

Gülen shows a capacity to adapt his discourses and speeches in variable secular contexts, having a talent to fascinate his supporters who are widespread among young university students and businessmen. Fascinating people by his tears during his sermons, his ability to make contact with his audience and to circulate his message reveals a new Islamic intellectual character that is shaped by Islamic discourse and by the emotional aspect of his spiritual dimension. Raised in a conservative and pious family, he received religious education and secular teaching. Having acquired knowledge in these two spheres, he has the possibility to speak about different themes.

After the secular project and the forced laicization and modernization undertaken by the new rulers of the Turkish Republic, the *ulama's* powers were delegitimized and reduced and were replaced by the new bureaucratic elites whose formation is culturally and socially different. In their classification of Muslim scholar figures, Gaborieau and Zeghal (2004: 7) propose an *alim-arif* framework that indicates a combination of *ulama* and *sufi* understandings of Islam.

A heuristic glance at Gülen's works and speeches enables us to define him as an *arif-alim* who intregrates two poles which are called *zahiri* (exoteric) and *batini* (esoteric). Gülen plays the double role and figure: *arif* and *alim*, spiritual and rational, sacred and profane. These two figures intermingle in an inextricable way. As noted by W. Montgomery Watt (1971), many Sufis were withdrawn from this world. At the same time a large number of Sufis were lawyers. This included, for example, Abu al-Qasim Abd al-Karim b. Hawazin al-Qushayri, a *shafite* lawyer born in 986 in northern Khurasan in Iran and author of the *Epistle on Sufism*, written in 1045 (see Al-Qushayri, *Al-Qushayri's Epistle on Sufism* [*Al-Risala al-qushayriyya fi 'ilm al-tasawwuf*], translated by Alexander Knysh, Lebanon, Garnet Publishing, 2007).

The famous sermons given by Gülen have an emotional aspect. In his sermons, his speaking and his voice are accompanied by tears and weeping. His language is made contemporary through the insertion of anecdotes in the sermon. In cassette recorded sermons, hearers are also observed to be very touched and freely to have wept when Gülen delivered a sermon that was shaped by Sufistic idioms and narrations. His voice as intoned in the mosque stirred people's emotions. Audiences listened carefully to the sermons through the emotional setting linked with an esoteric style of interpreting the Qur'an that Gülen refers to as a spiritual knowledge (*marifa*).

In the early years of Islam, *ma'rifa* was understood a secular knowledge. In time, *ma'rifa* became a Sufi term for the spiritual knowledge of God (see Chittick 1989: 149). For Gülen, *ma'rifa* is 'the special knowledge that is acquired through reflection, sincere endeavor, using one's conscience and inquiring into one's inner world. [...] The opposite of (scientific) knowledge is ignorance, while the opposite of *ma'rifa* is denial' (Gülen, 2004d: 135).

While he also emphasizes this Sufistic way of interpretation, Ramadan's discourse is framed by an academic-critical position. Tariq Ramadan was born in Geneva, a Swiss Muslim. His grandfather, Hasan al-Banna, was the founder of the Muslim Brotherhood in Egypt and his father was also a figure in that community and exiled to Switzerland. Tariq Ramadan studied philosophy, French literature, social sciences and Islamic studies. He is an advisor to many governments and teaches in many universities as a visiting professor. He is professor of contemporary Islamic Studies at the Oriental Institute of the University of Oxford. His works emphasize Islamic studies, theology and European Muslims, and he endeavours to reinterpret Islam on many issues. Ramadan's use of fluent English and French is very influential with young Muslims, especially among France's suburban young Muslims.

Ramadan's biography locates him as one of the Islamic intellectuals who emerge from secular educational institutions and who have a feeling for modern knowledge. Meanwhile Ramadan studied Qur'an and Hadith for many years and, in his books and speeches, he gives references to Muslim scholars. At the same time, he uses the same language and vocabulary as secular thinkers and even participates in debates with leftist and far leftist intellectuals, as in his book *L'Islam en questions* (2000) with Alain Gresh, the far leftist columnist of *Le Monde Diplomatique*.

This critical language and discourse is different from Gülen's discourse that emphasizes the mystical aspect of Islam. While Gülen's discourse outlines moral values through the formation of ethical principles and he is opposed to violence, his main aim is to develop the inner life of all Muslims. But in Ramadan's writings we see the critical approach that is the result of his academic background. Ramadan focuses on 'reforming' Islamic issues in relationship with European secular society. His latest books highlight the challenges that Muslims face in Western societies.

The Islamic faith-orientated views of these two Muslim scholars within mainstream Islamic orthodoxy can be understood as a continuum in the revitalization of Islamic concepts and notions. These efforts are identified as:

> a continuation of the radical *tajdid* tradition in Islam. In practice, they built on the accomplishments of the early Islamic modernists and the new-style Muslim associations. ... but at the same time, went far beyond the traditionalism of the remaining conservative *ulama* establishment (Esposito and Voll, 2001: 20).

Thus, Fethullah Gülen and Tariq Ramadan assume this role of the old traditional *ulema* left by secular politics and they also represent an orthodox modern Islam. In Turkey, at the end of Ottoman Empire, this new Islamic corps appears and starts from the *Tanzimad* period marked by the Young Ottomans who are identified as bureaucrat-*ulemas* (see Zaman, 2002). Within Europe, the search for interlocutors with the Muslim community has become a necessity for local authorities (see Dassetto, Ferrari and Marechal, 2007).

Ijtihad and Islamic renaissance

Ijtihad is an important element of renewal in Islamic history and tradition through which the *ulema* play a crucial role in determining the needs of modern times (Voll, 1983). They speak an about Islamic renaissance in the Muslim world and which the modern Muslim generation needs to develop consisting of the rediscovery, in a new manner, of human values and morals, knowledge, fine arts and religious thought. Gülen says: 'We are in search of an awakening of reason, as well as of heart, spirit and mind. Yet, it is not possible to assume a harvest of fruits of efforts and works resulting from this' (Gülen, 2005a: 458).

Thus, an Islamic renaissance in the modern world leads to an intellectual rebirth. Along with his positive approach to reformulation and a new way of understanding Islamic interpretation, Gülen outlines some of the hindrances and the reasons for why *ijtihad* has been forgotten and was lost: 'political oppression, inner struggles, the misuse of the institution of *ijtihad*, an extreme trust in the present legal system, the denial of reform, the blindness caused by the dominant monotonous present system of the time' (Gülen, 2005a). He says also that the door of *ijtihad* has never been closed (Yilmaz, 2003). After explaining some of reasons why the door of *ijtihad* was considered closed, Gülen expects a great revival of religion and religiosity in Islamic world.

A similar motivation is claimed and formulated in Ramadan's writings. He describes an open-minded and tolerant Islam that promotes the enlightenment of the Muslim world. He notes: 'a new, positive and constructive posture which relies on a fine comprehension of Islam's priorities, a clear vision of what is absolute definitively fixed and what is subject to change and adapting' (Ramadan, 1999: 132–4).

We have taken the example of *ijtihad* and the question of *dar al-harb* and *dar al-islam* that are reformulated by Gülen and Ramadan in order to understand how they apply Islamic knowledge to modern life. In Western societies, this traditional binary formulation does not correspond with Muslim needs. On this issue, Gülen uses the term *dar al-hizmet*. As this is explained by Yilmaz (Yilmaz, 2003: 234), 'If one's intention is to serve Islam by presenting a good example, then one can stay wherever one desires... wherever a Muslim is, even outside a Muslim polity, he or she has to obey the lex loci, to respect others' rights and to be just, and has to disregard discussions of *dar al-harb* and *dar al-Islam.*'

Before giving his reflection on *ijtihad*, Ramadan identifies the essential elements of Muslim personality and identity (Ramadan, 1999: 132–4). His treatment and analysis of the Muslim personality show why he supports a renewal of these binary opposite conceptions.

The first element is faith and spirituality manifested in several cases by practice which is the second element for Ramadan: practices that perform a Muslim's faith like praying and fasting. Third, the protection of human beings based on respect and toleration that provides a recognition of humankind. Freedom is also indicated as an important element. The fifth element is based on participation in social affairs which, for Ramadan, means to act in favour of one's society and environment. The analysis of these five elements of flowering Muslim identity is accompanied by rights and responsibility. The European arena appears to be a land and a space within which Muslims can profess their faith; participate in social affairs; and in which Muslims can take care of their social and political responsibilities. Ramadan emphasizes *Fiqh* and Islamic tradition in finding a way to preserve Muslim spirituality and identity.

He does not refer to the notion of *dar* (abode) and this old binary geographical representation. In Ramadan's formulation, Western societies have a crucial role and a specific space which leads Muslims to express their faith and Islamic message. Muslims need to create a way forward in this new space that avoids 'reactive and overcautious attitudes and to develop a feeling of self-confidence, based on a deep sense of responsibility' (Ramadan, 1999: 150).

Accordingly the formulation of his thought about Islamic reformism, Ramadan wants to know how Islam can find a place for itself in the European public sphere. For this reason, he underlines the new possibilities of interpretation of Islam. It is clear that the complexity of historical, economic and cultural issues about Muslims living in Europe can be a hindrance to finding a practical answer about how to deal with secularism and politics.

Ramadan argues that *ijtihad* is the most important instrument for the reinterpretation and reconstruction of Islam (Ramadan, 1999: 89). He urges the necessity of *ijtihad* in specific situations, giving Muslim Europeans examples in dealing with the participation of women in public life; distinguishing geographical boundaries as *dar al-Islam* and *dar al-harb*; foods; mosques; cemeteries; hospitals; schools and the headscarf which have occupied detailed points in the lives of Europe's Muslims.

The traditional debates about the definition of 'Muslim lands' and 'non-Muslim lands' are, in Ramadan's view, based on old conceptions and thinking which are not adequate to overcome the dilemmas presented by a binary vision of world. He argues that applying this binary model is a methodological mistake that increases the complexity of the problem (Ramadan, 1999: 127). Thus, Ramadan discusses old conceptions in a new context, examining their ability and utility in relation to new political, economic and social issues. He observes three consequences as the main reasons for developing a new thinking about Islam: Westernization as a model for the Muslim world; close ties between Muslim and European countries; and Muslims who live in Western pluralist societies.

Contrary to some *ulama* – such as those from the Hizb at-Tahrir or the Tabligh movement (who defend the continuing relevance and literal application of this old classification that distinguish *dar al-islam* and *dar al-harb)*, Gülen and Ramadan are in favour of a reformulation, or at the very least they are calling for a new debate about these concepts. After discussing these traditional terminologies, Ramadan suggests the importance of the concept of *shada* (testimony) which seems to him more applicable in a global period, and which permits Muslims to participate and to be involved in their society.

> This *shahada* is not only a matter of speech. A Muslim is the one who believes and acts consequently and consistently. 'Those who attain to Faith and do good works', as we read in the Qur'an, stresses the fact that the *shahada* has an inevitable impact on the actions of the Muslim whatever society he/she lives in. To observe the *shahada* signifies being involved in the society in all fields where need requires it: unemployment, marginalization, delinquency, etc. This also means being engaged in those

processes which could lead to a positive reform of both the institutions and the legal, economic, social and political system in order to bring about more justice and a real popular participation at grassroots level (Ramadan, 1999: 147).

In this sense, referring to the term *shada*, Ramadan is overlapping the ancient forms of binary opposition to demonstrate a further opening for Muslims. Analysing and classifying the conditions and qualities required to become a *mujtahid* and to make an *ijtihad*, Ramadan's position is rather more opaque than Gülen's. Nevertheless Ramadan does not claim that the gate of *ijtihad* is closed.

European Islam and citizenship

Muslims who have grown up in Western Europe, themselves think about the implications of their faith and daily practice that continue to form their lives. It is evident that Muslims encounter issues and in order to find a way forward with their dilemma of being European and Muslim they are increasingly searching deeply for new approaches to their questions (see Pauly, 2004).

As a so-called faith-inspired civic movement, the Gülen movement seeks to break out of the 'minority status' and isolation of Muslims in Western societies. In recent years, those who are inspired by Gülen's ideas have established non-denominational educational and dialogue activities all around world. Creating private schools, foundations, organizing inter-cultural and charity activities, they hope to make connections between Muslims and non-Muslims. Gülen encourages his followers and sympa-thizers to be exemplary Muslims, being devout and ascetic in their daily life. The essential element of integration used by the movement is education and schooling. Although these schools do not give religious courses, the essential orientation is based on the teaching of ethics and moral values such as devotion, hard work and responsibility (Agai, 2003: 49).

Gülen stresses the role of education in inspiring an 'ethical vision rooted in Islam but not limited in its expression to sympathizers of the *umma* (community)' (Michel, 2003: 82). The educational style of the Gülen-inspired schools aims to respond to the question of how to generate an ethical humanity with common values. Teaching is considered a holy duty (Agai, 2003: 58) and ultimately, through daily conduct, to demonstrate the right way in the ethical dimension of life (Özdalga, 2000). Scholars such as Balci (2003) and Michel (2003) note that the pupils come from different religious and ethnic origins. Gülen-inspired schools are chosen for their secular education, rather than religious Qur'anic schools, mainly in order to find common spaces with the host society that can diminish the negative profile of Muslims in the Western context.

Ramadan says that his first aim is reconciliation between two sides. He wants to show that Muslims can profess their faith and be loyal to secular principles, and also to show the compatibility between Islam and Muslim ethics in secular Western societies. Thus, Muslims can become actors in a public space where people share in debate and try to formulate things together for the common good. He opposes the more communal life of Muslims, and says that a Muslim has responsibility towards God and inalienable principles and that, 'As a result, the community of faith is essentially opposed to any form of "communitarianism"' (Ramadan, 2003: 147). He wants Muslims to be active citizens in Europe, to participate and to contribute to debates and socio-economic issues, engaging in more efforts to reconcile Western secularism and Islamic values (Ramadan, 2003: 143–4).

Like many liberal thinkers, Ramadan thinks that a religious citizenship is acceptable in the public sphere: thus Muslims can, with their beliefs, be involved and participate in political activities. But the political reality is more complex. Ramadan takes the European public sphere as a neutral space although that public sphere has, in fact, excluded certain groups throughout the nineteenth century – for example, women, the poor classes, immigrants, religious groups as revealed through Habermas' book on the evolution of public sphere in Europe (Habermas, 1991).

The visibility and the participation of Muslims matters in Europe, not their *communautarisme*. The French Republican model recognizes only the individuals, not the ethnic, racial and religious groups. Group-based identity politics is called *communautarisme*. In this sense, Muslims are defined as *communautaristes* who do not respect the *valeurs de la République*. Muslims' involvement in their practices is thus seen as a deviant in society.

The requirements of citizenship relate to a sense of belonging and loyalty to a political community. In his writings, Ramadan underlines that loyalty and argues that the Muslims of Western societies ought to strengthen their commitment through political investment, educational skills and inter-faith dialogue. He states that:

> A young Muslim ... is someone who is both French and Muslim and must find ways in which he can figure out how he is French and Muslim at the same time. It is a kind of realization, but one which requires a long process. The true Muslim comes to understand himself in the rigorousness of his conversation with God, and in the Muslim community by initiating dialogue with those who think differently from him. (Ramadan, 1997: unpaginated).

A meta-narrative discourse about Muslims that is largely based on a clash between Islam and West produces an Orientalist discourse that presents Islam as a violent religion which is incompatible with democracy, secularity and human rights (see Cesari, 2004: 21). The stigmatization of Islam at every level minimizes the effect and impact of Gülen's and Ramadan's ideas concerning civility, civic engagement and social participation.

A possible peaceful co-existence

The picture of Islam presented via events, the political situation, and manipulation raises a prejudicial meta-discourse about Islam and binary oppositions between Western societies and Muslims (van Koningsveld and Shadid, 2002: 176–80). To prevent this manipulation, Muslims should have a consistent dialogue with their neighbours to modify the negative image of Islam. Gülen-inspired dialogue and educational activities serve the recognition of Muslims in the host societies.

Gülen encourages inter-faith dialogue between different representatives of the religions. In an early text, 'The necessity of interfaith dialogue: a Muslim perspective', Gülen (2000: 4–9) demonstrates his interest in, and commitment to, inter-faith dialogue. In Turkey and via dialogue foundations, he has established a major force in dialogue. His writings, encouragement and concerns set out the principles for his followers to participate in dialogue and social action.

In terms of human responsibility, which is seen to transcend theological and civilizational differences and to be realized in a study of the common good, his endeavour is important for the notion of civility (Lamine, 2004). Lamine notes that in dialogue activities the main issues debated and the final target is mutual recognition of *altérite* which plays a central role in definition of the modern subject. In this sense, Gülen presumes that people, whatever their faith, race and nation, have much in common and can leave behind their ancient misunderstandings and conflicts. He gives an invitation to debate and finding solutions to overcome poverty, environmental questions, as well as in relation to inalienable human rights. This civic logic continues to be involved in society and to diminish borders with others.

Ramadan also urges that it is increasingly urgent for Muslims to rediscover the power of unity through intra-community dialogue (Ramadan, 1999: 220) but also that it is not sufficient to limit such dialogue to being between Muslims but rather, there is also an urgent need for engagement in dialogue and collaboration with others.

Conclusion

The participation of Muslims and non-Muslims in a constructive shared social project in Europe signifies the end of classical binary opposition between Muslim and non-Muslim lands. The new combination reflects an inter-subjectivity that also reveals religious diversity and pluralism as high human values. The two Islamic scholars explain how classical Islamic authority is, especially in Europe, renewed in the globalization and secularization process.

The multifaceted discourse of Gülen and Ramadan is judged by some to be 'double faced' (Favrot, 2004); 'making *takiyya*' (Fourest, 2004); 'having a hidden agenda' (Bulut, 1998); or being a 'hypocrite' (Çetinkaya, 2004). It is claimed that they threaten universal democratic values and human rights by hiding their real identity and strategy concerning the Islamization of people. To followers, they are people of dialogue and Islamic reformers who want to reformulate Islamic issues in dealing with new questions in the secular world. Both of them refuse the description of 'Islamist' and put a distance between themselves and 'Islamists' or political Islam. Such political vocabulary is not found in their approach.

Thus, this chapter has tried to analyse the views of these Islamic scholars, their typology and portraits as new pioneers of Islam in a secular context. Its aim has been to understand the emergence of new personalities that is quite different from the early twentieth century Islamist thinkers in terms of the evaluation of the West; nationalization; *ijtihad*; and co-existence between Muslims and non-Muslims. While the earlier generation's views and ideas (like those of Mawdudi and Al-Banna) emphasized anti-imperialism and were against Westernization, the second group of Islamic intellectuals speak about the co-existence between East and West; pluralism; democracy; and human rights. Familiarizing themselves with these notions, Muslims in Europe who follow the new Islamic scholars' ideas seek how best to accommodate in public-private life and to adjust religious principles in the social and economic fields.

The emphasis of Muslim intellectuals on democracy, human rights and rule of law is a sign of Islamists turning to new doctrinal strategies. In other words, it means turning from Islamism to 'post-Islamism' - a term that has been used to refer the shift in attitudes and strategies among Islamist movements and militants in the Muslim world (Roy and Haenni, 1999; Kepel, 2003). The term is used to describe the metamorphosis of Islamism in structural, ideological and practical ways. The term 'post-Islamism' is first used by Bayat. For him, post-Islamism represents a condition and project. It attempts to reconcile faith and democracy, Islam and liberty and is a result of inadequacies and contradictions that reinforce the Islamist militants in changing their discourse and strategies (Bayat, 2007: 10–11).

Yet it would also be wrong to label Gülen and Ramadan as 'post-Islamists'. This is because Gülen and Ramadan have just defended fundamental rights and universal values – not because of the failure of political Islam, but because Gülen and Ramadan do not ideoligize religion. In their writings, the attempted a reconciliation between faith and the secular; the sacred and profane; liberty and submission to God which are expressed through rediscovering Islamic texts in new circumstances. They endeavour to find possible links between the West and Islam and to intensify the interaction between Muslims and wider society. What one can observe is not the consequence of specific dominant institutional models of influence. It can be seen in the emergence of new Muslim actors in Europe who refuse Muslim exceptionalism and a discourse of victimization. They promote an inclusive attitude and a 'positive constructive dialogue' – a motto that appears in many Gülen-inspired dialogue centres such as Dialogue Society in London and Intercultural Dialogue Platform in Brussels.

6

Integration of Muslims in Europe and the Gülen movement

ARAKS PASHAYAN

Introduction

At the beginning of the twenty-first century, humankind faces a number of complementary tendencies related to the resurgence of radical trends in major religions, the increasing role of religion in the universal civilization, and cultural, ideological and religious diversity on global and local levels. In particular, the troubled integration of Muslims into European societies is evidence of a perceived incompatibility between Christian and Islamic traditions

In the face of these tendencies, the Islamic scholar and peace activist Fethullah Gülen argues that Christianity has much in common with Islam. Gülen insists that the world is becoming more global and both sides feel the need for a give-and-take relationship. The Gülen movement aims to promote creative and positive relations between the West and the Islamic world.

The Turkish community in Germany and Islamic identity

A 2009 study by the Berlin Institute for Population and Development found that even after 50 years and three generation in the country, Turks remained a people apart. They reside in what Germans have come to call 'parallel communities', a diplomatic term for what are in effect ethnic ghettos shunted off from mainstream German society. This exclusion exacts a heavy toll on new generations, many of whom do not know the native language. Reports of primary school classes where 80 per cent of children cannot speak German are testimony to the seriousness of the problem.

The Turkish immigrant group is one of the largest Muslim communities that have settled in Europe from the beginning of the twentieth century. There are around 10 million Euro-Turks living in the European Union countries of Germany, France, the Netherlands and Belgium. There are about 3.5 million Muslims (roughly 4 per cent of the population) in Germany. Most Muslims live in Berlin and the larger cities of former West Germany. However, unlike in most other European countries, sizeable Muslim communities exist in some rural regions of Germany, especially Baden-Wurttemberg, Hessen and parts of Bavaria and North-Rhine Westphalia. Most Muslims in Germany are Sunnis. Many Turkish Muslims are Alevis.

The Turks have formed their own special society within the Western societies. They always adhere to their national identity and leave impressions on native residents wherever they settle. The central element of their social life is the mosque, which often also comprises a cafe, a barbershop, food shops, a library and a lodge for wayfarers. Furthermore, many mosques have recently been equipped with modern means of communication like the internet and telecommunication lines.

Women, in particular, tend to stick to their distinctive outward appearance. Turkish women tie the *hijab* in a specific way. The merchants are always keen on displaying Turkish goods. The shops have names like Istanbul, Ankara, Emre, Mevlana and Turkiye, and display the same quantity and types of goods supplied in Turkey. No immigrant Turkish home lacks satellite dishes configured to receive Turkish homeland channels. Besides TV channels, Turkish daily papers are delivered to most immigrant Turkish doorsteps whether for free or by subscription. Most of these papers (including *Zaman*, *Turkiye*, *Hurriyet*) are distributed all over Europe. Other periodicals include European-language magazines and papers that specialize in Turkish affairs and the Turkish immigrant community, which attract only a small number of Turkish readers.

Charitable works are always carried out by Turkish residents. There are thousands of mosques that have been built with the donations from the Turkish immigrant community. They are also noted for seizing the opportunity to buy churches that are up for sale and then transforming them into mosques. They try to support Arab Muslim issues as well. Charitable giving makes them feel that they belong to the Muslim *ummah* (Nasreddine, 2004).

Islam is a visible religion in Germany and is the largest minority religion in the country. Although there were some small precursors, the contemporary history of Islam in Germany began at the end of the 1960s. The Turkish migrants remained invisible in their religious practices partly because they did not regard Germany as a new home. Their intention was to work only for a short period of time in Germany, and they were emotionally much more connected to political debate and public life in Turkey. They strongly believed that they would certainly return to Turkey. The first generation of migrants understood the practice of their religion as a homecoming. They practised it in their homes or in other intimate, invisible places, shielded from the outside because the outside was conceived of as foreign, as a foreign land, or – in Turkish – *gurbet*. The realities of migrants' lives – homesickness and ignorance – were characteristic of the so-called Gastarbeiter-Turkish literature until the beginning of the 1980s.

When, in the second generation, Turks in Germany had turned from being migrant workers into being immigrants it was not only their institutional dispositions that became transformed, but also their individual religious ones. For the first immigrants, the so-called Turkish 'People's Islam' was a formative influence for their practice of religion in Germany. The 'People's Islam' was orientated towards and shaped by the practicalities of everyday life and was defined by distinct phases of an individual's life (Nasreddine, 2004).

The 'People's Islam' was embedded into the Turkish culture at large, while in the diaspora, religion later became 'de-culturalized'. The migrants slowly began to study the Qur'an in Turkish, which was a radical change to their religious lives. Young Muslims in Germany often declare that they 'have discovered Islam for themselves'. The decision to wear a headscarf and model their lives individually, and out of their own free will according to Islamic principles, becomes the young women's means towards self-actualization and shapes their relationship with Islam.

When second-generation migrants left behind the idea of returning to their parents' home country, this not only changed their status as 'guest' to a status as immigrants, but also helped to shift the power balance between immigrants and Germany. Germany has been forced to meet the immigrant on a more equal level, consider him or her as a new citizen, and communicating with him or her in discussion about integration. In contrast with the first generation, which practised Islam defensively and invisibly, the second generation uses Islam as an instrument to give meaning to their everyday, individual lives. It has become a highly visible and irreversible part of German society.

The second generation does not only study the Islamic sources to find solutions to their everyday problems in Western society, but it also tries to counter Western discourses about Islam (American Institute for Contemporary German Studies, 2007). Applying Islam became a source of overcoming personal destruction, isolation and nihilism. The Islamic identity helped to identify a future. The religious factor allowed young people to find their orientations in German society (Tietze, 2004: 151–3).

Until 2001, migrants in Germany had not been perceived in religious terms, but in ethnic ones. Polls in the 1990s, for instance, indicated that about 3 million people with a Turkish background live in Germany. Within a couple of years, their identity changed – the majority society began to perceive them differently. Now they are no longer perceived in ethnic terms, but in religious ones: 3 million Turks became 3 million Muslims.

Turkish integration in Germany and Gülen movement

The discussions about Euro-Turks have been heated at a time during which Turkey has been given a perspective on full membership of the European Union. These discussions have also become embedded in the debates on 9/11; the killing of anti-Islamist political leader Pim Fortuyn and film director Theo van Gogh in the Netherlands; the cartoon crisis in Denmark; and the Pope's discussion about the Prophet Mohammad (Kaya, 2007). The relationship between Germany's largely Turkish Muslim population and the German national community was until recently conditioned by the political class's refusal to acknowledge that the 'guest workers' were there to stay. Since 2000, however, the German outlook and policy has changed: the reality of immigration and permanent settlement is now recognized and a new willingness, in principle, to extend citizenship has developed. However, the view that integration should precede naturalisation – the requirement that Turks and other Muslims should first integrate and demonstrate their 'German-ness' before they may acquire that citizenship – remains a brake on the process (International Crisis Group, 2007).

The German government has spent recent years working with immigrant groups and independent experts on a national integration plan. It sees integration as crucial to the country's future security and economic well-being. Discussions over the past years have shown that Germany has a long way to go before immigrants feel included in society. For decades, politicians had insisted that Germany is not an immigration country, but Chancellor of Germany Angela Merkel's focus on integration points to an important shift in German politics.

Whether Germany will become a multi-ethnic society will depend on a number of factors. First, some of the most severe social problems have to be tackled and the educational system has to be improved. Germany needs a lot of effort to enable underprivileged – German and non-German – young people to have a decent future, materially as well as emotionally. Even the outcasts, even right-wing extremists, have the right to get emotional support and help. This has nothing to do with approving their actions. On the contrary: only if a society stands firmly against violence, only if there is an obvious will to protect the weaker and to care for the victims, can a civil society survive in the long run (Weber, 1995).

There are social, economic and political barriers to integration presented by the host societies and there are many efforts among the Muslim population to promote its own visions and models for integration. Among these models is the Gülen movement, which is has embraced 'a modern, multicultural notion of political identity and community that is also deeply rooted in Muslim practice and traditions' (Irvine, 2006).

The debate over Turkish-Muslim integration in Germany has resolved around three main educational policy issues. The first involves religious instruction in schools. The second educational policy debate involves the establishment of private Muslim or Turkish schools. The third educational policy issue involves wearing of headscarves in schools. In contrast to France, German schools permit female students to wear headscarves in the classroom.

The issue of headscarves has been in a particular area of concern all over Europe, and in Germany as well. While, under the German Basic Law's freedom of religious expression clause, German students may wear headscarves in the classroom, the situation concerning teachers has been much more complex. Since teachers are representatives of the state, they have no permission wear a headscarf. The Gülen movement's approach to the issue is interesting. The movement prefers to avoid direct controversy and eschews a highly visible role in the current struggle over permitting teachers to wear the headscarf in the classroom.

Jill Irvine (2006) argues that such a stance is in keeping with the general goal of the movement in Germany to avoid highly charged political battles that could detract from its educational mission. The Gülen movement participants in Germany have founded a variety of educational institutions that operate throughout the country (Irvine, 2006). Despite the large Turkish population in Western Europe the Gülen movement took hold relatively late compared with other Islamic organizations. The institutionalization process of the movement started after the mid-1990s.

In the past decade, though all the difficulties, the movement in Germany has been building an educational infrastructure that aims to improve the social situation of Turkish residents and promote their integration into German society. They attempted to find 'middle way' between the cultural devastation implied by assimilation and the 'globalization' of a minority group living apart from the majority culture. Any solution to the challenges of integration must involve the give and take of cultural understanding and mutual enrichment. Turkish residents must become educated according to standards and become fully capable of operating at the highest levels of German professional society, but the key to integration is to provide the best possible education (Irvine, 2006).

Gülen movement participants in Germany have founded a variety of establishments. There are three main types of establishment: First, there are learning centres which offer particular courses in after-school groups to the students of the primary school by the college and private schools. Second, there are intercultural dialogue associations which organize intercultural events and meetings in order to promote cultural exchanges between the Turkish population and the native society. Third, there are entrepreneurial associations which assemble Turkish businessmen who financially support the movement (Demir, 2007).

The crisis of multiculturalism in Europe and the Gülen movement

Recently, one after the other of the leaders of the major European powers have expressed misgivings about multiculturalism. They have let it be known that multiculturalism shall no longer be the continent's doctrine of immigrant integration. 'The multicultural approach, saying that we simply live side by side and be happy about one another, utterly failed,' declared Merkel in a speech in October 2010. She observed that in light of the widespread failure of immigrants, particularly Muslims, to integrate – whether by learning the German language or by adopting German cultural and legal norms – the country could have no illusions about the success of its so-called *multikulti* policies in integrating immigrants (see http://www. guardian.co.uk, *17.10.2011)*.

As any mention of the untouchable issue of immigration tends do, Merkel's comments elicited furious condemnation in which the left-wing *Tageszeitung* dismissed her remarks as populist posturing. The *Financial Times Deutschland* insisted that such rhetoric 'cannot be excused'. Still other critics charged that Merkel was stoking 'xenophobia'. Yet the most notable aspect of Merkel's remarks is just how unremarkable they were.

Indeed, the most compelling criticism of her public renunciation of multi-culturalism is that it has come too late in Germany's immigrant crisis. When Merkel talks about the utter failure of multiculturalism, she has Germany's Turkish community in her mind. The chairman of the Turkish Society in Germany thinks that Germany never applied multicultural policies (see http://www.dunyatimes.com/en/?p=7948).

During a visit to Germany Turkey's prime minister, Recep Tayyip Erdogan told his compatriots that they should learn Turkish before German and resist assimilation into German society. He said, 'You must integrate, but I am against assimilation ... no one may ignore the rights of minorities,' adding that individuals should have the right to practise their own faith. Erdogan made an even sharper criticism of German immigration policy, stating that forced integration requiring immigrants to suppress their culture and language violated international law (see http://www.guardian.co.uk, 28.2.2011).

Thus Gülen and the initiatives inspired by his teaching challenge the tendency found among some Muslim groups to separatist withdrawal from the wider non-Muslim society. By contrast, they offer a basis for Muslim engagement with the wider society based upon a confident and richly textured Islamic vision. That vision also draws upon the historical wealth of a multicultural civilizational history to argue that neither Turkey nor the European Union have anything to fear, but have much to gain, from a future of full Turkish membership in the EU (Weller, 2010).

In his teaching and his writing, Fethullah Gülen emphasizes the importance of a shared humanity in striving for peace and the common good. Thus Gülen challenges the tendency found among some Muslims groups to separatist withdrawal from the wider non-Muslim society. By contrast, Gülen offers a basis for Muslim engagement with the wider society based upon a confident and richly textured Islamic vision – a vision that itself also draws upon the historical wealth of another multicultural civilizational history (Weller, 2010).

And so the vision of integration promoted by the Gülen movement centres is one of cultural exchange and enrichment rather than assimilation. Despite the denials of some German officials that there are Turkish ghettos in Germany many, if not most, Turks live a good portion of their lives separately from native Germans. Gülen movement centres and schools are attempting to build a bridge between the two communities. Integration also means a willingness on the part of the host population to understand and accept the values and experiences of the Turkish minority.

The Gülen movement's apolitical rhetoric has the potential to provide a positive identity to Muslim immigrants, which is necessary for peaceful coexistence. For European states and societies it is a legitimate channel of communication with the immigrant group. The Gülen movement has made a big contribution to improving mutual understanding between the adherents of different cultures and religions, taking into account that social marginalization and isolation are among the most important factors in the radicalization of immigrant groups in Europe.

Conclusion

Muslim communities, and Turkish communities in particular, are not adequately perceived by European societies founded on tolerance which has generated two tendencies within the communities. The first one is related to radicalization processes within the communities. The emigrants who encounter various social problems – especially unemployment – are subjected to discrimination which leads to their isolation. Suffering from psychological discomfort, they gradually become an alien element for the European society and they feel themselves as strangers. This fact leads to an increased consolidation within one's own ethnic group. The resultant ideological gap is bridged by Islam which functions as a uniting factor.

The second tendency is related to a newly established identity. There is a new generation which rejects isolation, tries to overcome stereotypes and is ready to integrate into European societies. These are the circles which have obtained European education, speak in the language of the given country and are well aware of the local culture. At the same time, they tend to retain their Muslim (or national) identity, and as a distinctive feature they choose religious identity, which is a more determining and powerful element in competition with the European/Christian civilization. These kinds of young people have decent prospects in German society.

The requirement of the institutional presence of Islam in European countries creates an immediate contradiction with the fundamental values of European societies. Europe is not willing to reject the liberal cultural and moral values, which constitute the basis for the Western civilization, even realizing that pluralistic multicultural community needs universal values. A Europe which faces demographic and socio-moral problems in some cases feels threatened by the manifestations of Islamic fanaticism.

It is not Christian and Islamic civilizations that clash in Europe but post-Christian secular/liberal values and Muslim traditional values. In this case, the only alternative to sectarianism, isolation and radical relativism is inter-faith and inter-cultural dialogue. As Gülen argues, to oppose and resent the 'West' will never benefit Islam or Muslims. He indicates the method of dialogue: forgetting the arguments of the past and concentrating on common points. He stresses tolerance as an extremely important virtue that should always be promoted. Everybody should be allowed to express themselves on the condition that there should be no pressure on others. Also, members of minority communities should be allowed to live according to their beliefs. The Gülen movement accepts Western civilization as a suitable foundation for material life while considering Islamic civilization suitable for spiritual life.

PART III

European contexts

7

From 'new man' to 'world citizen': the replication of Fethullah Gülen's renovation vision in the Dutch context

TINEKE PEPPINCK

Introduction

Modernization, secularism, democracy: they are all important issues for us in the Western world, but also in Turkey too. Even more than in Europe, modernization in Turkey was already an important issue and a necessity in the nineteenth century. This is because Turkey – at that time the Ottoman Empire – found itself in a difficult position. For centuries the Ottoman state had seemed to be powerful and unbeatable, but the tide was changing. With the industrial revolution in the West, the Ottoman Empire was confronted by a new Europe that had made a leap in the area of science and technology.

In a modernizing world non-professional spiritual renovation is a pre-condition for existing in the world, without being dominated by so-called 'civilized nations'. Modernization was the reference point in the ideology set up to liberate Turkey from Western domination: Kemalism, which was introduced through the leader of the war of independence and founder of the Republic of Turkey, Mustafa Kemal Atatürk. It is an Enlightenment ideology, with the goal of growing a generation that has free ideas, a free sense of consciousness and a free knowledge (Akşin, 1999: 17). According to Atatürk, this attitude was the foundation of 'Western' successes in the scientific arena and was now the key for success of Turkey as well. This success would guarantee her a place among the family of civilized nations.

Turkey as indivisible unity

The modernising Kemalist elite saw religion as the great obstacle. According to Kemalism, the dogmas coming out of religion would prevent people from engaging in critical and scientific reasoning. Besides it would lead to divisions, because during the Ottoman state era it had already been shown that the different societies (called *millets*) of which Turkey consisted would become open doors for foreign intervention.

Atatürk had concrete plans to deal with this threatening diversity stemming from religion. Under the influence of the European model of the nation state, it was decided that Turkey formed an indivisible unity with her land and nation, with Turkish as its national language. This ambition for unity was reflected in the religious field with the setting up of a Directorate of Religious Affairs. This decided what the correct explanation of Islam was, and from that point onwards, all appointments of all religious representatives were overseen by that Directorate. This means that all the holders of religious office in Turkey, even now, are government employees. As a result of this, it also highlights a question about what the separation of Church and state means in Turkey. This was clear for Atatürk as well: secularism means that the state is responsible for the explanation of Islam as the religion of understanding and reason of modern Turks. All other aspects of religious beliefs are limited to one's own personal conscience.

Is the movement a threat to democracy?

Although there are conspiracy theories about the way in which the Gülen movement educational institutions are financed, Fethullah Gülen has always made clear that these are an initiative and a result of generous Turkish citizens and of the self-sacrifice of volunteers, like teachers who are willing to work at (less then) a minimum wage (see Ebaugh, 2009). But what is this vision of Fethullah Gülen that appeals to so many people and that leads to such results? In fact in some respects, just like Kemalism, it is an answer to the dilemma of how do we hold our identity as Turks and safeguard our position in the world? In Gülen's vision the word 'Turk' encompasses mainly the Islamic community and refers the word 'identity' not only to being Turkish, but also mainly to the Islamic identity of Turks and the ethical values linked to this (Yavuz, 2003a: 24).

The Islam that Fethullah Gülen preaches is not a dogmatic Islam where religious rules are central (Bilir, 2004: 269). It is more of a mystical Islam, one that aims for personal development of the individual, a good human that develops those qualities that are appreciated by everyone, like loving fellow humans, courage, modesty and the willingness to do something for someone else out of self-sacrifice (altruism). Besides, for many people Fethullah Gülen is known as the face of tolerant and 'liberal' Islam. He is therefore presented as an advocate of dialogue with, and tolerance towards, people from other cultures and beliefs. Likewise he even visited the Pope in 1998, which can be seen as a good example of the principles he preached.

There was widespread amazement when, in 1999, tapes were broad-casted by the Turkish television broadcaster ATV, in which this widely appreciated 'hoca efendi' (respected teacher) seemed to be calling his disciples to wait for the right moment to seize power in Turkey. The public prosecutor opened a lawsuit investigation into Fethullah Gülen on the basis of accusations such as the founding of an illegal organization aiming to change the structure of the secular state, in order to found a state based on religious laws.

Are these well-grounded accusations, or is this hostility on the part of sectors of the Turkish state as argued by the members of the Gülen community? Considering these accusations, it will also be wise to realize that the Turkish state has always monopolized the explanation of Islam, along with other important concepts like democracy and secularism. In fact, Hakan Yavuz also argues that one of the reasons for the hostility from the side of the Turkish state could have been the establishment of the Journalists and Writers Foundation which is linked with the Gülen community. This Foundation seemed to have the ability to incorporate the Turkish cultural and economic elite through involvement in shared projects aiming for the formulation of a 'social contract' (Yavuz, 2003a: 42).

The fact is that Fethullah Gülen himself acknowledges the value of concepts like modernization, secularism and democracy. But he also attempts to discuss the content, because the meaning that he gives to the concepts proves to be different than that given by the 'Kemalists'. Likewise democracy is, for him, a meaning that is inherent in Islam. According to him, the Turkish people need a higher type of democracy than the present one; a democracy that offers more room for the spiritual (religious/Islamic) dimensions that, according to him, people are in need of. Secularism includes the principle that the state does not interfere with religious experience of its citizens, in order that it 'creates a climate where everyone can sow his ideas unhindered and harvest its crop' (Gülen, 2001b).

Fethullah Gülen's vision is actually an alternative form of modernization. As already explained, modernization seems to be the necessary condition for maintaining the right to exist in this world, without being oppressed or taken advantage of by so-called 'civilized nations', without having to relinquish one's own identity in exchange for a 'civilized culture'. This is the starting point of the Kemalist vision, as well as of that of Fethullah Gülen. Both want to avoid this, but their ideas about the way to do this differ greatly. Fethullah Gülen has a sharp critique about the results of the type of modernization that Atatürk instituted. Fethullah Gülen does not blame Atatürk for this, because according to Gülen, Atatürk had the same opinion as him, except that Atatürk has been both understood and presented in a wrong way to his people (Gülen, 1998).

Imitation of Western modernity

Conversely, according to Fethullah Gülen, the example of an ideal situation can be found in the situation as it was in the first centuries after the appearance of the Prophet Mohammed, and during the first centuries of the Ottoman Empire. According to him in those days the Islamic community was seen as the most ethical and developed in the world. It could develop a tremendous governing body because it was able to estimate the value of what Gülen (2003a) calls 'the tripartite foundation of inspiration, rationale and experience'. Their endeavours to be ethically perfect and their progressiveness in comparison to the times in which they lived, were due to the traditions and structures that made them pause in the face of the transitoriness of earthly life and the reality of eternity. Therefore people were focusing on immaterial values, like science, knowledge and the defence of law and justice (Gülen, 2003b). However, they invalidated their heritage by sacrificing their religion in the hope of more prosperity:

> In fact, we have made one of the most unforgivable mistakes of history, by sacrificing religion in turn for prosperity. We accepted a way of thinking in which this worldly life is superior to religion. Since that moment on, we are struggling to get out of the net of impossibilities in which we have been captured. Religion is long gone, but yet the expected worldly prosperity hasn't been obtained (Gülen, 2003a: 7).

According to Gülen, the result is a dependent position, because Turkey tries to please the 'West' at all costs. Also the Turkish nation finds itself in a miserable position because of its addiction to materialism. According to the Kemalist ideology a human can only be free if the influence of religion is not there. But Fethullah Gülen argues that the opposite is the case. Because of the missing influence of religion, modern humans become slaves to their own greed and primitive drives, and to the selfish fellow-humans who exploit them. The pursuit of more and more comfort consumes more and more energy from modern people and takes away the peace and calmness that, according to Gülen, finds its roots in a religious life. From a scientific point of view it does not make one more objective, because one who is ruled by selfishness will manipulate science to use it in order to serve one's own (material) needs (Gülen, 2003a: 20, 23).

What is the solution, according to Gülen? In many ways this solution resembles the goals of Kemalism, but the content is completely different: create a new generation of people who are free. Not free from the influence of religion in order to be able to think freely, but free through the notion that they are servants of God, who only have to obey his commands and need not bow before other kinds of power. Free because they are aware of the fact that the core of belief is to strive for God's approval, so they can free themselves from worldly desires. Free to do scientific research in an honest way, because in this they are not manipulated by their own interests, so they can use science for the good of the whole humanity. They have a broader perspective on science – a holistic view – because as well as the book of religion, during scientific research the book of the universe is consulted, so one can obtain deeper insight. Active, not because of chasing luxury, but because one strives for the approval of God, which is obtained through loving all creatures because of the creator himself, so one can become conscious of one's own responsibilities towards fellow men, society and the world.

The 'New Man'

Just like the Kemalist elite that implemented its own type of modernization in Turkey, it was also Gülen who has the conviction that the masses will not be able to implement far-reaching changes in the present situation. For this, people with insight are needed who will serve as pioneers. He expresses his expectations on this point as follows:

> Out of the masses that are wandering behind people without the capability of reasoning and sound thinking or following fantasies, as if they were sleepwalkers, a New Man will arise. This man will be able to think in a modern and rational way, and he will put his trust not only in the mind but also in his experiences and he believes as much in inspiration and consciousness as in those two (Gülen, 2003a: 17).

According to Gülen, what he calls the 'New Man' are those who are heroes, who are loyal to their own cultural and religious values, but are also developed in all fields and are in harmony with the time in which they live. They are people who, inside themselves, have realized a dialogue between elements that, in the present view, are seen as opposites to modernity: heart and mind, feeling and logic. They are people who focus on the present world and at the same time the next.

The 'New Man' deploys himself using all these elements, to be an enlightening example for others, both in social, scientific and technological areas. He does this through radiating both ethical values and professionalism at the same time. Because the 'New Man' is a 'peace-maker' he also goes into dialogue with the rest of the society, because it is his intention to unite the society around shared values like virtuousness, decency, diligence and being helpful. If he succeeds in this, a prosperous and peaceful society will emerge through dialogue and service providing an example.

If this works in the case of the Turkish nation, this nation can become an example for the rest of the world. It can show that Islam offers solutions where ideologies fail. Instead of being a child put aside, the Turkish nation can become the precursor that can unite the whole world around shared values, so that eventually also a peaceful world can exist; not because beliefs are being oppressed, but because through being a role model and being of service the hearts of others can be gained.

The emphasis that Gülen puts on the importance of education is completely in line with this kind of goal. He says that an ideal community, society or world consists of ideal individuals. Ideal individuals exist through self-development, but especially through the example that they receive from a teacher who radiates knowledge and an understanding of an almost perfect human (*insan-ı kamil*) and makes clear to his pupils the possibilities of following the same path.

Gülen's vision in the Dutch context

What is the relevance of this vision of Fethullah Gülen in the Dutch context? Can something be done in the Netherlands with this? Fethullah Gülen's vision seems to encompass an alternative to the type of modernization in Turkey with its rigorous secularism. The Netherlands is in that respect a very liberal country, offering much room for different beliefs. Let us not forget here: also in the Netherlands this was not achieved without effort. Influences from the French revolution meant that for a long time the Netherlands was striving for unity, in which King Willem I of the Netherlands gave the Reformed Church the task to nurture 'love for the King and Country' (Harinck, 2006: 107). This is quite similar to the way in which the present Turkish Directorate of Religious Affairs seeks to nurture especially an Islam that is serving the national consciousness.

In the Netherlands it was the so-called 'separatists' who were against this striving for unity and who were convinced of the fact that there is 'a dependency on God, which makes independent from the state' (Harinck, 2006: 109). Subsequently, Abraham Kuyper was one of the people who acted against attempts to drive away Christianity out of the public arena (Hooven, 2006: 36). He pleaded against uniformity in the public domain and for diversity, arguing that 'citizens would be rather loyal to a government that would allow them to live according to their own beliefs, than to a state that wanted to pour them into the same mould, and that therefore the public domain should be open to every philosophy of life and not only the reasonable ones' (Hooven, 2006: 36).

Ever since the Netherlands was divided into separate so-called 'pillars' (Post, 1989) within society, every belief had the opportunity to establish its own schools, foundations, hospitals, service organizations etc. During my research into the Gülen movement in the Netherlands, I was surprised to see that this subcategorizing spirit was, in particular, the very notion that the people whom I interviewed found awkward.

Of course, some people with whom I spoke in the Netherlands and who said that they were inspired by the vision of Fethullah Gülen, also stressed other problems that they believed the Dutch society was facing. One of the subjects of the conversation was that, from their perspective, the capitalist system ignores the spiritual nourishment and education of the people in the Netherlands; something that is reflected in the growing number of psychological problems among Dutch people, the growing number of divorces and the lack of respect for elderly people who are no longer productive. But the lack of openness and exchange was the main subject of the conversation. People in the Netherlands live alongside each other, isolated in their own little worlds, so that there are groups in a splendid diversity living along each other, but not together *with* each other. One of these groups is the Turkish community.

Tolerance and dialogue

What does this yet have to do with Gülen's vision? A parallel is seen with the situation in Turkey in terms of the lack of tolerance that different groups show at the moment a crisis occurs (for example, 11 September 2001 – 9/11). There are tensions between different groups (Kurds, Turkish Sunnis and Alevi Muslims, Armenians) because the government has imposed a uniform identity on the citizens, as if it wants to say: 'You will be Turkish and speak Turkish and you should never and ever divide our country because of divergent convictions.' The solution of Gülen for this is, as we have seen, to be tolerant through the love of God, expressing love and being of help to all creatures, and getting into dialogue to find out what is important for everyone, so that it can then be worked for collectively.

In the Dutch context everything seems to be worked out: everyone has the right of freedom of speech and there seems to be room for every possible conviction, even though this is not the ideal picture of integration in the eyes of everyone. From the point of view of Gülen's vision a few people were saying that people experiencing their own identity in their own subcategory undermines mutual tolerance and blocks an ideal of dialogue about joint problems and efforts for joint collaboration about shared goals, which can lead to unity while preserving one's own identity. Therefore, what they propose is: knowing one's own identity and engaging in dialogue that opens this identity into interaction (in an interview of 14 March 2007 with – pseudonym – 'Mahmut').

What is done with this ideal in the Netherlands? Some of my interviewees (for instance, an interview of 17 April 2007 with Gürkan Çelik) argued that development towards a perfect human being (*insan-i kâmil*) is the first priority. This was especially the case for the Turkish community and Muslims in the Netherlands who, according to the majority of my interviewees (including interviews of 26 February 2007 with Yusuf Alan; 13 March 2007 with Alaattin Erdal; 16 April 2007 with Ahmet Taşkan; and 14 March 2007 with 'Mahmut', a pseudonym), in comparison with the wider society, were hindered in reaching an equal level of development.

The ideal these interviewees (in interviews of 26 February 2007 with Yusuf Alan; 13 March 2007 with Alaattin Erdal; and 14 March 2007 with 'Mahmut') identified is that these people will understand the first command from the Qur'an (*iqra* in Arabic, which is translated in Turkish as *oku*, meaning not only recite, as is the case in Arabic, but also 'read' and 'study') as an exercise for themselves – namely, study and develop yourself through deepening in the book of the universe and the book of the religion, to become a human being who is developed with the heart, head and hands.

This includes the hands (acting), because of the importance of seeing one's own responsibility towards (Dutch) society, through awareness of the transitoriness of this life and the reality of the eternal, and the fact that a human being is not the owner of one's own qualities, skills and talents, but a manager who is supposed to offer these in service to humanity and not only to satisfy one's own material needs (in email correspondence of 31 March 2007 with Yusuf Alan about the article, *Kimim ben?* published on the internet at http://www.zamanhollanda.nl/haberdetay.asp?id=540). It was thought that development and consciousness at this level would probably also lead the Turkish and Muslim Dutch people to be of more help and service to their fellow Dutch people. From this position, they are more likely to be able to disseminate their message, because participation and the possibility of influencing the world around oneself seem to be two sides of the same coin.

Being an example

In all cases, being an example was the means to reach the primary goals. Being a role model is a recurring theme in Gülen's vision, which can also be found in independent foundations in the Netherlands in which people who are inspired by Gülen's vision are involved. One can find previous role models and 'mental coaches' in the student association Cosmicus and in a few educational centres in big cities in the Netherlands, who want to encourage Turkish young people to aim higher. One can find role models back in the Cosmicus primary-secondary school, who want to stimulate young people to develop themselves to be world citizens: people who have skills that can be appreciated all over the world (like being of help and altruism); who know their own identity but who also share their own story with the rest of the world.

One can also find role models in the *Zaman* newspaper who want to improve the participation of Turkish Dutch citizens by, on the one hand, making them aware of the Dutch actualities and, on the other hand, by motivating them to this participation by presenting role models to show what is possible – such as successful female Turkish entrepreneurs, academics and students (in 13 March 2007 interview with Alaattin Erdal).

By being active in this way, for the people who are inspired through the vision of Fethullah Gülen, it seems possible to bring together everything that the Dutch society expects from a Turkish Muslim. For example, in relation to the slogan of the new administration: 'Work Together, Live Together', the striving of these people gears seamlessly with this. Dialogue, tolerance, working together and participation are meanings that indeed are being appreciated universally. And because someone can join in so well, one has the space to give one's own content to these concepts, which gives one the possibility to make oneself heard and to keep one's own identity.

This means not only having a reason to exist in the Dutch society, but also even to become an example, hoping that this will also be followed by the Dutch, so that also they can participate in a dialogue and will no longer focus on their own interests, but will also be of service to, and self-sacrifice for, fellow human beings. If because of that, different groups in Dutch society can live peacefully together, it will be shown that this concept works because the Netherlands, with all its diversity, is a reflection of the wider world. Then the Netherlands will become a role model and a hope-giving example that can be followed by the rest of the world in the effort to build a peaceful world of living together (in 12 April 2007 interview with – pseudonym – 'Cemal'). Finally, all of this is on the basis of universal principles and values that, according to the Gülen movement, find their origin in Islam.

Concluding (personal) remarks

What to think about all of this? It very much depends on one's personal beliefs. As a Christian, this author recognizes in this story many of the elements of my own faith. I also discovered the influence of my 'Abraham Kuyperian' background upon my own way of thinking, because a uniform society or world conforming to the model of the nation state is my greatest fear. The Turkish and Dutch reality seem to have shown that the world and humanity are not 'built' to be uniform, but that they exist within the grace of diversity. A society where people are focused on knowledge and spiritual values instead of material things and personal interests, and one that is based on appreciating one's own identity, exchange and working together, seems much more attractive. Love, being of help and working together are indeed universal values that will more likely lead to a peaceful co-living than consumerism or national pride.

However, where I am critical about the vision is the fact that the important principles for peace within it seem to lack the basis that they have for me as a Christian. I cannot see Islam as the basic origin of these principles because for me they find their ultimate fulfilment in Jesus – for example, being of service (*Hizmet*), which makes one an example for others. The influence that being of service provides is much stronger and more real than the effect of top-down power.

But for me as a Christian, Jesus is the ultimate example of The One who rejected earthly power and chose the way of serving by choosing the cross in the interests of humanity; to make it possible that peace comes between God and humanity so that human beings can go in dialogue not only with one another but especially with God himself – in order that His Holy Spirit could come to live inside them as a 'mental coach' and to create a 'New Human' who can serve others according to His example (see Ephesians 2:13–20). Therefore for me, it is difficult to understand how one can be an example for others of the love of God if one has not first seen for oneself what the example of the love of God means. How can one sacrifice for the interest of others if one has not first experienced how God shows His love by sacrificing Himself for you.

However, I also would like to advise everyone, whatever belief he or she has, but who is concerned about the growth of the influence of the Gülen movement, Islam or whatever conviction in any way, to follow the example of the Gülen movement. Do not complain, but look into a mirror and ask yourself what you have done to put some effort with integrity into the well-being of humankind. This humankind will be more likely to be open to the influence of the one who earns this influence. In this way everyone's own view of life determines the way a vision like Fethullah Gülen's is received and interpreted, and perhaps this could be a fruitful subject for further research.

8

The emergence of a neo-communitarian discourse in the Turkish diaspora in Europe: the implantation strategies and competition logics of the Gülen movement in France and in Germany

EMRE DEMIR

The implantation process of the Gülen movement in Europe

Fethullah Gülen has always been a strong supporter of Turkish economic and political integration with the European Union (EU), while he has a sceptical attitude towards co-operation with Iran and the Arabic world. This pro-European attitude represents a differentiation in the Turkish Islamic scene. Since the 1970s, other leading Islamic groups such as Erbakan's National Outlook Movement appropriated an essentialist anti-Europe or anti-Western discourse (Kösebalaban, 2003: 170). Most of the Turkish Islamic community leaders considered EU membership to pose a danger of assimilation into the Judeo-Christian world. But Gülen affirms that Europe represents no danger to the Turkish-Islamic identity:

> We should be comfortable in our outreach to the world. We will not lose anything from our religion, nationality and culture because of developments like globalization, customs union or membership in the European Union. We firmly believe that the dynamics that hold our unity are strong. Again, we also firmly believe that the Quran is based on revelation and offers solution[s] to all the problems of humanity. Therefore, if there is anybody who is afraid, they should be those who persistently live away from the invigorating climate of Quran (Kösebalaban, 2003: 178).

Furthermore, in an interview in 1995, he assigns a particular task to the Turkish diaspora in Europe:

> Our people who live in Europe must come off from their old situation and become a part of the European society. Their children must be orientated to universities more then artisanal high schools. Also, they must transmit our cultural and religious richness to European society. In the future, they will constitute our lobbies which we highly need today. In the past, only the 2 per cent of the Turkish immigrant population was fulfilling their religious requirements. But today, 40 or maybe 60 per cent of the young population regularly prays in the mosques. Obviously, our people didn't undergo to an assimilation process, contrary, they impressed the host societies by their conviction and culture (Gülen in Akman, 1995: 2).

Despite the large Turkish population in Western Europe, compared with other Islamic organizations, the Gülen movement took hold relatively late and has been present in Europe now for about ten years. After researching Fethullah Gülen's old sermon records, it became clear that, at the end of the 1980s, Fethullah Gülen frequently visited some French and German cities. But the institutionalization process started after the mid-1990s.

Contrary to other Islamic movements, the Gülen movement didn't follow the Turkish migratory flow. We can explain this late arrival by two main reasons: first, the appearance of the Gülen movement in Turkey is itself relatively recent in comparison with other mainstream Islamic movements such as Milli Görüş and the Suleymanci communities. When the Suleymanci community and Milli Görüş started to institutionalize their European affiliates in 1970s, the Gülen movement was a little religious community in Izmir, a city located in the Aegean coast of Turkey. It was in the early 1990s that this religious-conservative community transformed into a transnational educational movement. Second, after the fall of Soviet Union, Fethullah Gülen gave a priority to the Turkic world in Central Asia. So he directed a major part of social and economic capital of the community to this region.

In recent years, the participants of the Gülen movement progressively transmitted their ideas in the Turkish Diaspora that lives in immigrant-populated cities such as Paris, Lyon, Strasbourg, Frankfurt, Stuttgart, Berlin and Cologne. In fact, the movement adapted its educational strategy to European conditions by initially creating learning centres. Generally, the Gülen-inspired associations prefer to establish private schools – as in Central Asia, in Africa and in the Balkan countries. But because of at least the perception of difficult administrative procedures being involved in the establishment of private schools in Europe, the Gülen movement adapted a different implantation strategy here. The participants who arrived first founded a learning centre, and after the institutionalization period, they took the initiative to form a private school.

Based on observation, it would appear that the community considers the learning centres as a 'preparatory period' for reaching the main goal, in other words, the private school. For instance, the movement participants indicated that the first learning centre – the BIL Learning House (Das Bildungshaus BIL) in Germany – was established in Stuttgart in 1995. After the BIL Learning Centre gained a considerable popularity among Turkish families and developed good relations with the local administration, in 2003 it was transformed into a private school.

Organizational strategies of the Gülen movement in Europe

The discursive and organizational strategies of the Gülen movement are differentiated from the other Turkish Islamic communities. The associational organization of Turkish Islam in Europe is based on two main axes: the construction and sponsoring of mosques and Qur'anic schools. In contrast with these two implantation strategies, the Gülen movement participants in Europe insist on the great importance of secular education and they do not build or sponsor mosques. They also do not focus on Qur'anic education for the youth as much as the Suleymanci community does. The mosques and Qur'anic schools led by Turkish Islamic movements play an important role in the transmission of religious and communal values to the new generation. But in the Gülen movement, the reproduction of the religious manner and communal values is realized by example (*tamsil*) without direct teaching.

Gülen movement participants in Europe have founded a variety of establishments, which operate in the major European cities. Essentially, we observe three principal types of establishments. First, there are learning centres which offer particular after-school courses from the college and private schools to the students of the primary school. Second, there are 'inter-cultural dialogue' associations which organize inter-cultural events and meetings in order to promote cultural exchanges between the Turkish population and the host society. Third, there are entrepreneurial associations which assemble Turkish businessmen who financially support the movement.

Learning centres, inter-cultural centres, entrepreneurial establishments and high schools are typically governed by a registered association. The members of the association, who are typically Turkish immigrant participants in the movement, choose a board of directors. (Irvine, 2006: 59). These centres typically serve about a hundred students at a variety of levels from secondary school grades to college-preparatory classes, offering courses such as English, French, German, maths, chemistry, physics and biology. In addition, the learning centres offer language courses for newcomer adults. Furthermore, the learning centres try to meet the needs of students primarily of Turkish background. The centres organize seminars for the students' parents 'to make them conscious about the importance of education'.

The staff in the learning centres comprise paid French/German teachers and volunteer university students of Turkish background. Although there are some exceptions (such as the Horizon learning centre in Mulhouse, France), the learning centres generally do not receive direct financial support from the state and local administrative institutions. In recent years, administrative staff of the movement's institutions in Germany established good relations with the local and national political leaders. In France, the relations with the local political authorities are at a minimum level because of the laïc context of France and the modest overall visibility of the movement in the public sphere. But we observed that learning centres in Strasbourg and Colmar have close relations with the deputies of their region and the local administrative institutions.

Gülen-inspired associations possess more than 100 learning centres in Germany and 16 learning centres in France. More recently, Gülen-inspired associations in Germany established three private high schools in Stuttgart, Berlin and Dortmund. The private schools offer a full college-preparatory curriculum to students primarily of Turkish background. These schools offer the same curriculum as public college preparatory high schools with the difference that they offer Turkish as the third language choice, after German and English. The Gülen movement sympathizers have recently inaugurated a private school in France. The Educative Secondary School in Villeneuve St Georges (a southern suburb of Paris) had 64 students in 2009 from different ethnic origins (Perrier, 2009: 3).

The Islamic organizations are usually managed by a head organization in Cologne, the city that became 'the capital of the Turkish Diaspora in Europe'. Contrary to the centralist organization of the other Turkish Islamic communities such as the National Outlook Movement and Suleymanci community, the inter-institutional relations between Gülen-inspired associations are loose and there is no single head organization or federation in Cologne. It is typically characteristic of the Gülen movement in Europe that it is highly decentralized. In Germany and France, each city or town is responsible for organizing and maintaining its own schools and centres. In an interview from 12 May 2007, the director of the Le Dialogue Learning Center in Strasbourg, Nihat Sarıer, said:

> We have no official relation with the other learning centres in France. Furthermore, we don't have a common strategy. Maybe, we are all inspired by the ideas of Fethullah Gülen but we are not controlled by a top organization which decides everything. Sometimes I discuss my problems with the directors of other centres in Paris, Metz, etc. and we share our experiences. But everybody lives in a different region or country, in different social and political circumstances; so everybody works with his own method.

Despite this decentralized structure of the movement, they have developed a loose network at the country, continental and inter-continental levels. First, the European edition of *Zaman* daily newspaper, which is located in Offenbach, Germany, plays an extremely important role in the communication between movement participants in different European countries. Every day, the journal publishes articles (particularly on its 17th page) about local activities of the Gülen-inspired associations and the educational success of private schools etc. In this way, a participant of the movement in Paris becomes informed about the activities in other French cities, or in Germany, Netherlands, and Belgium, etc.

Second, participants in the movement constantly organize tourist trips to other countries in Europe, and even in Asia or Africa. In these tourist trips they also visit Gülen-inspired educational establishments. For example, the local representatives of the *Zaman* daily newspaper in Metz recently organized a visit to Turkmenistan and Krygizstan for entrepreneurs of Turkish origin who financially support the local establishments of the community. They also visited the Gülen-inspired schools in these countries.

Third, according to information given by Hüseyin Gülerce, a columnist of *Zaman* and Fethullah Gülen's close friend, every city or town in different European countries sponsors Gülen-inspired educational activities in African countries. As a result of these strategies, the participants feel themselves to be not only participants in a local association in one's own city but also part of the worldwide educational movement.

The learning centres: quest for normalization?

In contrast to the worldwide implantation strategy of the movement, the participants in the movement in Europe encounter some difficulties around the procedures for establishing private schools. These difficulties are not just because of the administrative procedures themselves; they also arise because of the prejudices against Muslim immigrants and the rise of xenophobia-Islamophobia in the old continent. The Gülen movement in Central Asia or in the Balkans always sought direct contact with the host society. In contrast with the other regions, the participants in the Gülen movement in Europe encounter a big Turkish population that had become an object of negative characterizations and stigmatizations. Therefore, the Gülen movement implements a new immigrant-orientated strategy to gain legitimacy in the host societies.

Erving Goffman's (1963) concept of 'stigma' provides one means of understanding the normalization strategies of the Gülen movement and immigrant-origin youth in the host societies. Stigma refers to an individual sign, to social information the individual transmits about oneself that disqualifies a person and creates an obstacle to being fully accepted by society. A stigma therefore designates an attribute that profoundly discredits the individual. But we must emphasize that the 'normal' and 'stigmatized' are not persons, but viewpoints. These viewpoints are socially constructed by the mainstream values of the society (Goffman, 1963: 61). According to Goffman, ethnic, racial, religious or national identities are also the particularities that can create a distance from the 'normal'. Goffman named these types of stigmas as the 'tribal stigmas'.

The young population of the Turkish community who are separated from their peers by characterizations such as 'the suburban youth' and 'immigrant-origin youth' etc., are victims of an alterity. They suffer from stigmatization because of the negative image (delinquency, drug, urban violence, religious extremism, etc.) associated with the suburbs/ghettos in which they live. The majority of the young generation experiences school failure from an early age and they are orientated towards non-qualified work. Even when they have reached an adequate school level for qualified employment, they face discrimination because of the 'tribal stigmas', which they carry. According to Lorcerie's essentialist categorization of Goffman, stigmatized persons adopt five principal strategies to correct their stigma (Lorcerie, 2003: 34).

First, they can try to correct the essence of the stigma or to dissimulate the stigma signs and to deny its influence: to search for assimilation. Second, they can try to show that their difference from being 'normal' persons does not prevent them from being successful in society, or from excelling at school or in their work – things that are difficult to achieve even for the 'normal' persons. Third, as a reaction to the disrepute in which they are held by the 'normal' ones, they can try to perform a personality that is bound to their social, cultural or ethnic identity. Fourth, they can try to cash in on their stigma; seeking to instrumentalize it. Finally, they can try to redefine their difference as reason of pride and advantage over the 'normal ones' (as in the assertion of negritude or 'Black is beautiful').

The first and third strategies go through a process of 'self-devalorization', while the second, fourth and fifth strategies are experienced by a process of 'self-valorization'. According to Goffman, all the strategies except the last one can be led by a collective action (Lorcerie, 2003: 37). Moreover, 'normal' persons can perceive the first, second and fourth strategies as manoeuvres. The practice of all these stigma-correcting strategies can be observed among Turkish immigrant youth. But the young students who participate to the educational activities of the Gülen movement adopt the second strategy. They try to excel in the host society via educational success and differentiate from their friends and other stigma carriers.

It is the same for the Gülen movement itself. The administrative staff of the Gülen-inspired institutions frequently complain about the host society's perception of the learning centres as an 'Islamic association', a 'communitarian association', or an 'ethnic association', etc. During an interview (12 April 2007, in Paris), one of the leading actors of the movement in France noted:

> We did not come to Europe only for the Turkish immigrants. We want to serve the French society. But when we talk about our private school project with the local administrative responsible or politicians, they maintain a sceptical attitude to this idea because of the negative image of the Turkish community in France. They evoke the poor situation of Turkish students at the school. It is really very saddening! So, firstly we will focus on the educational problems of our children. If we achieve to break this negative image, we will have a chance to start a dialogue between equals and we can realize our private school project.

The movement participants think that they are victims of an alterity as a result of juxtaposition of the Turkish community in France and a movement of Turkish origins. Because of the stigmatization of Gülen-inspired associations, in Europe the participants of the Gülen movement are primarily focused on the problems of the Turkish population in Europe. The reintegration of Turkish students into the educational system of the host societies is defined as a first goal.

A double strategy of normalization can be observed. On the one hand, the immigrant youth appropriates the communal values of the Gülen movement, which legitimates the second correction strategy. On the other hand, the administrative staff are disturbed by the negative perception of the host society and are in a search of success and excellence in their occupation – i.e. the educational activities. During the implantation process in Europe, the movement also adopts the second correction strategy.

The invisible religion: towards secularization in the public sphere?

During our observation period at the learning centres in France and in Germany, no religious propaganda or proselytism was observed. This secular education policy in Europe is a by-product of the worldwide strategy of the Gülen movement. The school curricula are prepared in accordance with the national education requirements of each country and they are totally secular and scientific. Even the Muslim students, who demand a place to practice their prayers in the school, are not authorized to do it (Balcı, 2003: 69). Elizabeth Özdalga notes that:

> The main objective [of the education provided in these schools] is to give the students a good education, without prompting any specific ideological orientation. One basic idea of Gülen's followers is that ethical values are not transmitted openly through persuasion and lessons but through providing good examples in daily conduct (Özdalga, 1999: 19).

The total absence of religious discourse in these educational establishments constitutes the most interesting and paradoxical point of this movement. By borrowing the concept of Pierre Bourdieu, we suggest that the religious manner constitutes the 'doxic' experience of the movement. Doxa are the fundamental and unthought beliefs that inform an agent's actions and thoughts within a particular field (Bourdieu, 2003: 22). A doxic experience is one in which members of a society share a common sense that is transmitted by a series of implicit assumptions and values that appear as a matter of fact, as a truth (Bourdieu and Passeron, 1970). Through the concept of *Hizmet*, which can be described as any volunteer service or work done for the community, Gülen sacralizes secular education. What is essential in this 'faith-based social movement' exists implicitly in the body of the community (Kömeçoğlu, 1997: 47).

Although the religious visibility of Gülen-inspired activities is relatively weak, the participants in the Gülen movement in Europe do not encounter big difficulties in inculcating religious values among the participants due to their conceptualization of *Hizmet*. For instance, in Strasbourg we observed that some of the parents of the students are influenced by the idea of *Hizmet* and believe that the secular education in Gülen-inspired establishments will help their children to be successful not only in life but also in the hereafter. *Hizmet* promotes the appropriation of individual piety and Islamic ethical (*adab*) values in the private sphere and an active participation in the modern secularized world in the public sphere. In this way, participants of the movement voluntarily or 'involuntarily' revalorize a secularization process in the public sphere. They offer a new communitarian identity to the Turkish community by appropriating secular codes in the public sphere and appropriating religious codes in the private sphere.

But the Gülen movement must not forget that for European Muslims, Islam was largely considered as a 'clannish' (*communatauriste*) reinvestment. Clannish reinvestment refers to the valorization of religious or ethnic identity instead of French or German citizenship (see Cesari, 1997: 97). As a characteristic of diasporic Islam, 'religion' and 'ethnicity' march hand in hand in Europe because they construct 'the compensatory refoundation of an "us" lost in the dangers and reversals of immigration' (Bastenier, 1998: 197). The associative institutionalization of Islam in Europe fulfils many complementary functions such as a wish for identity, a community-centred life and fidelity to the ethnic group. Therefore, Islam in Europe is 'more culture (than faith) and more tradition than belief' (Dialmy, 2007: 70–1). However, despite the accentuation of Turkish identity in the Gülen movement, Fethullah Gülen's conception of Islam is closer to the universalist orientation of Islam than to an 'ethnic-clannish' one. As Dialmy (2007: 70–1) puts it, the movement in France and in Germany 'seeks to find a "middle way" between the cultural devastation implied by assimilation and the "ghettoization" of a minority group living apart from the host society culture' But the community faces the risk of losing the 'fine balance' between the diaspora's community-orientated conception of Islam and the movement's more universalist Islam and integrationist stance.

This balance is threatened by two main factors, First, in spite of its relative success, the Gülen movement's relatively 'liberal' and renewalist interpretation of Islam causes some critiques from its participants. For instance, the Director of Le Dialogue Learning Centre, Nihat Sarıer, explains that parents of the secondary school students strongly object to mixed education in the learning centre: 'When I talk about the importance and necessity of mixed education in the classes, the parents say "No, This is a Turkish association. We don't want a mixed education here"' (in Irvine 2006: 56). As another example, a visit of the Gülen-inspired inter-cultural dialogue association in Paris, Plateforme de Paris, to a Catholic church evoked criticism from some movement participants.

Second, although it is important to note a declining youth participation in the community-orientated Islamic movements such as Suleymanci community or fundamentalist movements like Kaplanci community, the large variety of Sunni Islamic associations still constitute a considerable 'religious market' in the Turkish diaspora. These associations (which have maintained their own clientelist networks) criticize the integrationist, less community-orientated and liberal discourse of the Gülen movement. For instance, the Milli Görüş community harshly criticizes the inter-faith dialogue activities of the Gülen movement in Europe, while the Alevi community and the nationalist group, Ulkucus, strongly opposes the Gülen model of integration.

Consequently, the socio-political problems and economic vulnerability of the Turkish diaspora in Europe transform the strategies of the Gülen movement. If the schools in Central Asia, in the Balkan countries or in Africa are considered, then the implantation strategy of the movement is not dependent on the Turkish immigration waves throughout the world. In different regions, the participants of the movement always seek to make contact with the host societies. In contrast to the evolution of the movement in Central Asia or Balkans, etc. in Turkish-populated Western European countries, the movement does not focus on the host societies.

As a result of our qualitative research, we observed that the participants of the Gülen movement act according to two different logics. On the one hand, they strive to have a larger share of the religious market of the Turkish diaspora by producing a new religious discourse, as they did in Turkey. On the other hand, they seek to gain legitimacy in Germany and France by building an educational network in these countries, as they did in Central Asia or in the Balkans region. Due to this synthesis of two different logics, a reinvented and reorganized community developed in Europe.

The Gülen movement seeks out an ethno-religious reference among movement participants. Therefore, this 'fine balance', is procured by a *reciprocal compromise* between the 'social reality' of the Turkish diaspora and integrationist stance of the movement, which is why I would argue that, in Europe, the Gülen movement became a neo-communitarian movement.

The discursive strategies: Gülen movement participants in the lands of dar al-hizmet

Many scholars specializing in European Islam build their analysis on the traditional Islamic contrast between *dar al-Islam* (House of Islam) and *dar al-harb* (House of war) which presents an historical antagonism from Islam towards non-Muslims. But the conflict is merely one facet of the complex relationship between Muslims and 'Western' society (Henkel, 2004). For a great part of the Muslim population in Europe the *dar al-Islam* and *dar al-harb* distinction is not a pertinent method to define the relationship with non-Muslim societies. In Germany and France, 'many religious Muslims have recently undergone a significant shift toward a more "integrational" stance' (interview with Nirhat Sarier, Director of the Le Dialogue Learning Centre, 12 May 2007).

The movement employs the term *dar al-hizmet* (country of service) (Yilmaz, 2003: 234) when operating in the Turkish diaspora. Gülen stresses a Muslim who lives in a non-Muslim society has to obey the *lex loci*, to respect others' rights and to be just, and has to disregard discussions of *dar al-harb* and *dar al-Islam* (Yilmaz, 2003: 234). The conceptualization and practical use of the term *dar al-hizmet* looks like a 'practical solution' offered by Gülen, more than a new politico-legal contribution to the Islamic law.

The essential idea of the Gülen movement with regard to the Turkish diaspora is for it to become a recognized part of the main society without losing its 'Turkish-Islamic' identity. During our research, we observed that the concepts such as *dar al-hizmet* and 'renewal of intention' (*tashih-i niyet*) are frequently used by the disciples of the Gülen movement in Europe. As a matter of fact, Turkish immigrants mainly migrated for economic reasons. The Gülen disciples in Europe advise movement participants to renew their intentions. This specific term means not to justify their presence in European countries for purely economic reasons, but to live as a good Muslim in order to represent the 'true Islam' to their entourage. A Turkish (small entrepreneur) movement participant who lives in Frankfurt-Germany says (2006):

> We all came here (Germany) with an economic motive – to gain more money and have a more comfortable life. Nobody can deny it. But after 30 years, we became the members of this society. We cannot continue to live in our small communal worlds. Fethullah Gülen advises us to renew our intentions. That means we are not here just for a more comfortable life, but also be a good example for our entourage and work for the good of this country.

Despite the 'politically correct' aspect of this declaration, it indicates a discursive change with regard to the host society. Consequently, by eliminating the contrast between the *dar al harb* and *dar al Islam*, the term *dar al hizmet* especially allows the youth of immigrant origins to express their will to be recognized individually and collectively in the host society, not only as a diasporic-passive subjects, but also as 'veritable subjects' (Touraine, 1997: 13) and, 'who are searching a constructive role in the host society, as the autonomous authors of their trajectory and as the producers of their existence' (Bouzar, 2003: 74).

Conclusion

The moderate, apolitical and dialogue-orientated Gülen movement undertakes a new task in Europe by readapting a particular implantation strategy orientated to the Turkish Diaspora. The more recently arrived Gülen movement assigned 'the reintegration of Turkish youth to the educational system of the host societies' as a first goal. The community is in a search of a mediator role, willing to influence the Turkish youth to a transition from the diasporic (stigmatized) condition. They aim to establish a fully secular educational network in Germany and in France, which can attract the *Banlieue,* or ghetto youth, to the schools.

By differentiating from other Islamic organizations, they could gain the confidence of the host society states. It is too early to speak about a success or failure of the movement because it is has not yet reached a very tangible size in Europe. But the main reason for a possible failure in the future could be the loss of the 'delicate balance' between clannish pressure of their social base and their innovative and integrationist discourse.

9

The Gülen movement as an integration mechanism for Europe's Turkish and Muslim community: potentials and constraints

M. FATIH TETIK

Introduction

This chapter endeavours to analyse the potential contributions of the Gülen movement to the integration process of the Turkish community in Europe in the medium term, and in the long term the whole Muslim community, as well as the feasibility of this process with reference to existing restrictions in the composition of these communities. However, prior to giving a historical account of Muslim immigration to the West and possible functions that the Gülen movement can contribute to this process, it is imperative to highlight why Gülen and the movement inspired by him were selected, although Gülen is the first or sole pioneer of dialogue in the Muslim world.

The distinctiveness of the Gülen movement derives, first, from its existence as an embodiment of Gülen's ideas; and second, the capability of this movement gradually to influence its surrounding environment. In other words, in the Muslim world there have been certain Islamic scholars prior to, or contemporary with, Gülen who have formulated certain ideas related to inter-faith dialogue and/or integration to host societies. What makes Gülen significant is the presence of a movement or people that are at least sympathetic to his ideas and puts them into operation. His ideas do not remain in the world of ideas but become a charter or an action plan pursued by the participants of the movement. Therefore, while initially the personal, then communal, organizational and finally societal acceptance and realization of these notions are required for the other scholars, Gülen's ideas almost bypass the first three phases and function in order to be recognized at the societal level.

From empire's children to imported employees

The two world wars and ensuing political events created a brave new world for Muslims in which three great empires of the sixteenth century were carved up into 44 nation-states. This separation led to one-third of the Muslim population living as minorities in non-Muslim countries. The number of minorities has noticeably been augmented after Muslims voluntarily migrated to the Western world as well as Australia and New Zealand in expectation of a new and better life. According to estimates of the National Intelligence Council (NIC), based on contemporary fertility rates European Muslims will, over then next 15 years, double their population. Although European countries experience social-political problems with their minorities, they have to continue with the 'minority importation' in order to sustain the economic growth of the continent. In spite of not being welcomed by Western society, immigration, therefore, seems not to be stoppable and to be an irreversible aspect of the continent.

In the early decades of immigration, the majority of the immigrant workers were young men from rural regions who had a low level of education and very conservative opinions about religious and/or other social concepts. They were not only deficient in knowledge of Islam but they were also very unskilled in social issues such as the language or culture of their new society (Sander, 1991: 82). These factors, nonetheless, were not so difficult for them because their aim was to return home after saving sufficient money for their living expenses in the homeland. Therefore, they were only 'guest workers' without any intention of residing permanently in Europe (Anwar, Blaschke and Sander, 2004: 19).

By the 1970s, the sense of temporariness started to fade away following the family reunifications that altered and broadened the context of workers' relations with their surrounding society. With the arrival of their families, the minorities began to interact with a wide range of social institutions, such as education and social welfare (Nielsen, 1991: 43), which forced them to address how they were also going to preserve their traditions. In other words, the transition from individual workers to families (or from foreign workers to immigrants) triggered the formation of safeguarding institutions for traditional values (Pauly, 2004: 99).

Even so, these institutions were not established to facilitate an integration process or to enhance communication with the host nation but to protect their society from external impacts. In other words, Muslims were pursuing an isolationist and defensive policy. For Joly (1998), this was 'not simply the predominance of another religion which caused concern to Muslims; they wanted to safeguard Islam from the growing secularisation' of the surrounding European social order. Arguably, this was not a genuine consciousness about the preservation of their religion, but was a protective reflex in relation to aspects of their traditions that made them different even if they did not live the tradition. This is because, as Darsh (1980: 51) argues, the majority of immigrants were not very well educated people whose 'own culture, way of life and religious beliefs were mocked, derided or desecrated'. This formation of traditional and religious bodies, however, is not an independent process. On the contrary, existing European political, economic, social and religious structures have a determinative effect on the profiles, nature and stream of this formation (LeVine, 2003: 101).

Today, immigrants are concentrated in the *banlieus* of the big cities in Western Europe (Nielsen, 1991: 34). With illegal immigration in the 1980s and 1990s, refugees from the revolution in Iran, the Iran–Iraq war, the Palestinian conflict and Kurds from Middle Eastern countries, not only the numbers of immigrants but also the national and sectarian variety of the immigration greatly intensified. Religion often upholds its position in the social milieu by acting as a protector of cultural identity – or by being protected in the customs – and providing a sense of unity and similarity. This characteristic of religion is vital, particularly in a Western social context, because for a worker with an Islamic background religion is the only support and 'it is the only thing that belongs to him and that he can master' (Elsas, 1991: 175). For instance, as Yilmaz examined in the daily practice of the Turkish community in Britain, '[T]he traditional homeland Turkish culture, identity and diversity are, to a great extent, reproduced and reconstructed in the British context' which even gives rise to the emergence of the Anglo-Turkish Muslim law (see Yilmaz, 2004).

Being a Muslim in Europe

Scholars articulate a range of quite distinct categorizations for being a Muslim in Europe. In what follows, this chapter uses five categories. First, those who choose to remain distant from the religion and the religious establishments; second, those who prefer personal piety and devotion but are detached from religious organizations; third, those who join moderate/mainstream Islamic organizations seeking improvement in the religious consciousness of their members; fourth, those who adhere to organized missionary groups; and fifth, those who adhere to militant affiliations.

Depending on their stance, in the new social framework Muslim organizations could either comprise groups formed by the immigrants themselves who were concerned with the conservation (or reconstruction) of essentials of traditional culture and collective continuity and reproduction in the European environment, or emerge as branches or extensions of movements or organizations from various countries of origin (in other words, groups formed with the same objective of the previous category but opting to operate under tutelage of a powerful organization based in the country of origin). Finally they could be formed by governments or state-led agencies – in other words, as groups or organizations formed in order to control a national Muslim minority in Europe and to prevent them from connecting with informal religious movements considered as rivals. But, whatever their mode of organization and their strategies, in the course of restructuring the religious community within a secular society they try to find a point of equilibrium between total assimilation and total rejection.

For most, the equilibrium point is found by reconstructing 'a home away from home, or *desh pardesh*' (Ballard, 1998: 5). A growing number of the older generation of Muslims and their European-born offspring are continuing to find substantial inspiration in the resources of their own cultural, religious and linguistic inheritance, which they have actively and creatively reinterpreted in order to rebuild their lives on their own terms. They have become an integral part of Western society. However, 'they have done so on their own terms' (Ballard, 1998: 8). As skilled cultural navigators, Muslims, along with other ethnic minorities, have been meeting the demands of different cultures and laws. Ballard (1998: 31) explains this phenomenon:

> [J]ust as individuals can be bilingual, so they can be multicultural, with the competence to behave appropriately in a number of different arenas, and to switch codes as appropriate […] they are much better perceived as skilled cultural navigators, with a sophisticated capacity to manoeuvre their way to their own advantage both inside and outside the ethnic colony.

However, due to the socio-political turmoil in both former and new habitats, the economic, cultural and intellectual backgrounds of the Muslim community inevitably struggle against a set of overwhelming difficulties that deeply damage the integration process. It is worth noting that the validity and intensity of these problems are spatial although some of them stem from the intrinsic qualities of migrating and receiving cultures. These are listed in the following text.

A high degree of fragmentation

The Muslim minority in Western Europe suffers from sectarian (e.g. Sunni vs. Shiite), cultural, national, linguistic, political heterogeneity and 'intra- and inter- community rivalry and split' (Ballard, 1998: 81). It seems that these problems will possibly not be resolved in near future due to the absence of working 'socialization agents'. As Pauly (2004: 147) rightly describes it, in our day, 'there are as many as Islams as there are Muslims'. Even mosques and prayer halls are organized as national entities. This is partly because chain migration and village transplantation led to people with same origin gathering in the same area in the Western Europe, but it is mostly sectarian and ideological differences which grounds contention and resentment among the Muslim community.

Incompetence

According to surveys and opinion polls in Western Europe, Muslim migrants represent a cluster which is socio-economically marginalized, geographically dispersed and internally split, and does not have a constructive asset to share with the mainstream European community. The first generation and considerable proportion of their children are not properly competent in terms of the formal education, vocational skills and language of the host country.

Obviously this generalization is rather harsh and one-sided, but that does not mean there are no reasonable grounds for it. For example, school drop-out rates among students with a migrant background are more than two times higher than among non-migrant groups; and the percentage of people who are officially suspected of a crime is 2.9 per cent among first generation non-Western immigrants and 4 per cent among second generation non-Western immigrants, but 1.2 per cent for the total population. These ratios are noteworthy not only because they show first generation's adaptation crisis but also because they suggest the expected future socio-economic position of the second and (more importantly) third generation.

Guidance crisis

In the absence of traditional social settings such as family, acquaintances and neighbourhood, and of a healthy social infrastructure and environment in which Muslims could express themselves to the mainstream society, the functions and significance of the *imam* and the mosque have become central in communities. Not only by offering religious services but also by generating a network of solidarity that redresses the discomfort of isolation, the mosque became an indispensable intermediary institution for Muslims (Leveau, 1988: 114). Nonetheless, the insufficiency in the capacity and number of *imams* relative to the number of the growing Muslim population necessitated importing *imams* from the countries of origin. But most newly recruited *imams* could not help their communities since they did not have the necessary know-how – either about Islam or about the new society and language. Hence, new *imams* have usually been more helpless than the people whom they have been supposed to be guiding (Elsas, 1991).

Generation gap

Today, the West has a large number of the younger generation of Muslims trying to live in their new homelands. Wherever their parents came from, they experience Islam in a very distinct manner. Islam as a part of the social order was not taken for granted, and neither their environments nor their practices justify/affirm it. This situation leads to a generation gap between parents of traditional background who fail to transmit Islamic identity in an acceptable mode and children who interact with society and suffer from the incompatibility between conventional values and Western life. At that juncture, they prefer to learn what they understand to be genuine Islam from the original sources and to construct a hybrid identity as a combination of Islam and Western culture.

As Elsas (1991: 183) aptly expresses it: '[T]he majority of Muslim youths choose a bicultural option with regard to integration: to become full members of the encompassing society without complete identification with its norms and values.' In France, for example, despite the assumptions of many sociologists of religion who once forecasted secularization as the inevitable upshot of individual choice, 'a number of young Franco-Muslims are choosing strict religious observance, rather than wholesale abandonment of Muslim attachments, as an expression of personal autonomy' (Cesari, 2002: 42).

They abandon neither Islam nor their social roles; because, on one hand, Islam represents a protection or a shelter from assimilation into a secular and foreign culture: and on the other hand, their social roles are everything they have in their new homelands. Features of this hybrid identity vary according to the state's policies towards Islam and public perception of the religion. In a small number of cases, the search for a 'true Islam' may later channel them to embrace a radical form of Islam if they are guided to this direction.

Nevertheless, it should be noted that while young Muslims secularize at an individual level, they perceive religion as the *sine qua non* of their identity. For example, although more than half of the first generation in France regularly performs daily prayers, this percentage drops to only 3 per cent in second and third generations. But the latter group sees Islam as the primary element of their identity and downplays French citizenship (see Cesari, 2002: 43).

Perception of 'minorityness' and reciprocal perspective of 'the other'

Today, not only do a number of Muslims evaluate the West in the light of the experiences of colonial times but also some European states and individuals consider Islam according to parameters remaining from the Crusades. The West for Muslims and Muslims for the West symbolize a very distinctive 'other', a religio-political force that they engaged with for centuries within a heritage of salient confrontations and clashes. This reciprocal perception at best inevitably slows down, and at worst obstructs, the process of Muslim integration in the West.

For the West, the resultant stereotypes have kept negative images of Islam and Muslims alive or even caused them to be perceived as 'a threat and a problem' (Esposito, 2003: 12). From this perspective, to some degree the West's principal cultural puzzle is not only how different cultures will be integrated into the secular society or Islam's compatibility with Western lifestyles, but also how secular society will develop *vis-à-vis* Islamic existence.

However, Allievi made a remarkable contribution to the problem of the perception of Islam by Western society and by Muslims themselves. As he portrayed it, the situation in Europe, 'resembles much more the Meccan than the Medinese situation. Specifically, the society and the situation in Europe nowadays, from the religious point of view, resemble that of Mecca before the *hijra*' (Allievi, 2003: 142–3). In the Meccan context Muslims were a minority not a dominant clique, or even an influential one. Normally, that is the expected situation when the novelty of Muslim settlement is taken into consideration. What he sees as a contextual dilemma is that although the current situation for Muslims is more Meccan than Medinese,

> the common comprehension of Islam by non-Muslims, as well as by Muslims, is often much more Medinese than Meccan. The whole idea of *shari'a* (Islamic law) and *fiqh* (Islamic jurisprudence), as well as the idea of political power influenced by religion, and in many respects the entire Islamic theology [...] simply presupposes that Islam is a majority in the population as well as a majority in power (Allievi, 2003: 142).

By contrast, for Kettani the reason behind this attitude is not that they see themselves in power but that they are highly exposed to the external socio-political system, or the sense of 'minorityness'. Islam, he argues, 'insists on the health and wellbeing of a community, conditions guaranteed by social and political empowerment' (Kettani, 1979: 3). Hence, Muslims must not collude with minority status as a long-term situation in which they accommodate and submit to those in power. Their 'minorityness' is to be understood as a challenge to the community in order to seek methods to correct such a condition and surpass it. To Kettani (1979: 3), if a minority Muslim community faces repression and cruelty and is not tolerated in the observance of its faith, then its members have the options of either *jihad* or emigration. Put differently, Muslims should never accept being under the rule of non-Muslims.

For some Muslims in Western countries, these assertions constitute the intellectual backbone of their resistance. However, particularly for the younger generations, and contrary to their predecessors, the implication of these perceptions is not to isolate or ostracize themselves from the society but to adapt to the environment in which they live (Shadid and van Koningsveld, 1991: 91). They have even redefined their religious doctrines (probably not only for the sake of religion) and reoriented the way they carry out social and cultural activities.

Turks in the diaspora

For Turks, as the initial locus of the Gülen movement, the picture is also not so encouraging. As previously mentioned, at the beginning of the formal era of immigration, the first generation were a not an especially educated population who had a rural background of Eastern and Western Anatolia. Following the initial shock experienced when they first came to the Western context, based on an instinct for protection they began gathering in Turkish ghettos. As with others, they had no intention to stay permanently. Thus they did not feel the necessity to integrate into the wider society.

To begin with, religion did not have any role in the Turkish community. Particularly prior to the 1980s, and in parallel to Turkish politics, the majority of Turkish associations could be categorized according to their position on the continuum of the extreme political poles of Turkish society. Turkish political competition, both official and underground, became reflected among the Turks in diaspora. But the transition from temporary migration to permanent settlement, family reunification and Turkish political developments increased the significance of religion in the Turkish community.

However, religion in the Turkish community is neither strong enough to mobilize people nor is it a monolithic entity. The Turkish community is divided into many parts due to sectarian and ethnic diversity. In terms of sectarian variations, the Turkish population is mostly Sunni with 88 per cent and Alevis with 11 per cent – with not much interaction between them. No Alevis live in Sunni-dominated areas and, as was shown earlier, the differences are reproduced in the composition of the various associations and organizations. The Alevis and the laïcists are unlikely candidates for Islamic religious movements. Moreover, in an ethno-national sense, the main division occurs among people with Turkish and Kurdish origins (Başyurt, 2004).

Whereas the total number of Turks in the diaspora (including unofficial migrants) reached nearly 4.5–5 million, the majority remained surprisingly uninformed about, and indifferent towards, them and their religion. In Germany alone there are two thousand four hundred mosque associations but their members do not reflect Muslimness in the pure theological sense of the definition (Başyurt, 2004). They are mostly 'cultural Muslims' who adjust their religious practices towards 'folk Islam', and are not very interested in the theological/ideological issues. By and large (and contrary to other Muslims) there is a tendency to join the nearest mosque, no matter which view it represents. Their Islamic way of life is a mixture of 'popular religiosity, national customs, Islamic rules of conduct, mysticism, folk knowledge, folklore and magic with Islamic elements' (Thomä-Venske, 1988: 78).

Members of the first generation, particularly, define themselves as Muslims although this is not because of their firm adherence to an Islamic faith but because they merge the notion of nationality and Islam. In other words, they are Muslims because Islam was taken granted with 'Turkishness'.

Today, as the newcomers, the Turkish community outside Turkey suffers from very serious deficiencies that not only obstruct a healthy integration but also threaten the Turkish community itself. Lack of formal and vocational education, critical deficiencies in communication in the native language, social isolation, animosity and anxiety towards the societal environment and involvement in crime have already reached a very critical level. For example, in German prisons alone there are 25,000 Turks and more than this number are involved in street gangs. In Britain, 40 per cent of Turks and 60 per cent of Kurds have no formal education (Bradley, 2005); 75 per cent of Turks in Germany live in 'ethnic enclaves' without any interaction with the mainstream society and this problem increases as new generations arise; 81 per cent of the Turkish workforce in 1981 were unskilled and the unemployment rates among the Turkish community is up to three times the average (Pedersen, 1999: 155).

Even though Germany's economic and occupational structures have undergone significant changes, most of the Turks that were originally hired as unskilled or semi-skilled labour have remained in unskilled or semi-skilled jobs. For some, the worst problem is that the Turkish community does not feel it necessary to integrate with the surrounding society and shows no effort to realize this. In fact, the situation is not as desperate since a fair proportion of the second and third generation now struggles to eliminate this disadvantaged status. Nowadays, for instance, it is even common to observe 'shining examples' of the Turkish youth in a Western context who have achieved academic or professional excellence in nationwide examinations.

Theoretical incentives of the Gülen movement for integration

Initially – and perhaps the most importantly – Gülen's redefinition of the West and Western civilization in religious terms is an attempt to replace the conventional dichotomy of *dar al-Islam* (abode of Islam) and *dar al-harb* (abode of war). Not only does he attempt to alter Muslims' assessment of the West as a natural enemy and of its countries as natural places of destruction, but also he seeks to substitute the classifications, which give temporal reconciliation, with an standard of unconditional accord or peace.

For instance, besides the *dar al-Islam* and *dar al-harb* dichotomy, Islamic jurisprudence has utilized different concepts such as *ikrah* (duress), *darura* (necessity), and *maslaha* (public welfare), and has produced some concepts, such as *dar al-ahd* (country of treaty, covenant), *dar al-aman* (country of security), *dar as-sulh* (country of peace) and *dar al-darura* (country of necessity), which denote that 'Muslims can live according to their religion in non-Muslim lands perhaps with difficulty but peacefully'. (Yilmaz, 2003: 234) Quite the reverse, Gülen's term of *dar al-hizmet* (abode of service) requires Muslims to *ad infinitum* perform peaceful manners in their societies to demonstrate Islam's 'true character' (Yilmaz, 2003: 234).

This term, without any reservation, charges the believer with a new duty to portray a good example in their everyday lives (*temsil*). It stresses not only the necessity but also the obligation of a Muslim to obey legal settings of the new country, not just in receiving benefits from the political setting (for example, pensions), but additionally in performing civic duties (e.g. taxes) and in fairly recognizing the other's rights. According to Yilmaz, Gülen stresses that:

> [W]herever a Muslim is, even outside a Muslim polity; he or she has to obey the *lex loci*, to respect others' rights and to be just. In Gülen's understanding, *umma* is more of a transnational socio-cultural entity, not a politico-legal one. He hopes that this socio-cultural entity will be instrumental in bringing general universal peace. (Yilmaz, 2003: 234).

Thus, by these words, he nullifies the conventional evaluation of the Western context, even those giving a conditional status of peace but which are prone to change according to conditions. And quite strikingly, in terms of Islamic theology he also changes the emphasis placed on the previously mentioned peaceful manner. In the classical dichotomies, the terms do not belong to the essence of the faith. But Gülen has repositioned the peaceful method and obedience to the host country to the centre of a Muslim's personal and religious life and requires him/her to re-designate the complete way of life similar to the commands of the religion. Hence, for him integration becomes an intrinsic or integral part of the religion.

Second, and parallel to the first set of logic, the values of Western civilization such as democracy and modernity, and the re-evaluation of the West's development, occupy one of the focal points in his logic. He does not observe the West and its civilization from the perspective of 'our eternal enemy'. Thus he denies the rejection of its values just because 'they are Western'. He sees Western dominance as the result of their obedience to the Divine laws that are valid in nature through pursuing scientific knowledge and by developing a well-structured methodology. Gülen emphasizes his concern for the basic tenets of Islam, but he also professes the backwardness of today's Islamic interpretation and livelihood in relation to the requirements of the era. For him, that is why the West dominates the Muslim world, while latter fails to understand and perform Islam properly, and disregards the scientific investigation undertaken by the former (Gülen, 2005b: 251).

He promotes this notion with his understanding of *takwah*, which is generally understood as preservation from sins. But he sees *takwah* as a systematic rapprochement with the creation, as the fulfilment of all the requirements of this world (for example, from science to economics) and that these are all consistent with having a pious and otherworldly character. It seems that this is not a mere justification of modernity and a pursuit of a 'middle way' between being Muslim and being modern; because he accepts Islam itself as the middle way. In this regard, Gülen is searching for an interpretation of Islam that is compatible with, and at the same time critical of, modernity and tradition. In other words, it is not an effort to graft Islam onto modernity and obtain a hybrid identity: 'What he does is reveal a dynamic interpretation of Islam that is both compatible with and critical of modernity and Muslim tradition' (Kuru, 2003: 130).

Third, his re-reading of dialogue in which dialogue is the natural result of the practice of Islamic ethics sets him apart from most Islamic scholars. For him, Islam does not reject interaction with diverse cultures on condition that the essence of Islam is not challenged. For all other conditions, dialogue is not a superfluous endeavour, but an imperative that is inherent to the faith. For him,

> love, respect, tolerance, forgiveness, mercy, human rights, peace, brotherhood, and freedom are all values exalted by religion ... [and are

the parts of] the messages brought by Moses, Jesus, and Muhammad, upon them be peace, as well as in the messages of Buddha and even Zarathustra, Lao-Tzu, Confucius, and the Hindu prophets (Gülen in Ünal and Williams, 2000: 43).

On the contrary, opposition to diversity or attempts to take measures against the emergence of diverse ideas are, indeed, against God's creation and historical fact.

Conclusion: what can the Gülen movement offer in practice?

In the Western context, given the theological incentives and its physical and intellectual potential, the movement has the ability to promote the Turkish community's process in the medium term; and in the long-run, it can support the integration of the majority of the Muslim community even if that requires them to undertake a communal re-identification. As religion is the principal identifier for most Muslims, Gülen's realignment of an individual's role and the re-positioning of host countries in a religious context would gradually benefit them in having civic values that are compatible with the prerequisites of modern states.

From education to the media they can diffuse to all levels of everyday life and influence the population more effectively and efficiently. Especially when the movement's success in Turkey is taken into consideration – where the basis for its operation is so limited because of a fierce rivalry from the pro-*status quo* state elite – in a Western context that is characterized by freedom and social rights it can be claimed that the movement is fairly promising.

With its moderate approach that contains tolerant and friendly messages for the Western world, it can lessen the radical messages of ideologies coming from Saudi Arabia and Iran. In the larger context, it can also weaken the impact of radical and pro-violence Islamisms in the Muslim world. Partly, this process contributes to the democratization of Turkey and the Islamic world, respectively, through Muslim citizens within European states. And in any possible accession of Turkey to the EU, the community can significantly facilitate Turkey's adaptation process. The democratization process of the whole Muslim world will undeniably take quite a long time, but even in this situation Turkey can function as a buffer between liberal and democratic Europe and the Middle East which absorbs the shock coming from both sides of the alignment and, hence, can lessen the political and cultural resentment for both sides.

The movement's educational principle that favours integration into the modern world can assist the second and third generations of Muslim minorities who face severe educational, vocational and language problems. In the Netherlands, for example, one of the countries where the movement is well established, many civil society institutions founded by Turks exist and whose co-operation definitely affects the integration process. The positive outcome of the movement's actions also contributes to Turkish participation in national politics.

In the Dutch parliament there are several MPs with Turkish origins. Additionally, with their emphasis on education, it is expected that, by 2015, the educational level of the Turkish minority will be equal to the level of the native students (Başyurt, 2004). Therefore, on the one hand, with the movement's specialization in education, it can improve the educational level of Turkish children by paying special attention to their specific problems. On the other hand since, in the education progress, it does not refer to any religious and ideological orientation, the young generations would not be constrained in terms of interaction with the mainstream society. As Özdalga (2003: 436) puts it, the Gülen movement 'may be seen as a training ground, a transition zone in the formation of values and identities suitable for integration'.

To date, the Gülen movement has proved itself successful particularly in its educational and dialogue activities around the world. But it is noteworthy that the rest of the world is not Europe in relation to political, social, financial and cultural characteristics. Until recently, with some exceptions, the countries where the movement opened educational or social institutions have been relatively underdeveloped compared with Turkey. From 1990 onwards, participants of the movement have built and opened many facilities, such as colleges, universities and dormitories from Turkic Republics in the former Soviet Union to African countries and to Indo-China. Opening institutions was financially and politically challenging, but to be recognized by the host countries was not so difficult by reference to a successful educational background in Turkey.

The real challenge, however, was to prove the merit of the movement first in Western Europe through success in education and with a representation of their commitment to Western values; and second, in the Muslim world as Muslims – because in both regions, states and societies are expected to be more reluctant to welcome it. As stated, on the one hand the West may be unwilling to recognize the genuineness or sincerity of the movement due to the West's history with Islam and its Islamophobic reflexes. On the other hand, the Muslim world may see the movement's faith-based principles as being at best unorthodox, if not deviant or abnormal according to Islamic precepts.

In addition, the Turkish minority's economic, social and intellectually disadvantaged position might cause an unwillingness to assist or participate, or their shortcomings (such as incompetence in native language) may hinder their efficient participation. At this point, it should be noted that the history of the movement in Europe and in the Muslim World is quite short.

But as a beginning it has made a good start in the Netherlands with almost all kinds of institutions and activities; in the USA with a striking rise in the number of state-financed 'charter schools'; and in Kurdish-controlled northern Iraq with seven schools, despite the unstable ground for developing the movement's operations there.

10

An exploration of the strategic dimensions of dialogue in a Gülen movement organization in Northern Ireland

JONATHAN LACEY

Introduction

Did you hear the one about a Muslim man in Northern Ireland? The policeman stopped him and asked: 'Are you a Catholic or Protestant?' The man replied: 'I am a Muslim.' The policeman then asked: 'Are you a "Catholic Muslim" or a "Protestant Muslim"'?

The above 'joke' serves to illustrate the traditional division in Northern Ireland between Catholics and Protestants. The society has been so focused on the two separate primordial articulations of identity that it was difficult, until recent years, to think outside of this dual paradigm. For so long the two communities lived separately and antagonistically. Thousands have been killed in a 'civil' war that has spanned decades.

A peace agreement was signed in 1998, which has led to relative peace in the region. This more benign environment is pregnant with potential for lasting peace. The reconciliation has also led to increased migration to the region, which now hosts more than twenty thousand people from minority ethnic backgrounds (for an early cartography of minority ethnic religious communities in Ireland see Ryan, 1996) including roughly 300 Turkish people. As such the reality that there are more than just two identity communities in Northern Ireland becomes more visible.

This chapter focuses on an unlikely actor in dialogic relations in Northern Ireland, namely the Gülen-inspired Northern Ireland-Tolerance, Educational and Cultural Association (NI-TECA). This chapter explores the Gülen movement through the endeavours of this association drawing on fieldwork and qualitative interviews I conducted with members of NI-TECA. The chapter begins by describing the current situation in Northern Ireland. I argue that the form of democracy practised in this region, namely 'consociational democracy' (for a review of the literature on this topic see Andeweg, 2000), is a flawed system and has served to entrench ethnic divisions further in Northern Ireland. Along with an increase in racist incidents, this is the situation in which NI-TECA is attempting to bring its style of dialogical practice. Through the various events NI-TECA promotes, I argue it engages in strategic dialogue, creating platforms where it can challenge the negative representation of Islam and promote Gülen's ideas. I use concepts developed in social movement theory, namely identity deployment and framing, to capture the strategic nature of these dialogic engagements.

Consociational democracy, parity of esteem and minority ethnic groups in Northern Ireland

At this early juncture it is necessary to describe the current situation in Northern Ireland in order to situate NI-TECA in the appropriate context. In 1998, after three decades of violence in Northern Ireland, the Good Friday Agreement (GFA) was signed by the elites of the two major opposing parties in an attempt to bring stable governance to the region. Consociational Democracy was adopted as the model for governance. At the heart of this system is the 'grand coalition'. This entails a number of various antagonistic segments (potentially hostile) sharing power in a grand coalition and attempting to cooperate and run the government together. One of the architects of consociational theory, Arend Lijphart, maintains that because the stakes are so high in a plural society (i.e. winner takes all) 'a grand coalition is therefore more appropriate than the government-versus-opposition pattern' (Lijphart, 1977: 27). Presently Sinn Féin and the Democratic Unionist Party (DUP) represent each community in the grand coalition in Northern Ireland.

There are disputes by academics and politicians as to whether this form of government is a step forward or a missed opportunity. It is my contention that it was a missed opportunity as it institutionalizes the notion of primordial identities that necessarily perpetuates the conflict (albeit in a largely non-violent form). Literary theorist Declan Kiberd praised the GFA, claiming that 'it offers a version of multiple identities ... open rather than fixed, as a process rather than a conclusion?' (cited in Finlay, 2004: 4). In this sense Kiberd is claiming that there is recognition in the GFA that identities are constructed and open to change. However, Andrew Finlay rightly points out that Kiberd's reading of the GFA is selective. Read as a whole, the document promotes 'parity of esteem' for two communities only, namely 'British or Irish, unionist or nationalist' (Finlay, 2004: 5). Furthermore, Finlay insists: '"parity of esteem" [necessarily] depend[s] on an implicit essentialism' (2004: 23). This echoes the logic of consociational theory that fixes, reifies and objectifies identities that in reality are much more fluid and changing.

There is evidence to suggest that since the signing of the GFA in 1998, there has been an increasing abyss developing between communities in Northern Ireland. By 2002, there were at least 27 'peace walls' dividing potentially antagonistic 'communities'. Such 'peace walls' are a euphemistic name for walls in Northern Ireland that are of up to and over 1 kilometre in length and up to 6 metres (20 feet) in height, and were built specifically to keep apart 'warring factions'. But in 1994, the year of the Provisional Irish Republican Army ceasefire, there were only fifteen such 'peace walls' (Jarman, 2002: 23; Wilson and Wilford, 2003: 3). This is not to suggest that consociational democracy (epitomized by power-sharing by two conflicting 'segments' in society) has created this abyss between the two 'communities'. Of course, these problems were already in existence. However, it is contended that this form of democracy has led to its exacerbation and consolidation.

The people of Ireland, particularly Northern Ireland, were exhausted with the violence and havoc of the previous 30 years. They were ready for radical transition in 1998 when the GFA was signed. However, the adoption of consociational democracy represents a missed opportunity and in my view was myopic. The physical barriers of the 'peace walls' are mirrored by a growing pessimism towards the possibility of concordance among the different 'communities'. This has been documented by the Northern Ireland Life and Times Survey of Public Attitudes, which discovered that the people of Northern Ireland are very cynical about the future of peace (cited in Wilson and Wilford, 2003: 2–3).

So, Finlay is correct to suggest that the GFA (guided by the tenets of consociational theory) 'remains resolutely bicultural in the way that it privileges the rights of two indigenous communities, each of which is presumed to have its own cultural identity, conceived in essentialist terms' (Finlay, 2004: 24). In this context one must ask what the effect is on other ethnic groups in Northern Ireland that do not fall into the bi-cultural model of the GFA. Lentin and McVeigh (2006) note that despite Northern Ireland's slack economy it is attracting a sizeable number of migrants. While the GFA caters for, and promotes, the two 'segments' in society, it ignores other minority ethnic groups. McGarry and O'Leary (2004) dispute this claim, insisting that in Northern Ireland law provisions are made for individual human rights complaints through the European Convention of Human Rights and the Northern Ireland Act, 1998. In theory, of course, they are right. However, it is my contention that due to the state-sanctioned divisions and institutionalizing of mistrust between the two major 'segments' in Northern Irish society, mistrust of all ethnic groups has penetrated throughout the region.

Deepa Mann-Kler is an Indian woman living in Belfast and a community activist in Northern Ireland. She maintains that 'One of the many legacies of the Troubles has been the denial of the existence of racism in Northern Ireland' (Mann-Kler, 2002: 63). She notes that there are more than 20,000 people of minority ethnic background living in Northern Ireland and they are largely 'non-recognised' (see Taylor, 1994) by the state and consequentially inequality towards these groups is endemic. More recently, Gabriele Marranci (2005), Ronit Lentin and Robbie McVeigh (2006) and Robbie McVeigh and Bill Rolston (2007) have pointed out the rise in racism in Northern Ireland. In 2005 the prominent German magazine *Der Spiegel* claimed that Belfast was 'the most racist City in the world' (cited in Lentin and McVeigh, 2006: 145). Lentin and McVeigh (2006) make the point that this claim is both complex and disputed. Nevertheless, the aforementioned commentators provide evidence for growing intolerance in Northern Ireland.

Bottom-up approach

Though I have outlined several criticisms regarding the model of democracy practised in Northern Ireland, it is beyond the scope of this chapter to analyse alternative models. I do, however, join Cochrane and Dunn (2002: 4), who insist there is a dire need for an empirical focus on the bottom-up approach of actors involved in peace-building. They recognize that the overwhelming majority of research focuses on the top-down approach of the elite representatives rather than those working on the ground.

Cochrane and Dunn provide some interesting research vis-à-vis grass-roots organizations in Northern Ireland. Their focus is on indigenous groups such as the 'Families Against Intimidation and Terror' (FAIT) and 'Quaker House' (QH). My focus is somewhat different, centring on a non-indigenous group – namely NI-TECA, which promotes dialogue in a tense post-GFA climate. However, to construe NI-TECA as simply a migrant-led grass-roots organization would be a mistake, as it is connected to the transnational Gülen movement, and therefore has access to the movement's human, informational and material resource pools. Furthermore, as will be demonstrated throughout this chapter, NI-TECA's main aim, like other Gülen-inspired organizations around the world, is to challenge the pejorative (re)presentation of Islam and promote Gülen's ideas. Dialogue provides a platform where these organizations can (re)present Islam in accordance with their ideology (the term ideology being loosely used here to refer to an 'action oriented system of beliefs' as defined by Daniel Bell, cited in Sypnowich, 2010).

NI-TECA: a Gülen-inspired organization

In his survey of Islamic organizations in Western Europe Jørgen Nielsen (2004: 121) identifies three dominant forms of establishment; first, groups that emerge from the diaspora to cater for the needs of the community; second, groups that are established by the government; third, organizations established as branches of a movement in the country of origin. Due to their access to various forms of resources, it is these latter groups that often come to figure as the most prominent Muslim organizations in Western European contexts (Nielsen, 2004: 124). Examples include the Pakistani-originated Jama'at-i-Islami, the Süleymancis and Milli Görüş from Turkey, and the Muslim Brotherhood from Egypt.

In order to gain state support, Muslim organizations in Europe often have to adapt their organizational structures to align with standard organizations in the country of settlement. This often involves adopting an hierarchal system with committees, management etc. – a tradition alien to many Islamic groups. Due to the proven organizational capability of large transnational Islamic movements, their organizational extensions are likely to best adapt to these conditions. Nielsen importantly points out that regardless of the organizational form a Muslim group in Europe adopts, their country of origin shapes them. In most Muslim countries, Islam is enshrined in the everyday activity and practising Islam is relatively effortless in comparison to a country where Islam is a minority religion.

So when most Muslim migrants reach Europe they will have had little experience of initiating organizations to help them live as practising Muslims. Nielsen rightly points out that Turkey is an exception in this context, because ever since Atatürk's cultural revolution, Islamic organizations had to develop strategies to promote the teaching and accommodation of Islam in Turkey (Nielsen, 2004: 124). In this sense many Islamic movements in Turkey are likely to be particularly well endowed with organizational skills and accommodation strategies with a secular state that may be hostile or indifferent to Islamic groups.

As an organization inspired by Gülen and connected to the broader transnational Gülen movement, NI-TECA can be considered among the third group of Islamic organizations mentioned earlier and has access to resources that would be unavailable to entirely autonomous groups. NI-TECA was initiated in 2004 by a number of Turkish migrants living and working in Northern Ireland, who already had previous experience volunteering in other Gülen organizations in various countries.

These movement entrepreneurs are committed followers of Fethullah Gülen, well read in his work and committed to his ideology. Though the founding members claim to have migrated to Ireland mainly for economic reasons, it is likely that Gülen's call for his followers to migrate in order to become ambassadors for Turkey (Yilmaz, 2003: 35) and the movement was also a motivating factor. While NI-TECA is aligned with the wider movement, it remains relatively autonomous and is not a professionalized movement organization but rather relies on a variety of different voluntary contributions.

In its earliest form, NI-TECA began to cater for the small Turkish diaspora living in Northern Ireland, but soon began to reach out to the Northern Irish public, engaging in various social and cultural activities, including inter-faith Ramadan dinners and conferences, and subsidized guided trips to Turkey. A brief look at websites belonging to Gülen organizations around the world demonstrates the relative uniformity of activities practised by movement organizations.

Having secured economic stability for themselves and initiated NI-TECA, movement entrepreneurs sought to grow the organization and recruited movement volunteers from Turkey and Central Asia. These participants are invested with the responsibility of challenging biased attitudes towards Islam and promoting Gülen's ideas, predominantly among non-Muslims, in attempts to gain influence rather than new members. NI-TECA recruits both full-time and novice volunteers to consolidate the organization in Northern Ireland. These movement participants typically stay for a few years before moving back to their country of origin.

Volunteer commitment

Gülen-inspired constituents display a great degree of commitment to promoting Gülen's ideas and show little concern for entering potentially hazardous situations. I asked one short-term NI-TECA volunteer how he felt about coming to Northern Ireland. He admitted that he had heard that it was a troubled place. Some of his friends exclaimed: 'Oh it's not a good place in Northern Ireland. It's not safe.' Despite this warning he made the trip to Belfast and has now been working voluntarily with NI-TECA for three years. The important point is that he believed Belfast to be an unsafe place to live and he still showed the courage to go there to work voluntarily. He now feels that these warnings were naïve and feels very safe living in Belfast.

Another participant from Turkey speaks humbly about his experiences working in troubled spots around the world such as Albania and Kosovo, where he was director of a Gülen-inspired school. He claims that these Balkan countries share hundreds of years of history with Turkey from the Ottoman era and he therefore felt at ease in these regions despite the conflictual situations surrounding him. He also noted that there were still many Turkish-speakers there. Many other participants of the movement have entered into potentially hostile regions, especially in Central Asia and the Balkans over the years in order to promote their ideals. Given the experiences of these volunteers they were largely unflustered by the violent history of Northern Ireland and the thought of entering into an apprehensive post-GFA atmosphere.

The work undertaken by members of NI-TECA is voluntary. I asked members of the association what motivated them to give up their time to engage in these social endeavours. One member of NI-TECA said:

I think it is a responsibility. It is not a hobby ... If I don't do it I will be irresponsible according to my religion. It is one of the major requirements of my religion ... You can't sit down in your house all the time. If Islam is good you have to live it ... You must be proactive, especially in this part of the world ... [where] dialogue is needed (2007).

This opinion is widespread in NI-TECA and indeed among other participants of the Gülen movement I interviewed in Dublin, London and Istanbul. Participants believe it is their responsibility as 'good Muslims' to carry out 'good works'. They insist that though prayer, pilgrimage and asceticism are core components of Islam, so is engaging in social endeavours to make the world a more peaceful place. They see dialogue as a vehicle through which change can be made, but it is primarily changing negative attitudes to Islam that followers of Gülen are interested in.

By establishing dialogue events, NI-TECA and other Gülen-inspired organizations around the world establish platforms where they can challenge negative (re)presentations of Islam and promote Gülen's ideas. Furthermore, by initiating dialogue events they also get to set the terms of dialogue and to a large extent control the parameters of discourse. One leading NI-TECA member states:

We are not following others in dialogue practice ... we want to be leading dialogue. To be part of other dialogue activities is not enough for us. We have the resources, we have the courage, we have everything to lead the way here in Northern Ireland in dialogue (2007).

Despite the small scale of the movement in Northern Ireland, the above respondent demonstrates the confidence of movement organizations. Drawing on the wider pool of the transnational movement resources (knowledge, experience, manpower and financial) they are better equipped than autonomous groups engaged in such practices. The next section of this chapter discusses some of the ways movement participants engage in strategic dialogue.

Strategic dialogue and identity deployment

> Inter-faith dialogue is a must today, and the first step in establishing it is forgetting the past, ignoring polemical arguments and giving precedence to common points, which far outnumber polemical ones (Gülen, cited in Ünal and Williams, eds. 2000: 244–5)

In an era when Huntington's (1996) mediatized thesis arguing for the inevitable clash of civilizations is gaining strength, Gülen insists that dialogue should replace the potential clash. The phrase 'Dialogue of Civilizations' has become a slogan for the Gülen movement and a mantra for Gülen's followers. Dialogue, Gülen argues, can only be accomplished by side-stepping the most antagonistic and apparently irreconcilable differences and instead focusing on the similarities among disparate groups, which he insists far outweigh the differences. The demonstration of commonalities between different faith groups is central to the NI-TECA's activities in Northern Ireland and serves as a key movement accommodation strategy.

NI-TECA hosts annual symposiums celebrating the commonalities of the Abrahamic religions, inviting academics, clerics from different faiths and local politicians. One member of NI-TECA (2007) explained the reasoning behind these conferences:

> It is important to share and discuss the common values ... We believe in the Abrahamic religions. At the basic principles all the religions are the same. As a Christian you cannot tell me that being a thief is good behaviour; no you cannot say this ... The Muslim people believe that all of these Abrahamic religions ... are from the same light ... The origin is the same ... When we are organizing this [conference], the aim is not to compare the religions and it is not to talk about the differences. I think if we come together and talk about the differences we will not solve our problems. You are a Christian. If you are a good Christian you are happy and I am happy. You should be a good Christian and I should be a good Muslim. But while I am being a good Muslim, I should be aware of you and learn about you and your traditions ... the aim is not to convert or to make them Muslim or Christian.

In 2006 NI-TECA held a conference focusing on 'Mercy in the Abrahamic Religions', inviting speakers from the Jewish and Christian community in Northern Ireland. In 2007 they organized a symposium – namely, the 'Fundamentals of Peace', where there were speakers from the three faiths again, who talked about the universal principles of 'truthfulness and trustworthiness'. These conferences attracted up to 100 attendees from a variety of religious backgrounds, including Jewish, Catholic and Protestant. As the previous interviewee states, NI-TECA is not interested in converting non-Muslims to Islam; instead, it draws attention to the similarities in the Abrahamic religions while sidestepping obvious theological inconsistencies between the different faiths.

A display of commonalities is also practised in another activity organized by NI-TECA. Each year members distribute a dessert known as 'Noah's Pudding'. In collaboration with Catholic and Protestant churches, they dispense these puddings to those leaving church on Sunday mornings. They also include a leaflet describing the reason for distributing the puddings and details of the ingredients. The leaflet narrates that when the Prophet Noah survived the flood, his family gathered all the remaining food on the ship and made a pudding. NI-TECA members replicate this symbolic gesture in order to remember the Prophet Noah. This endeavour, they argue, is also an act of dialogue. They claim that 'Sharing food offers a way to re-affirm unity and the essential relationship of humans to one another, regardless of faith background and belief' (http://www.NI-TECA.org.uk).

Like the symposiums celebrating the Abrahamic religions, the distribution of the puddings is aimed at emphasizing the figure of Noah as a common character in all the Abrahamic faiths. This strategy is aimed at aligning Islam with the other dominant faiths in the region. By emphasizing the similarities between the different faiths, it is hoped that Islam will be perceived in a more positive light. Hosting these events then takes on a de-stigmatizing tone as NI-TECA members attempt to challenge pejorative (re)presentations of Islam by emphasizing sameness.

Social movement scholar Mary Bernstein argues that movements often deploy their identity in the public sphere in strategic ways, at times celebrating difference, while at other times electing to suppress divergence and emphasize similarities, depending on the audience they are intending their message to resonate with. She notes how the civil rights movement in the USA emphasized similarities with the majority population in a strategic attempt to secure policy reforms. This is a useful strategy as it tactically aligns one's goals with the values of the majority by expressing the premise of similarity. However, at other times, such movements deployed their 'radical racial identities' in an effort to mobilize black communities and contest dominant American culture, resonating with a different target group (Bernstein, 1997: 352).

In the context of the Gülen movement, Berna Turam (2004: 268) identifies a contrast between how movement participants behave in private and public sites. She argues that while movement participants display 'liberal discourses on tolerance and individual liberties in the public sites. The private sphere displays homogeneous moral ways of life and pious worldviews that impose rigid restrictions on individual liberties.'

Several other scholars have pointed out the conservative nature of the Gülen movement and the strict moral code in movement lighthouses and other institutions (see for example, Yavuz, 2003b: 35). It is not that movement constituents do not believe in tolerance and dialogue but they choose to make salient or accentuate certain features of their identity in public that will resonate with a target population in their attempt to accommodate the movement to a new context. In the Central Asian context, Turam (2003) demonstrates how the Gülen movement strategically engages in 'ethnic politics' in an attempt to gain influence in the region. Rather than emphasizing the Islamic facet of their identity, which may be treated with suspicion, movement participants accentuate the ancient ethnic affiliation between the Turks of Anatolia and the Turks of Central Asia. In the case of Northern Ireland, emphasizing similarities between different faith groups helps to gain recognition for the movement organization and serves as a consciousness-raising activity.

Strategic dialogue and framing mechanisms

Muslims should say, 'In true Islam, terror does not exist.' In Islam, killing a human is an act that is equal in gravity to unbelief. No person can kill a human being. No one can touch an innocent person, even in time of war. No one can give a *fatwa* (legal pronouncement in Islam) in this matter. No one can be a suicide bomber. No one can rush into crowds with bombs tied to his or her body. Regardless of the religion of these crowds, this is not religiously permissible (Gülen, 2004c: 1).

The above is an unambiguous condemnation of terrorism by Fethullah Gülen. One cannot be a Muslim and a terrorist, he insists. Shortly after the 9/11 attacks in New York (in 2001), Gülen also took out an advertisement in the *Washington Post*, denouncing terrorism. This attitude inspired NI-TECA to organize a conference with the Police Service of Northern Ireland's (PSNI) Community Safety Branch and named 'The Necessity of Dialogue to Prevent another 7/7'. It was a closed conference whose attendees were solely from the PSNI, including the Chief Constable of Northern Ireland and a number of police officers working in the field of community relations.

The conference featured a speech by a member of the Gülen-inspired Dialogue Society in London and a short documentary produced by the same society. The documentary was entitled *Peace Through Education and Dialogue: Initiatives of the Fethullah Gülen Movement* (see http://www.nids.org.uk). It was first presented by the Dialogue Society to the House of Lords on the first anniversary of the 7/7 attacks. It involves a single narrator, and the storyline cites the causes of terrorism and offers ways to overcome radicalization. The documentary provides what social movement scholars refer to as a collective action frame.

Benford and Snow (2000: 614) argue that 'Frames help to render events or occurrences meaningful and thereby function to organize experience and guide action. Collective action frames also perform this interpretative function by simplifying and condensing aspects of the "world out there"...' Through frames, movement organizations interpret and construct meanings and events in ways that are likely to resonate with a target population, whether this be potential adherents, bystander publics or elites. In this way movements are continually in the process of re-signifying meanings to suit their aims and objectives. Benford and Snow identify three core framing tasks – namely, 'diagnostic framing', 'prognostic framing' and 'motivational framing' – only two of which I will discuss here.

First, movements construct 'diagnostic frames', where they identify a problem that needs to be challenged or rectified and attribute blame. In the aforementioned documentary terrorism, and the popular association between terrorism and Islam, are identified as problems. A large section of the documentary involves disassociating Islam from terrorism, arguing that, 'In fact terrorism is not rooted in any one religion, or race, or cultural tradition.' It goes on to relay the virtues of Islam, arguing that peace rather than violence is paramount in Islam:

> For Islam is a faith whose very name means Peace: a faith that commands peaceful relations with all regardless of creed or race or nationality: a faith that tells us that life was created out of compassion a faith that states the 'Unjust killing of one person is like the killing of all humankind' ... What an absurdity it is that a faith centred on peace and compassion is associated by terrorists with their commitment to destruction and death. But the radicalised attitudes behind terrorism are capable of hijacking any faith in order to justify the unjustifiable (see http://www.nids.org.uk).

Having identified terrorism as the problem and disassociated the principles of Islam from violence, the short film goes on to blame structures rather than individuals for terrorism, claiming that 'backwardness, poverty and isolation' are to blame for the rise of terrorism. Having diagnosed the problem and allotted blame, the documentary goes on to construct a 'prognostic frame'. Prognostic framing involves the proffering of solutions to a problem and concomitant strategies to achieve such goals.

The narrator in the documentary states: 'If the root problem is rightly identified as backwardness, poverty and isolation, the answer surely lies in sustained opportunities for education, social justice and dialogue.' The short film then demonstrates the Gülen movement's activities around the world, particularly in arenas of education and dialogue. The Gülen movement subsequently, according to this frame, becomes part of the prognosis. Its activities and outlook are promoted as part of the challenge, particularly to the root causes of 'Islamic terrorism'.

Like the previous events discussed, this symposium with the PSNI can be considered as another example of strategic dialogue. In the name of dialogue, participants try to challenge the relationship between Islam and violence, presenting Islam as anathema to terrorism in line with Gülen's statement earlier. This dialogue platform also serves as a space where movement participants can disseminate Gülen's ideas and attempt to increase his popularity. It also helps to raise the profile of NI-TECA among state officials and other minority ethnic groups in Northern Ireland

Discussion and concluding remarks

The examples of NI-TECA'S activities discussed in the previous section demonstrate the various ways in which they strategically engaged in dialogue. They are different in many ways to the traditional organizations working for dialogue and peace in Northern Ireland. Members of NI-TECA are obviously non-indigenous, while the vast majority of groups engaged in dialogical practice in Northern Ireland are natives to Ireland. They also have their own agenda, which is aligned with the broader Gülen movement and whose ideology and outlook infuses all of their events.

Most indigenous groups in Northern Ireland act locally and think locally. They work at a grass-roots level to try and bring peace to the region. Their thoughts are focused on peace in their local area and region and they are unlikely to envision their modest work as having a global impact. NI-TECA, on the other hand, engages in an explicit form of what sociologists refer to as 'glocalization'. This concept has its origins in marketing culture whereby global corporations adapt their products and managerial practices to local conditions and tastes (Robertson, 1997). Roland Robertson generalizes this concept to refer to the inter-penetration of the global and local in any given context.

In a very practical way members of NI-TECA act locally and think globally, always positioned delicately and concurrently in the two contexts without incongruence. By thinking globally (in their capacity as Gülen Movement volunteers) they always heed the messages and principles of Fethullah Gülen and are loosely connected to other Gülen-inspired groups around the world in a global circuit. They largely work in unison with the same aims and objectives but adapt their dialogical methods to local situations, working with various different faith-groups, including Catholics, Protestants and members of the Jewish faith. Additionally, they have adopted a conscious strategy of inviting local academics and clerics to speak at their conferences, grounding the movement in the locale, while at times electing to draw from their international reservoir of 'sister organizations' to bring in spokespeople to represent the Muslim opinion on a variety of issues.

Their emphasis on localism largely extends to funding too. NI-TECA members insist they get most of their funding from local Turkish business people and other funding from the City Council, though they also have collection boxes in local shops to help with their fundraising. They maintain that finances are regularly tight but they do not let these obstacles deter them. They do however occasionally 'go global' in an attempt to gain funding for some activities. Members, for example, acknowledge that they get some financial assistance from business people in Turkey to help subsidize an annual trip they organize to Turkey for indigenous people from Ireland.

Given the difficult history of ethnic and religious intolerance in Northern Ireland and the current nervous post-GFA environment, one may question whether another ethnic and faith group in Northern Ireland could exacerbate tensions rather than contribute to dialogue. In response, it is clear that we now live in a globalized world, and one corollary of this is an increase in migration and, furthermore, an unprecedented mixture of cultures and religions.

As previously mentioned there has been a relatively dramatic increase in migration to Northern Ireland in recent years. The Turkish community is among these migrants. They do not claim to represent all Muslims in the region but do espouse views of tolerance and, through Gülen's conceptualization of *dar al-hizmet* (Yilmaz, 2003: 234), they obey the laws of the land and offer a contribution to society based on their system of beliefs that avowedly has service to humanity at its core. By hosting various functions and inviting different ethnic and faith groups, including Catholics and Protestants, NI-TECA may act as a conduit by setting up platforms which may be interpreted with suspicion if they were initiated by either of the previously mentioned Christian groups.

In this sense the neutrality of Islam vis-à-vis the different Christian groups may serve as their strongest asset in promoting their dialogue platforms and indeed their own agenda. Furthermore, it has been well documented that some migrants isolate themselves in their host country. This is often exacerbated by restrictive and assimilationist tendencies of the host government (for discussion see Castles et al., 1984; King, 1993; Castles and Miller, 2003). NI-TECA has shown that it is willing and indeed actively engaged in promoting integration into the mainstream in Northern Ireland, combating potential problems of isolation and discordance.

Cochrane and Dunn (2002: 178) note that it is difficult to assess the quantitative influence of small bottom-up organizations working for peace in Northern Ireland. They claim that it is only when you see the cumulative effects of all of these organizations that you realize the importance of each small group. Similarly, NI-TECA's work is certainly small in scale. However, to view it in isolation from the larger Gülen movement would be a mistake. It can be considered a node in the transnational Gülen movement. Their input to the movement is certainly humble though added to the hundreds of other Gülen-inspired associations around the world, the cumulative effect is considerable and has helped to turn a religio-social movement peculiar to Turkey into a global movement.

PART IV

Challenging terrorism

11

Robustness and civility: themes from Fethullah Gülen as resource and challenge for government, Muslims and civil society in the United Kingdom

PAUL WELLER

Introduction

Government, many Muslims and the wider civil society were shocked by the 7/7 (2005) London Transport bombings in which 52 people were killed and 700 injured. Subsequently, the 'multiculturalist' policy consensus that had shaped UK public policy for several decades became subject to increasingly intensive questioning. Politicians and some parts of civil society challenged a perceived 'separatism' among Muslims in the light of which an already previously evident trend to emphasize a need for shared values and social cohesion was accelerated and the promotion of 'moderate Islam' and 'moderate Muslims' was advocated.

However, it is the argument of this chapter that legitimizing simplistic distinctions between 'good' (understood as 'liberal' or 'modernist') and 'bad' or 'suspect' (understood as 'traditionalist', 'radical' or 'fundamentalist') Muslims and forms of Islam does not ultimately help in combating terror in building a properly inclusive society. Rather, such reactions run the risk of eliding the condemnation of acts of terror conducted on religious grounds into the criminalization, or at least social marginalization, of religious conservatism and/or radicalism. In contrast, it is argued that what is needed are authentically Islamic approaches that can offer both a resource and a challenge to government, Muslims and the wider civil society.

Finally, it is suggested that such approaches can be found in themes from the Turkish Muslim scholar Fethullah Gülen who, on Islamic grounds, condemns terrorism in the name of religion. But Gülen's contribution is not only one of critique. Rather, being rooted in a confident Ottoman Muslim civilizational heritage, it also offers constructive impulses and, emerging from the context of the modern history of the Turkish Republic, it is one that has developed and matured through engagement with both ideological 'secularism' and political 'Islamism'.

7/7 and the British bombers

Prior to 7/7, 'mainland' Britain, and especially London, had previously experienced high levels of violence designed to inculcate terror and advance a political cause – namely that pursued by the Provisional IRA (Irish Republican Army) in pursuit of British withdrawal from the North of Ireland.

However, in contrast with the PIRA bombings experienced by Belfast, London, Birmingham, Manchester and other cities during the 1970s and 1980s, the 7/7 bombers acted without regard to their own personal safety and security. Indeed, from videos later made by the perpetrators of the bombings, the fact that these bombings brought death to themselves as well as to others was something not to be avoided but embraced, being understood as an act of martyrdom. Indeed, these attacks were the first instance of 'suicide bombings' to occur in Europe and that were later (in a 1 September 2005 video broadcast on the Arabic television network Aljazeera) officially claimed by al-Qaeda.

Second, while bombings of this kind had been carried out in the name of Islam in other parts of the world, the bombings were perpetrated not by people coming from outside the country and whose experience might have been directly shaped by the horrors of war and destruction experienced by Muslims living in the conflict zones of the world. Rather, they were carried out by young men brought up in the UK and who were, to all outward appearances, integrated members of British society.

On 1 September 2005, a tape featuring one of the bombers, Mohammad Sidique Khan, was broadcast on the Arab satellite TV station Aljazeera (see BBC News Channel, 2005). In this tape, he explained that he and others saw themselves at war and were giving up everything for the sake of what they understood as avenging and protecting their Muslim sisters and brothers. He also warned that people in the UK would continue to be a target of others like him until the government they had elected stopped what he described as its attack on Muslim people.

'Multiculturalism' and social policy

The realization that young Muslims brought up in Britain were seeing the world in this way and drawing consequences to inform actions of this kind merged with an earlier current of questioning that had already, a few years earlier, begun in relation to 'multiculturalist' consensus that had been the basis for UK public policy on ethnic and religious plurality ever since the passage into law of Britain's second Race Relations Act, in 1968.

In relation to the thinking that informed that Act of Parliament, the Labour Home Secretary, Roy (now Lord) Jenkins set out (Jenkins, 1967: 269) what later became a classic formulation of the multiculturalist vision when he explained that: 'I do not think that we need in this country a melting-pot, which will turn everybody out in a common mould, as one of a series of someone's misplaced vision of the stereotyped Englishman', clarifying that government policy was aiming for 'integration' (understood in those days as the opposite of 'assimilation' defined as: 'equal opportunity, coupled with cultural diversity, in an atmosphere of mutual tolerance').

However, already by the time of the controversy that surrounded the publication of Salman Rushdie's (1988) book *The Satanic Verses*, and in what was a sign of things to come, Lord Jenkins himself (1989) was already recorded as saying that, in retrospect, politicians might have been more caution about the creation of substantial Muslim communities in Britain during the 1950s.

In the aftermath of the summer 2001 disturbances in the northern English mill towns involving youth of Muslim background, and even more so following the 9/11 attacks on the World Trade Center and the Pentagon in the USA, such sentiments became more widespread amid heightened security fears (see Allen and Nielsen, 2002). Such fears intensified especially following the arrest of Richard Reid, the British so-called 'shoe bomber', who was arrested on 21 December 2001 for an attempt to destroy an American Airlines Flight from Paris to Miami through setting off explosives hidden in his shoes.

This gave a warning signal that UK Muslims might be being caught up in the emergence of a global struggle, as had also the involvement of suicide bombers of Muslim background from Britain, including Omar Khan Sharif from the author's home city of Derby, in the 30 April 2003 attack on a bar in Tel Aviv, Israel (see BBC News Channel, 2003). The change of approach to social policy that accompanied these developments was highlighted in a statement released by the Chair of the former Commission for Racial Equality, Trevor Phillips, on 22 September 2005. In this, Phillips (2005) argued that:

> [T]he aftermath of 7/7 forces us to assess where we are. And here is where I think we are: we are sleepwalking our way to segregation. We are becoming strangers to each other, and we are leaving communities to be marooned outside the mainstream.

At government level, and in some contrast with a former celebration of 'diversity', an emphasis on 'cohesion' and of a new forms of 'integrationism' (see Kundnani, 2007) was gathering pace, the meaning of which was closer to the 'assimilationism' rejected in Roy Jenkins' original vision than to the kind of 'integration' it had advocated. In this context, the government announced the creation of its Commission on Integration and Cohesion which produced a report under the title of Our Shared Future (Commission on Integration and Cohesion, 2007).

'Moderation', 'radicalism', 'extremism' and 'terrorism'

In a speech to the Los Angeles World Affairs Council, the former British Prime Minister, Tony Blair (2006) argued that, 'We will not win the battle against this global extremism unless we win at the level of values as much as force ...'. In this context, Blair referred to 'an elemental struggle about the values that will shape our future' and argued that, 'It is in part a struggle between what I will call reactionary Islam and moderate, mainstream Islam'. In the light of this, there was an attempt on the part of government and other public bodies to promote a 'moderate Islam' and 'moderate Muslims' and to marginalize by association with terrorism what can be seen as 'radical', 'fundamentalist' or 'extremist' Islam.

A good example of such an approach – and which this chapter argues tends to confuse rather than to illuminate – can be found in the kind of public discourse that followed the 30 June 2007 attack on Glasgow Airport (see BBC News Channel, 2007). Following the attack, the then new Security Minister, Admiral Sir Alan West was interviewed on Independent Television News on 8 July. That interview was reported in the on-line media service, *BTYahoo News* (2007) under the headline of 'Tackling *terror* [my italics for emphasis[will take 15 years'. Having, in its headline, introduced the theme of 'terror', in an assumed continuity of reference although using a change of language the report then went on to state that, 'Tackling *radicalization* could take 15 years, Gordon Brown's new Security Minister has warned.' The report then went on to say that: 'Admiral Sir Alan West conceded the government was finding it hard to get its anti-terror message across, but stressed that preventing people from being recruited to *extremism* [again, my italics for emphasis] was central to beating terrorism.'

From this it will be seen how easily the editorial voice slides from 'tackling terror' to 'radicalization' to 'extremism'. While there can certainly be some linkage between these phenomena, it is also very important they should be clearly distinguished. Not to do so will result in additional difficulty in trying to isolate those who are prepared to use indiscriminate and criminal terror in pursuit of their goals from those who may share some aspects of their understanding of the world, but who would not resort to criminal violence in pursuit of it.

In other words, 'radicalized' Muslims are not necessarily 'extremists', and 'extremist' Muslims are not necessarily going to undertake terror actions. Depending on one's starting point, the designation of others as 'extremists' can simply be a way of marginalizing people from engagement, but without seeking to understand the context and/or content of their views. Etymologically and also in religious reality 'radicalism' can be understood as something that is concerned with going back to the roots, and which entails a critique of traditionalism for its own sake. Thus the issue at stake is not 'radicalization' per se among Muslims, but the *forms* that such radicalization takes and also in what it *results* (see Abbas, 2007).

Such a distinction is very important to draw for democratic politics in a world where naked power and military violence seem to be stacked against many predominantly Muslim countries and people. In this context it should not be surprising that these factors might lead many young Muslims in the UK, along with their own experience of minority status as one in which religious discrimination and disadvantage (see Weller, Feldman and Purdam 2004; and Weller 2006a), are relatively common to form perceptions of the world in which the prevailing economic, cultural and military powers that will, at the very least, be robustly questioned.

In the light of this, simplistic distinctions between 'good' (understood as 'liberal' or 'modernist') and 'bad' or 'suspect' (understood as 'traditionalist', 'radical' or 'fundamentalist') Muslims and forms of Islam should not be legitimated. Such reactions run the risk of eliding the condemnation of terrorist crimes against humanity conducted on religious grounds into the criminalization, or at least social marginalization, of religious conservatism and/or radicalism.

Some 'tendencies' among Muslims

By contrast, what is needed is a more sophisticated and grounded understanding of the tendencies among Muslims that goes beyond the ephemera of political rhetoric and media reportage. In his book *Western Muslims and the Future of Islam*, the European Muslim scholar and reformer, Tariq Ramadan, identified what he calls 'six major tendencies among those for whom Islam is the reference point for their thinking, their discourse and their engagement' (2004: 24–30). All such categorizations can, of course, be questioned and alternatives offered. Thus, with regard to the organized forms that Islam has taken among Muslims of South Asian origin who comprise the majority of Muslims in the UK (see Robinson, 1988; and Andrews, 1994) there can be other forms of categorization. However, those suggested by Ramadan are included here for the illustrative purpose of underlining the diversity as well as unity that is found among Muslims.

Ramadan argues that what he calls 'Scholastic Traditionalists' have a distinct way of referring to the Qur'an and Sunnah by strict and sometimes exclusive reference to one of the classical schools of jurisprudence, relying on scholastic opinions that were codified between the eighth and eleventh centuries. He (Ramadan, 2004: 25) says, 'There is no room here for *ijtihad* or for a rereading, which are taken to be baseless and unacceptable liberties and modernizations' and that 'They are concerned mostly with religious practice and in the West do not envisage social, civil or political involvement'.

Of 'Salafi Literalism', Ramadan (2004: 25) explains that, although those from this tendency are often confused with 'Scholastic Traditionalists', they reject the mediated interpretation of traditional schools and scholars: 'The Qur'an and the Sunnah are therefore interpreted in an immediate way, without scholarly enclaves' and also that this tendency 'refuses any kind of involvement in a space that is considered non-Islamic.'

What Ramadan (2004: 26) calls 'Salafi Reformists' have significant differences among them, but what unites them is a 'very dynamic relation to the scriptural sources and a constant desire to use reason in the treatment of the Texts in order to deal with the new challenges of their age and the social, economic, and political evolution of societies'. In terms of social engagement, Ramadan (2004: 27) observes that: 'The aim is to protect the Muslim identity and religious practice, to recognize the Western constitutional structure, to become involved as a citizen at the social level, and to live with true loyalty to the country to which one belongs.'

'Political Literalist Salafists', Ramadan says, are 'essentially born of the repression that has ravaged the Muslim world'. Their approach is 'a complex blend that tends towards radical revolutionary action ... the discourse is trenchant, politicized, radical and opposed to any idea of involvement or collaboration with Western societies, which is seen as akin to open treason' (2004: 27).

'Liberal' or 'Rationalist' Reformism is born from the influence of Western thought in the colonial period. According to Ramadan, this tendency has presented itself as 'liberal or rationalist', and has 'supported the application in the Muslim world of the social and political system that resulted from the process of secularisation in Europe' (2004: 27). Of this approach, Ramadan says, 'In the West, supporters of liberal reformism preach the integration/ assimilation of Muslims from whom they expect a complete adaptation to a Western way of life' (2004: 27).

In relation to 'Sufism', Ramadan says that: 'Sufis are essentially oriented toward the spiritual life and mystical experience' and that, 'There is a call to the inner life, away from disturbance and disharmony' (2004: 28). However, Ramadan also notes that 'This is not to say that Sufi disciples ... have no community or social involvement; the contrary is often the case' (2004: 28).

An Islamic resource for civility

Against such a varied background, it should be clear that defining the issues in simplistic ways is more likely to undermine the development of inclusive approaches to the common good. In particular, it can be counter-productive for government overtly to try and define and, even more so, to try to create what it might see as a 'good moderate British Islam' over against a 'bad radical Islam'. This is especially so because of the high level of distrust of government that exists among Muslims in the context of British foreign policy, and especially the military actions in Afghanistan and Iraq.

But it is also important to bear in mind the evidence that exists concerning the experience among Muslims in the UK of discrimination and unfair treatment on the basis of religion (see Runnymede Trust, 1997; and Weller, Feldman and Purdam, 2004) that can be expressed in terms of what come to be known as Islamophobia (see Weller, 2006a), as well as the impact (see Fekete, 2004) that a growing security apparatus 'reach' among Muslims in the UK can have among Muslims' own sense of security as well as on the perceptions of them by others and, in turn, their own perception of these perceptions (see Kundnani, 2009; House of Commons Communities and Local Government Committee, 2010).

Therefore, even from a pragmatic perspective, the best possibility for combating the attraction of young Muslims to understandings that see the world in highly dichotomized ways, is to identify authentically Islamic approaches to make a contribution that can offer both a resource for civility and a challenge to government, Muslims and the wider society alike. One such resource can arguably be found in the teaching of the Turkish Muslim scholar, Fethullah Gülen (See Hunt and Aslandoğan, 2006).

Gülen does not fit any of Ramadan's categorizations of Islamic tendencies. While some have argued that he can be seen as a Sufi, as Saritoprak (2003: 169) has argued, 'Strictly speaking, Gülen is not a Sufi' – although he has what might be called a '*tasawwuf*-style' of living. At the same time, his teaching and the movement that has developed around it are oriented towards *tajdid*, or the 'renewal' of Islam. As Gülen himself puts it (in Ünal and Williams, 2000: 53), reflecting on why Islam is often seen as a pre-modern religion and Muslim societies are often in disarray, 'Since Islam is misunderstood, implemented incorrectly, and perceived as a simple religion belonging to the past, today the Islamic world is in a pitiful state' and therefore that:

> As Muslims, we must ask ourselves why? Taking the Qur'an and Sunnah as our main sources and respecting the great people of the past, in the consciousness that we are all children of time, we must question the past and present. I am looking for laborers of thought and researchers to establish the necessary balance between the constant and changing aspects of Islam and, considering such juridical rules as abrogation, particularization, generalization, and restriction, who can present Islam to the modern understanding (in Ünal and Williams, 2000: 53).

Thus while rooted in a confident Muslim and Ottoman Turkish heritage, Gülen does not take refuge in an invocations of an idealized past as a solution to the contemporary weakness of the Muslim community and polities. Rather, he seeks to provide a clear analysis of the kind of global and historical context that has led some Muslims into seeing the world in terms of an epic, militarized global struggle of almost Manichean dualism between *dar-al Islam* and *dar-al harb*. Thus Gülen (2004e: 239) has observed that:

> Islamic societies entered the twentieth century as a world of the oppressed, the wronged, and the colonized; the first half of the century was occupied with wars of liberation and independence, wars that carried over from the nineteenth century. In all these wars, Islam assumed the role of an important factor uniting people and spurring them to action. As these wars were waged against what were seen as invaders, Islam, national independence and liberation came to mean the same thing.

In describing this historical development, Gülen recognizes the factuality of what has occurred in the interaction between Islam and the broad currents of global politics, economics and military power. But he also identifies the roots of a current concern in which, for many, Islam has become a political ideology bringing with it what, he argues, are damaging consequences for Islam, Muslims and the world.

An Islamic challenge to terror

Gülen (in Ünal and Williams, 2000: 248) does not question the objectivity of the current situation in which Muslims often experience injustice, but he also argues robustly that:

> When those who have adopted Islam as a political ideology, rather than a religion in its true sense and function, review their self-proclaimed Islamic activities and attitudes, especially their political ones, they will discover that the driving force is usually personal or national anger, hostility, and similar motives. If this is the case, we must accept Islam and adopt an Islamic attitude as the fundamental starting point for action, rather than the existing oppressive situation (Ünal and Williams, 2000: 248).

Without such a robust self-examination and re-evaluation among Muslims, Gülen argues that, 'The present, distorted image of Islam that has resulted from its misuse, by both Muslims and non-Muslims for their own goals, scares both Muslims and non-Muslims' (in Ünal and Williams, 2000: 248). Indeed, on Islamic grounds Gülen clearly condemns terrorism in the name of religion. Thus he says:

> In Islam, killing a human is an act that is equal in gravity to unbelief. No person can kill a human being. No one can touch an innocent person, even in time of war. No one can give a fatwa (a legal pronouncement in Islam) in this matter. No one can be a suicide bomber. No one can rush into crowds, this is not religiously permissible. Even in the event of war – during which it is difficult to maintain balances – this is not permitted in Islam (Gülen, 2004c: 1).

In his 'Message concerning the September 11th terrorist attacks' Gülen (2004e: 261–2) went further to state clearly that, 'Islam does not approve of terrorism in any form. Terrorism cannot be used to achieve any Islamic goal. No terrorist can be a Muslim, and no real Muslim can be a terrorist', while in his piece entitled 'Real Muslims cannot be terrorists', Gülen explains this further in the following way:

> The reasons why certain Muslim people or institutions that misunderstand Islam are becoming involved in a terrorist attacks throughout the world should not be sought in Islam, but within the people themselves,

in their misinterpretations and in other factors. Just as Islam is not a religion of terrorism, any Muslim who correctly understands Islam cannot be or become a terrorist (2004e: 179).

Specifically in relation to the al-Qaeda network, Gülen is quoted (2004c: 4) as saying about Osama Bin Laden that: '[H]e has sullied the bright face of Islam. He has created a contaminated image. Even if we were to try to repair the damage that he has done, it would take years to repair' and that 'Bin Laden replaced Islamic logic with his own feelings and desires'. In relation more generally to those who invoke Islam and yet take the pathway epitomized by Bin Laden, Gülen (2004c: 5) argues for a self-critical approach and for the need to recognize that, 'It is our fault ... A real Muslim, one who understands Islam in every aspect, cannot be a terrorist ... Religion does not approve of the killing of people in order to attain a goal.'

British Muslims post-7/7

In a question originally posed in the Turkish context, but also touching a raw nerve of sensitivity among the elders of the Muslim community in the UK, Gülen (2004c: 5) asks 'What kind of responsibility did we take in their upbringing so that now we should expect them not to engage in terror?'

Of relevance to this, in a piece in *The Guardian* (9.7.2007) newspaper, the journalist Madeleine Bunting (2007) wrote of the reaction of Muslim leaders gathered in London immediately following the 7/7 bombings. Of these leaders, Bunting noted that many had refused to accept that the bombings might have been perpetrated by people of Muslim background. Because of this, she noted that the discussion had frustrated the younger generation of British-born Muslims because their elders had not understood how the youth of the community, especially, had been caught up in a global political conflict interacting with a generational conflict and crisis of identity in the UK.

By contrast with that period, after the attempted central London and Glasgow airport bombings of 30 June 2007, full-page adverts were taken out in national newspapers, and on 7 July *imams* and activists from across the country gathered to tackle extremism. The Islam is Peace (2007) organization's 'Not in Our Name' campaign adverts stated clearly that: 'The Muslim communities across Britain are united in condemning the attempted bombings in London and Glasgow'; that 'Islam forbids the killing of innocent people'; and that 'We reject any heinous attempts to link such abhorrent acts to the teachings of Islam'. In light of this, Bunting noted that Britain's Muslims were now acting in a concerted way; that in contrast to a previous fear of 'washing one's dirty linen in public' such subjects were now being aired in public, including in discussion with non-Muslims; and that Britain had become the context for one of the most impassioned debates about Islam to be found in the world.

Islamic analysis

If Bunting was correct, then the opportunity that at present exists for resources such as those offered by Fethullah Gülen and the movement inspired by his teaching to make a positive impact is underlined. What is particularly important about Gülen's contribution on these matters is that it is based not on mere condemnation of terrorist activity, but also on a realistic understanding of the dynamics of the world, and on a deep understanding of Islamic tradition.

Thus, while clearly condemning the 9/11 attacks on the USA, Gülen also warned about the kind of response that the USA might make, and of the likely consequences that could flow from that. Addressing this in words, the force and resonance of which are only underlined by what has occurred since then, Gülen (2004e: 262) said:

> Before America's leaders and people respond to this heinous assault out of their justified anger and pain, please let me express that they must understand why such a terrible event occurred and let us look to how similar tragedies can be avoided in the future. They must also be aware of the fact that injuring innocent masses in order to punish a few guilty people is to no one's benefit; rather, such actions will only strengthen the terrorists by feeding any existing resentment and by giving birth to more terrorists and more violence.

Sadly, the prescience of Gülen's warning can be seen all too clearly in the continuing instability of Afghanistan; the quagmire of death and destruction that Iraq became; the tangled metal and bloody aftermath of the train bomb in Madrid in March 2004; and the London Transport bombings of July 2005. As Shezad Tanweer, one of the 7/7 bombers, expressed it, the voters of Britain may have wondered what they had done to deserve such bombing attacks, but he pointed to government support for what he called the 'genocide' of more than 150,000 innocent Muslims in Fallujah and in other places, stating that there would be no peace until these policies change because he and other Muslims dedicated to their cause loved death as much as others love life (see BBC News Channel, 2006).

In the face of such deep-seated rage, articulated in a way that clearly undermined the government's oft-repeated mantra that these terror actions are nothing to do with foreign policy, what is needed is not only a clear differentiation of Islam from terrorism, but also a form of Islamic teaching, and even more so, an embodied practice in which authentic Islam can itself become a resource for Muslims themselves to engage with the issues and challenges of the modern world, such teaching and practice also needs to be capable of communicating in a serious way with people of other religious faith, as well as those of secular perspectives.

In other words, in order to contribute to the growth of civility in our multi-ethnic, multicultural and multi-religious society, the actions and perspectives of the bombers need robust challenge from Islamic resources that draw upon the deep wells of Qur'an and Sunnah; are informed by the rich history of multicultural Islamic civilization; and yet are also fully engaged with the contemporary global realities of modernity.

Gülen's teaching can offer such resources because, as the editor of Gülen's book, *Towards a Global Civilization of Love and Tolerance*, M. Enes Ergene (in Gülen, 2004e: viii) explains it in his Introduction to that book: 'Gülen's model is ... the essence of the synthesis created by the coming together of Turkish culture with Islam'. It is especially a development of the Sufi tradition that:

> re-generates this tolerant interpretation and understanding of Muslim-Turkish Sufism within contemporary circumstances, albeit highlighting a broader, more active, and more socially oriented vision ... Gülen opens up this framework and vision to all societies in the world, transforming and broadening it.

South Asian Muslims and Islam with a Turkish face

Of course, the influence of Gülen's teaching in the UK is limited by the fact that the primary face of Islam and of the organized Muslim community groups in the UK is a South Asian, rather than a Turkish (or an Arabic) one. These groupings are shaped by a strong minority consciousness arising from the experience of British Imperial India (see Hardy, 1972). Such a consciousness can feed creatively into the contemporary minority experience in the contemporary UK. But, as compared with the heritage of those Muslims whose background is shaped by more a confident majority history, many from within this heritage have been less self-confident in interaction with the wider public life, and more concerned with preserving Islam in a sea of alien cultural influence.

By contrast, Islam in the Turkish context – and as reflected in Gülen's teaching – is rooted in a confident Ottoman Muslim civilizational heritage that is characterized by a greater ease with diversity that was part of that heritage. Furthermore, since the Kemalist revolution in Turkey this tradition has also, of necessity, had to learn to engage with both modernity and secularity and also with currents that go beyond secularity alone also into stances of ideological secularism.

During the period of the Turkish Republic, and in very polarized social contexts that have included three coups (1960, 1971 and 1980) and periods of community violence and military rule, Gülen and the community that has emerged around his teaching have had to chart a course that both engages with, and differentiates itself from, the twin challenges that arise from ideological 'secularism' and political 'Islamism'. Forged in this crucible, Gülen's teaching offers a critique of the political instrumentalization of Islam while arguing for an active Muslim engagement with the wider (religious and secular) society in ways based on a distinctive Islamic vision characterized by robustness and civility which could make a positive contribution in the present UK context.

Neither traditionalism nor reformism

Thus Gülen's teaching offers the possibility of finding an alternative path that is reflected in the title of Ahmet Kuru's (2003: 115–30) essay: 'Fethullah Gülen's search for a middle way between modernity and Muslim tradition'. Of course, 'third ways' are often fraught with difficulty. They have also sometimes been viewed with a certain scepticism on the basis that, in the end, they have turned out not to have been 'third ways' after all, but rather variants on one or other dominant ideology.

There remains a possibility that this may become the fate of the movement inspired by Fethullah Gülen's teaching. However, what is significant and potentially creative with regard to Gülen and his teaching is that the 'middle way' that he advocates is not a road of mere 'compromise' but is one that is rooted in a particular understanding and application of traditional Islam in which Islam is itself identified in terms of a 'middle way'. As Kuru (2003: 130) argues:

> Gülen does not try to create an eclectic or hybrid synthesis of modernity and Islam or to accommodate the hegemony of modernity by changing Islamic principles. What he does is reveal a dynamic interpretation of Islam that is both compatible with and critical of modernity and Muslim tradition.

Thus, Gülen employs what might be called a 'textured hermeneutic' which is more in line with the classical traditions of the interpretation of Islam, and is quite different from the 'flat' approach of modern Islamists. As Hakan Yavuz (2003a: 29) summarizes matters more generally: 'Gülen's views on the precepts of Islam are pragmatic and contemporary without being liberal.'

It is precisely because it is not 'liberal' in the populist or modernist sense that Gülen's teaching can resonate with those Muslims of more traditionalist orientation. At the same time, the contextual sensitivity of his teaching contributes to the conditions that can facilitate dialogue between traditionalists and those of a more contemporary and secular outlook, as well as with those of other religions.

At one time Gülen himself was not a stranger to concerns about the impact on Islam of Western influence and a perspective in which the 'secular' is almost automatically equated with the 'immoral'. But in a 2000 interview with Hakan Yavuz (2003a: 45), Gülen acknowledged:

> We all change, don't we? ... By visiting the States and many other European countries, I realized the virtues and the role of religion in these societies. Islam flourishes in Europe and America much better than in many Muslim countries. This means freedom and the rule of law are necessary for personal Islam.

On the basis of this re-evaluation, rooted in an openness to learning from experience, Gülen critiques the kind of superficial reading of religion in European and Western societies that can be found among many Muslim traditionalists, observing that:

> Some people might be tempted to say that religion has no place in the life of society in developed countries such as America and those of Western Europe. We must immediately point out that such a statement is in no way correct and that these countries have been and are attached to their religions. Just as we have expressed earlier, although religious values may have been weakened over the last two centuries throughout the world, humanity today is again searching for religion, and is once again inclining toward it. Even though the population may be indifferent to religion, to a certain extent in Western Europe, those in the administration seem to be, on the whole, rather religious. Among these, there have always been religious people at the highest levels of administration, and there still are today. Moreover, though secularism is the rule in all these countries, there has never been a mentality dictating that the guidance of religion should be abandoned in social or even in the political life of a country (Gülen, 2004e: 244),

In making these observations, Gülen contrasts a civil society understanding of the 'secular' that aims to facilitate the participation of citizens of all religions and none in the public life of a society with an ideological form of secular*ism* that is concerned to promote positivist philosophical positions and their philosophical consequences (see Weller, 2006b).

What Gülen argues for is a society in which support for a rich and deeply-rooted religious integrity can challenge the sorts of dichotomous and Manichean views of the world that lead to actions of indiscriminate terror. It is a perspective that is able, though its robust integrity, to promote the development of an inclusive civility. As summarized by Sahin Alpay (1995), 'Hodjaefendi opposes the use of Islam as a political ideology and a party philosophy, as well as polarizing society into believers and nonbelievers.' Such a contribution can also challenge government and the wider society to continue to work on negotiating a way forward for British society that continues to draw on the distinctive strengths of its component parts rather than requiring Muslims to lose what makes them who they are as a price for full participation.

Islam for civil society, religious freedom and dialogue

Traditionalist Muslims often highlight a tension, if not an outright incompatibility, between *dar al-harb* (referring to territory that lays outside the sway of Islam) and what is called *dar al-Islam* (referring to those lands in which Islam has taken root). Others – of which Ihsan Yilmaz (2003) sees the movement inspired by Gülen's teaching as an example – are more concerned with what Yilmaz identifies as *dar al-hizmet*. This reflects a development away from an instrumentalization of religion in politics to a public life of service based on religious motivations and contributing to civil society as one contribution alongside others.

This contrasts with the approach of those of whom Gülen (2006e: 40) says: 'There are those who are uncomfortable with other people's freedom of conscience and religion. While saying "freedom of conscience and religion", there are people who perceive it as only their own freedom. There are such fanatics and bigots.' Thus the deep-seated commitment of Gülen's vision, and of the practice of the movement inspired by his teaching, to inter-religious dialogue offers another important resource. As Bekim Agai (2003: 65) points out:

> Although many Islamic leaders may talk of tolerance in Islam, it may be problematic to put it into practice. Gülen himself has shown that he has no fears of meeting leaders of other religions, including the Pope and the representative of the Jewish community in Istanbul. He also crossed the borders of Islamic discourse to meet with important people in Turkish society who are atheists. These activities were not easy from a religious perspective because Islamic discourse in Turkey has definite boundaries that do not appreciate close ties to the leaders of other religions and nonreligious persons. Also, his support for the Alevis was not very popular among most Sunni-Islamic groups.

In a compact and accessible way, the main contours of Gülen's thinking on dialogue can be found in his article on 'The necessity of interfaith dialogue:

a Muslim perspective' (in Ünal and Williams, 2000: 241–56) and in his piece on 'At the Threshold of a New Millennium' (in Ünal and Williams, 2000: 225–32). It should be noted that these were written before the global religious and political shock of 9/11 and its aftermath, thus underlining that Gülen's advocacy of dialogue is not merely reactive and pragmatic, but is rooted in his vision of Islam and the contemporary world. Gülen stands against ways of thinking and acting that promote what can all too easily promote the illusion that the uncomfortable plurality of the contemporary world can simply be abolished. Against such illusions he (Gülen, 2004e: 249–50) warns that:

> [D]ifferent beliefs, races, customs and traditions will continue to cohabit in this village. Each individual is like a unique realm unto themselves; therefore the desire for all humanity to be similar to one another is nothing more than wishing for the impossible. For this reason, the peace of this (global) village lies in respecting all these differences, considering these differences to be part of our nature and in ensuring that people appreciate these differences. Otherwise, it is unavoidable that the world will devour itself in a web of conflicts, disputes, fights, and the bloodiest of wars, thus preparing the way for its own end.

Reflecting on the history of violent conflict in Turkey that preceded the military coups in 1971 and 1980, Gülen (2004c: 7) said:

> Everybody was a terrorist. The people on that side were terrorists; the people on this side were terrorists. But, everybody was labelling the same action differently. One person would say, 'I am doing this in the name of Islam'. Another would say 'I am doing it for my land and people'. A third would say, 'I am fighting against capitalism and exploitation'. These were all just words. The Qur'an talks about such 'labels'. They are things of no value. But people just kept on killing. Everyone was killing in the name of an ideal.

Towards the future: resource and challenge

Madeleine Bunting's *Guardian* article previously referred to was published under the headline, 'Hearts and minds of young Muslims will be won or lost in the mosques'. In it, Bunting pointed out that 'around 90 per cent of Britain's male Muslims attend Friday prayers making it a key arena for connecting with the Muslim core constituency'. In contrast to what she argued was the 'self-defeating' approach of those who argued that the government should withdraw from engagement with organizations that have historical links to 'Islamism', she cited the work of the Metropolitan

Police Muslim Contact Unit which understood that the best chance of drawing extremists away from violence was through the influence of those who know how to argue the case on Islamic grounds and so could redirect the religious fervour of 'hot-headed young men'.

It is precisely because Fethullah Gülen is one who does know how to argue the case on Islamic grounds that his teaching has the possibility to redirect the religious fervour of 'hot-headed young men' from violent confrontationalism towards self-critical renewal. Gülen's teaching is not 'modernist'. So it cannot, with integrity, be denounced as a 'sell-out' to secularism, nor is it 'reformist' in the sense that many mean by this. Instead, Gülen's teaching offers a contribution that is devout, and looks for the renewal of Muslims through deeper engagement with the sources of Islam.

At the same time, this Islamic depth calls for deployment of an appropriate *ijtihad* that is directed towards Islamically faithful engagement with the realities of the current historical and geographical and socio-political contexts. All of this, together, is then directed towards *tajdid* or 'renewal' of Islam and of Muslims that can actively develop and enrich both the 'bonding' and 'bridging' social capital (see Weller, 2005b) that religions can offer to the wider civil society.

As Yilmaz (2003: 208–37) puts it in the title of a paper on the movement that has been inspired by Gülen's teaching, what Gülen's teaching stimulates is an '*ijtihad* and *tajdid* by conduct'. As one whose vision and practice of Islam was honed in modern Turkey within the cauldron of conflict between 'Islamist' and 'secularist' visions, Gülen's integrity, robustness and civility can contribute towards the laying of more secure foundations for civility among Muslims. At the same time, his contribution can also bring to the wider Christian, secular and religiously plural society the challenge of the rich religious and civilizational heritage that is Islam, in the forms in which it took shape in the Ottoman Turkish and Sufi Muslim heritage.

In view of the increasingly important role of Turkey vis-à-vis the European continent and its possible future entry into full membership of the European Union (Bilici, 2006), this heritage in itself is likely to play a more important part in emergent Muslim identities in Europe. And in the setting of the transitional context for Islam and Muslims that is Britain post-7/7, the teaching of Gülen can offer a secure and robust Islamic basis for challenging the equation of Islam and Muslims with terrorism and extremism.

In all these circumstances there is a conjuncture of factors in which there can be a resonance with Gülen's teaching. His teaching and the movement that is inspired by it, can positively contribute to the development of a 'style' of Islam in the UK in which Muslims are open to being informed by the strengths of the broader British and European culture and inheritance, while also themselves being confident enough to continue to make a distinctively Islamic contribution that is characterized by both robustness and civility.

12

A Sunni Muslim scholar's humanitarian and religious rejection of violence against civilians

Y. ALP ASLANDOĞAN AND BEKIR CINAR

Introduction

This chapter discusses the unconditional rejection of violence against civilians by the influential Sunni Muslim scholar, Fethullah Gülen, on humanitarian and religious grounds.

We first consider forms and contexts of violence because terrorism is an extreme form of political violence. In other words, 'political violence is either the deliberate infliction or threat of infliction of physical injury or damage for political ends, or it is violence which occurs unintentionally in the course of severe political conflicts' (Wilkinson, 1977: 30). This violence is perpetrated under a religious, ideological or nationalistic rhetoric that is part of a larger picture which includes various forms of violence that usually stem from frustration under adverse political conditions and have political goals.

After reviewing the general views of Gülen on violence, we examine Gülen's rejection – on both humanitarian and religious grounds – of violence against civilians that is perpetrated under a religious rhetoric. Gülen has consistently voiced his condemnation of terrorism. We provide both summaries of Gülen's views as well as direct translations [translated by Cinar and Aslandoğan] from the original Turkish of quotations from his works published in that language. We also touch briefly upon some of Gülen's comments on the political conditions that provide the breeding ground for terrorism.

Forms and contexts of violence

The term 'violence' obviously concerns a great variety of social phenomena and its meaning is vague (Chwe, 2001). Historically, 'the use of violence to effect political change is a generalized phenomenon around the world' (Boix, 2004: 197). In general terms, violence is a product of an individual or a group that acts unilaterally in order to impose its opinion, and there is no space for negotiation because the power of each side is not equal. The violence can be linked to specific places or times and can be sustained and reproduced in social structures. Davis says that 'violence is shown to be negatively related to the availability of alternative means of acquiring political goods and to the availability of alternative economic opportunities' (Davis, 1999: 2).

One of the aims of political violence (Davis, 1999) is to alter the political and economic status quo, because this is seen as maintaining injustice and unfairness. The injustice and unfairness are subjective and a reflection of the perceptions of people who claim to be suffering from them. Therefore, they are also relative, not absolute.

This idea will be examined within 'the deprivation theory of civil violence' (Wilkinson, 1974: 126). According to Wilkinson:

> [T]here are at least four models of relative deprivation: rising expectations may overtake rising capability; capabilities may remain static while expectation rise; general socio-economic malaise may actually bring about a drop in capabilities while expectations remain constant; and finally there is the classic J-curve phenomenon in which, for a period, capabilities keep pace with rising expectations and then suddenly drop behind (Wilkinson 1974: 126).

Davis suggests that 'political violence results from the social frustration that occurs in the wake of relative deprivation' (Davis, 1999: 13). Individuals or groups may feel that the deprivation causes the problem, and the use of violence 'becomes more attractive to those that are excluded from the state apparatus – the prize of victory raises with inequality' (Boix, 2004: 199).

In order to understand the extreme form of violence which is terrorism, we should look at the essential characteristic of politics itself that requires 'conflict between the desires of different individuals' (Crisp, 1990: 5) in finding a right balance among the interest groups of the society: 'This is why the heart of politics is often portrayed as a process of conflict resolution' (Heywood, 2007: 4). If the political system is not a liberal democratic system, then the opposition may not be in a position to express its ideas and alternatives as much as those holding state power. This could lead it to respond on a different level. If the state actors respond in turn with the use of force, this might be countered with force of a similar nature.

When such a dispute involves disagreement about the appropriate source of legitimation the conflict may be more than usually intractable, for the standard democratic procedure of majority vote by the legitimating 'people' is fatally flawed when the question at issue is who 'the people' are. The more intractable the dispute, the more likely, other things being equal, that dissent will take illegal or terroristic forms (Crisp, 1990). Thus, throughout history, peace is the end product of freedom, achieved through political communication defined as 'the ability of people to express their views, thoughts, and beliefs freely, without the fear that they will be imprisoned as a result' (Sharansky, 2002: 12). Further, he states that 'we must understand that it is not only individuals who are equal, but also the nationalities of this world that are equal. They all deserve to live in democracy, to live under a government that depends on them (Sharansky, 2002: 13). Windsor agrees with Sharansky and states that 'promoting democratization in the closed societies of the Middle East can provide a set of values and ideas that offer a powerful alternative to the appeal of the kind of extremism that today has found expression in terrorist activity, often against U.S. interests' (Windsor, 2003: 43).

Such a political system is a democratic political one, in relation to which, as Windsor notes, 'democratic institutions and procedures, by enabling the peaceful reconciliation of grievances and providing channels for participation in policymaking, can help to address those underlying conditions that have fuelled the recent rise of Islamist extremism' (Windsor, 2003: 43). Further, Dermer argues that it has been 'the lack of freedom in many parts of the world that was the greatest threat to peace and stability' (Sharansky and Dermer, 2006: i). In the context of the Middle East, for instance, Gause argues that,

[T]here is no reason to believe that a move toward more democracy in Arab states would deflect them from their course. And there is no reason to believe that they could not recruit followers in more democratic Arab states – especially if those states continued to have good relations with the United States, made peace with Israel, and generally behaved in ways acceptable to Washington (Gause, 2005: 69).

However, keeping the political structure of the Middle East as it is will not obviously solve the problem. As Sharansky says, 'I am convinced that all peoples desire to be free. I am convinced that freedom anywhere will make the world safer everywhere' (Sharansky and Dermer, 2006: 17). Therefore, without freedom of choice, expression and belief, security is not possible.

Identifying and analysing forms of violence and responses to forms of violence requires one to focus on the role of representation, sovereignty and identity in conflict, as well as the role of the state system in reconstructing some of the essential conditions of asymmetric warfare. Without analysing the implications of the conditions and nature of the peace and order, as well as important elements of the violence, one cannot reach a proper result in identifying the violence.

Frustration, civil disobedience and violence

Civil disobedience is often an effective means of changing laws and protecting liberties. It also embodies an important moral concept that there are times when law and justice do not coincide and that to obey the law at such times can be an abdication of ethical responsibility (Starr, 1998).

According to the theory of frustration-aggression, '[H]umans only become violent if they are frustrated in their efforts to attain a particular goal: severe frustration leads to anger and anger to acts of aggressive violence' (Wilkinson, 1977: 35). This theory 'maintains that aggression is always a consequence of frustration' (O'Brien, 2004: 101). Frustration results from unfulfilled needs or unresolved problems such as 'worsening deprivation, injustice or oppression' which can be seen as 'a major precondition of political violence' (Wilkinson, 1977: 36).

We witness two types of political violence in politics. One of them is national scale political violence that becomes unavoidable in an unequal society in which assets are not distributed fairly among people. Then, the potential rebels can apply violence to overturn the existing political and economic system (Boix, 2004). The other is international scale political violence that is perpetrated against real or perceived entities responsible for injustices or suffering. In short, political violence is an end product of political injustice and unequal treatment of human being on a national or an international scale. Therefore, despite the lack of consensus over the definition, terrorism is an extreme form of political violence that may be defined as the use of violence for political aims.

Especially during the last few decades, acts of violence have been carried out by individuals with Muslim names or by groups claiming to have Muslim identity. While each such action or information about their possible perpetrators has made headline news, Muslim reactions to such actions and their tragic consequences were given a disproportionately smaller space by the news media. In the following, as a case study, we will examine the views of an influential Muslim scholar on violence.

Roots of terrorism

Here we will discuss the political roots of terrorism and the role ideology or religion might play in the promotion of a terrorist agenda among the masses.

Political roots of terrorism

No human is born a terrorist and the decision to get involved in terrorism does not happen overnight. Therefore, an important realization here is that terrorism is a process (Silke, 2001) and 'terrorism is a choice; it is a political strategy selected from among a range of options' (Walzer, 2002: 5–9). The process of terrorism has a historical background, which involves people who rightly or wrongly perceive that the political system is treating them harshly. This harsh treatment may even stretch back to their ancestors. The action of terrorism is an end product of the process. This process moves through several stages until the overt terrorist action takes place. Only at the action stage of terrorism does it become noticeable and is named by people. From the initial genesis of terrorism to the action itself, each individual stage requires careful determination and planning.

Terrorism can be likened to a cancerous cell in an existing political system. If the political system works perfectly, this cancer cell will not be visible within the political system; if the system does not work perfectly, it will be visible and grow and spread into the whole political system (Cinar, 1997: 247). In his parallel views, Wilkinson states that:

> [R]evolutionary violence stems directly from conflicts within and between a country's political institutions. Revolutionary violence is seen as basically the product of conflict about legitimacy, political rights, and access to power. It often results from the refusal or incapacity of a government to meet certain claims made upon it by a powerful group or a coalition of groups (Wilkinson, 1974: 129).

Examination of an existing political system and its governance may provide the required information about the root causes of terrorism. Such an investigation, however, should start at least from forty years before the present day. Ethnic terrorism may be a product of a 'nation-state' (Rotberg, 2002: 90) because nationalism means that the dominant ethnic groups in the country have been prized above others who have been subordinated in the country's political, economic and social life for a prolonged period. Today, it is difficult to see any colonial power in any country, but many minority ethnic groups within the nation-state see the dominant ethnic group or government as a colonial or occupying power.

In addition to seeing terrorism as the product of the nation-state, one may see it as a product of the political systems of repressive regimes; economic systems which are corrupted and produce poverty and no job opportunities; educational systems which are lacking in decent education and training; and the never-ending conflicts within a society.

Another type of political system is the international system, and, in particular, the current balance of power within it. Thus within the international system, the imbalance of power in places such the Middle East, Iraq, Afghanistan, Chechnya and Kashmir is a factor in the escalation of violence. This violence is not only in these places but also in the threat that it poses to other parts of the world.

Ideological roots of terrorism

It is stated that 'terrorism is not an ideology as such. It has no united political agenda. In principle, almost any ideology could be claimed by a terrorist' (Kullberg and Jokinen, 2004: 1). However, 'terrorism needs an all-encompassing philosophy, a religion or secular ideology, to legitimize violence, to win recruits to the cause and to mobilize them for action' (Kumar, 2007). Thus, human beings seek to justify whatever they do. The justification can be informed by an ideology or a religion cast into an ideological form (Shadid, 2002: 228). People who belong to different groups in a friction-stricken society feel forced to position themselves in relation to two opposing poles. The opposing concepts of the others have such powerful meanings that they tend to supersede other conflicts and determine how these conflicts are interpreted, mobilized around and fought over (Tore et al, 2004).

Religion and terrorism

Mark Juergensmeyer (2005) states that:

> The scholars agreed that while religion has been a major factor in recent acts of terrorism, it is seldom the only one. Religious ideologies, goals, and motivations are often interwoven with those that are economic, social, and political. A group's decision to turn to violence is usually situational and is seldom endemic to the religious tradition to which the group is related. Islam does not cause terrorism, nor does any other religion with which terrorist acts have been associated. ... As John Esposito explained, usually 'political and economic grievances are

primary causes or catalysts, and religion becomes a means to legitimate and mobilize'.

Ian Reader stated that even in the case of Aum Shinrikyo, the Buddhist movement implicated in the Tokyo nerve gas incident in 1995, the religious factor 'would not have been enough to take the group in the direction that it did' (Juergensmeyer, 2005: 27). Terrorism can be the means used in the name of some ideology by terrorist groups, but that ideology is not terrorism (Kullberg and Jokinen, 2004:1). One points out that:

> Interviews with terrorists often reveal that their sense of frustration bred of failure. Religion provides them with a means of dealing with these personal issues in a way that address their particular inadequacies by making them part of a more powerful movement and promising ultimate victory (Richardson, 2006: 91).

In short, religion may enable people to deal with their frustrations, but it is not the root cause of those frustrations, or their decision to engage in terrorist action. A striking study supporting this point is the study by Pape (2005: 23) that draws on conclusions from 23 years of data collected by the Chicago Project on Suicide Terrorism and which demonstrated that, rather than religious orientation, the best predictor of suicide terrorism is the occupation of territories claimed by a group. Pape found surprisingly weak correlation between religion and suicide terrorism, even including the case of al-Qaeda-related groups. Out of the 315 separate attacks within the 23 years between 1980 to 2003, 301 of them were perpetrated as part of a 'large, coherent political or military campaign' against an entity perceived as a 'foreign occupier' (Pape, 2005: 4). Pape lists nine such cases – the Lebanon, West Bank and Gaza, Sri Lanka, southeast Turkey, Chechnya, Kashmir, Punjab, Iraq and the Arabian Peninsula – that account for 95 per cent of the suicide terrorist attacks in the aforementioned period. He also shows that in the past 20 years a group with Islamist rhetoric was responsible for less than 35 per cent of suicide attacks.

Gülen's opinions on political violence

Fethullah Gülen has been recognized for his consistent stance against the use of violence with a religious rhetoric. More specifically, he was the first Muslim scholar who publicly condemned the attacks of 9/11 with an advertisement in the *Washington Post*. He also helped publish a scholarly book on Islamic perspectives on terror and suicide attacks, condemning such acts on humanitarian and religious grounds. What is more, he did not express these views just to Western readers but voiced them in mosque sermons among thousands of Muslim audience members. He unequivocally rejects suicide attacks, regardless of location or conditions, and has given interviews to Turkish, Japanese, Kenyan and American newspapers categorically condemning acts of terror for political, ideological and religious reasons. He has also appeared on numerous national television shows publicly condemning such acts.

Throughout his career as a preacher and teacher, Gülen has maintained a consistent stance against the use of violence for political means, especially against civilians. In Gülen's view, economic conditions, corruption in the state, or ideological reasons cannot justify violence. He is on the record numerous times for encouraging his listeners or readers to respect the rule of law and to find a peaceful solution to any conflict between individuals or between the individual and the state. Besides its illegitimacy, Gülen views violence as producing the very opposite of what its perpetrators aim to achieve, especially in the case of inter-group conflicts arising from difference – as experienced in Turkey during the 1970s. According to Gülen (in Baskan, 2005: 853) 'the problems of difference among people can be solved by means of tolerance. If these differences are respected, there will be a chance of benefiting from everybody's ideas without discriminating against anyone.'

His first published article in the popular magazine *Sızıntı* (a monthly magazine on literature, science and story which began publishing on 1 February 1979) states that his methods and mission are stopping 'the crying of children by sharing their unhappiness and agony, and helping them to be happy and helping them reach their highest level of human soul' (Gülen, 1979: 1–2). With this mission, he states one of his principles as avoidance of political and ideological conflict (Hermansen, 2007: 4). Institutions that have been established by participants of a civil society movement inspired by his works have made non-violence a key principle in their activities (Altunoğlu, 1999: 60). Altunoğlu states that according to Gülen, whatever is achieved by violent means will inevitably collapse (Altunoğlu, 1999: 94). Violence cannot be seen as a means of achievement. Moreover, Gülen expresses that 'it is obvious that you could not and cannot achieve anything by violence and bad temper. It is needless to emphasize that when you knock with love, respect and affection, doors to the paths of dialogue are opened and that you can have the opportunity to explain the values that you represent' (Gülen in Camcı and Ünal, 1999: 140).

Gülen's rejection of violence on humanistic grounds

The first component of Gülen's response to violence against civilians is a rejection on humanitarian grounds. As will be illustrated below, Gülen declares acts of violence against innocent civilians including women and children as inhumane. He uses clear statements in categorically condemning killing of innocent civilians, the elderly, women and children. The following is an excerpt from his condemnation message which was published by Gülen in the *Washington Post* following the September 11 attacks.

> We condemn in the strongest of terms the latest terrorist attack on the United States of America and feel the pain of the American people at the bottom of our hearts. Islam abhors acts of terror. A religion that professes "He who unjustly kills one man kills the whole of humanity". Cannot condone senseless killing of thousands. Our thoughts and prayers go out the victims and their loved-ones.

During late 1990s Turkey suffered from the terror activities of a group who called themselves 'the party of God'. This group went to such extremes as to torture and kill Muslims who they declared as being hypocrites or conspirers of enemies of faith. The Turkish daily newspaper *Zaman*, which is known for its sympathetic editorial position toward Gülen, used a headline on 17 January 2001 that gave a new name to this group: 'The party of savagery'. In multiple interviews given to *Zaman* daily, *Milliyet* daily, Kenyan and Canadian newspapers, Gülen also clearly stated his condemnation of Bin Ladin, his accomplices and their actions (Gülen, 2004a).

It is important to note that Gülen both declares perpetrators of terrorist acts as evil as well as questioning their humanity. In other words, in Gülen's views these individuals have lost their inner capacity to function as human beings through their conscious and persistent involvement in acts of terror against humanity. On the one hand, by condemning terrorist acts as cruel as inhuman, Gülen shows his solidarity with humanity and his common stance against terror as a fellow human being. At the same time he also appeals to the human side of his audience, who are primarily Muslims. But Gülen completes this appeal with a religious component and for an important reason. After all, the appeal and justifications of the terrorist groups such as Bin Ladin's is based on both suffering of individuals and nations, as well as their religious conscience.

Gülen's rejection of violence on religious grounds

Gülen's opinion about violence, including political violence, is based on mainstream traditional interpretations of the basic sources of Islam, such as the Qur'an, the prophetic tradition, as well as particular interpretations of certain aspects of those same sources as shaped by the Central-Asian and Anatolian experience. His opinion has provided a powerful approach to spiritual change not only in Turkey but also many parts of the world through educational institutions and dialogue activities.

There are three components of Gülen's religious response to violence against civilians. The first is the rejection of *self-declared wars*. The second is the reiteration of an important principle of Islamic jurisprudence: *individuality/personal responsibility of crime* and the rejection of harming women, children and other non-combatant civilians under any circumstances. The third is the rejection of 'they have no other means' rhetoric and of the philosophy that 'the *ends justify the means*'. Gülen supports this position by pointing to the Leninist roots of this philosophy and to the lack of precedents in the lives of the Prophet of Islam (peace be upon him) and his companions.

Gülen (2006b) states that 'all kinds of unjust murders are great sins' referring to some of the central concepts of justice and peace in the Qur'an, both of which are the current essence of the modern legal system developed to protect life, capital and reproduction. Other verses to which Gülen alludes in this context include, 'Deal fairly, and do not let the hatred of others for you make you swerve to wrong and depart from justice. Be just, for that is next to piety, and fear God' (*Qur'an*, 5:8); and 'He who kills a soul unless it be (in legal punishment) for murder or for causing disorder and corruption on the earth will be as if he had killed all humankind; and he who saves a life will be as if he had saved the lives of all humankind' (*Qur'an*, 5:32)

According to Gülen, no political reason could justify killing innocent civilians and causing disorder and corruption on the earth. In contrast, he highlights that 'loving and respecting humanity merely because they are human is an expression of respect for the Almighty Creator. ... If we can raise a community upon this perspective, people will eventually recover and they will manage to compensate for whatever they have lost' (Gülen, 2006c).

Gülen's first categorical response to violence against civilians is the *rejection of self-declared wars*. The following quotation summarizes this point: 'The rules of Islam are obvious. Individuals cannot declare war; this includes a group and an organization. War is only declared by the state that has legal and legitimate authority' (Gülen, 2004b). Another quotation reiterates this principle and alludes to the rules of conduct during war, which we will elaborate below: 'An Islamic authority can do war only within the framework of such definite principles, and only a legal and legitimate state, not certain individuals or organizations, can decide a war' (Gülen, 2004c).

Elsewhere, Gülen states that if a person or group believe that their government does not represent their views, then it is their duty to influence the government or otherwise induce social change through non-violent means (Gülen, 2003c). Gülen also highlights a point of confusion among both Muslims as well as non-Muslims, with regard to those principles that regulate a soldier's conduct during the time of war and encourage active defence in the protection of five important entities: life; freedom; family/progeny; property; and sanity/health. Gülen also underlines the principle of individuality of crime, and the rejection of the approach that the ends justify the means.

The earliest recorded stance of Gülen against violence occurred in the midst of ideologically driven armed conflicts in Turkey during the 1970s. Various ideological groups such as communists of Turkey (Marxist, Leninist, Maoist, as well as sympathizers of the Albanian leader, Enver Hodja) and ultra-nationalists used both propaganda as well as violence to pursue their agendas. Clashes among the youth groups (it was a form of terrorism) claimed the lives of thousands of youth as well as members of the security forces, intellectuals, teachers and politicians. Armed groups would demand that students boycott classes and the shopkeepers close down shops, in order to disturb normal life in the country. During this troubled period (an account of Gülen's years in Izmir can be found in the biography by Erdoğan, 2006: 94–158), Gülen consistently promoted non-violent resistance to the demands of these groups. The Marxist-Leninist-Maoist groups were especially keen on provoking resistance from the faithful and hence drawing them into armed conflict. When communist fractions marched across the street from the mosque where Gülen was preaching, he is reported to have said the following:

> Those people who chant agitating slogans today may one day come into the mosque and shoot me. If any of you in this audience react violently, let it be known that I do not approve or condone it. If I am assassinated, despite all your angers, I ask you to bury my body and seek for order, peace and love in our society. Regardless to what happens; you should say that 'we, believers should be representatives of love and security'.

His second noteworthy stance was during the first Gulf war. While Saddam Hussein was sending missiles to Israeli cities, Gülen declared publicly in a mosque sermon ('The Exemplary Morals and Conduct of Our Prophet' given in 1990) attended by thousands of Muslims: 'Today, I am equally sad for the Israeli children who are under the threat of deadly missiles, as I am sad for the dying Iraqi children. Killing innocent children has no place in our faith.'

The third component of Gülen's religious response to violence is perhaps the most significant. This is the rejection of the philosophy that 'the ends justify the means'. In a recorded address after London Transport bombings and amidst suicide bombing events in Israel, Gülen (in 'Hosgoru, bombalar ve azinliklar' – 'Tolerance, bombs and religious minorities', available online in Turkish at http://www.herkul.org) criticized a Muslim authority who condoned acts of suicide bombings for Palestinians:

> Unfortunately some condone acts of suicide bombing with the rhetoric of 'they have no other means'. If this (referring to suicide bombings) is

the only means Muslims have, let that means be buried deep into ground together with the one who uses it.

Gülen continues that the combination of certain non-religious motives and the lack of a holistic perspective allow people to pick and choose what part of the religious tradition they would use in justifying violent acts:

> The problem today is that Islam is not understood properly, in a holistic manner. Islam has always been respectful of plurality of worldviews and this point needs to be understood well today. Islam is an authentic religion and it should be lived true to its spirit. While striving toward an Islamic life, it is self-contradictory to use illegitimate means. Just as the ends should be righteous, the means should also be righteous. A Muslim cannot hope to please God by killing humans. Killing humans can not be a means of pleasing God (Gülen, 2004a).

Gülen also offers explanations for misinterpreted verses and prophetic sayings which are abused by those who justify acts of violence. He states that the reasons why certain Muslim people or institutions that misunderstand Islam are becoming involved in terrorist attacks should be sought not in Islam, but within the people themselves, in their misinterpretations and in other factors (Gülen, 2001a).

The verses in the Qur'an that specify conditions for *jihad* have been misinterpreted by others and taken as the fundamental aim of Islam. In essence, these people, who have failed to grasp the true spirit of Islam, have been unable to strike a balance between the broad and finer points. This, when coupled with the fact that they have been consumed with hatred, has led them to misinterpret Islam. The heart of a genuine Muslim community is full of love and affection for all of creation.

Gülen's opinions on political roots of terrorism

In the political perspective, while discussing misunderstandings, misrepresentations and abuses of religious texts, Gülen hints at the presence of individuals, ideology or interest groups, and other entities that benefit from friction and armed conflict. He points out that the possibility should be considered that some individuals have been manipulated and deceived or even hypnotized through special drugs to carry out actions they would not otherwise carry out. Gülen does not deny that political conditions are sources of political violence and terrorism, but he insists that people should not use those conditions in order to justify their unlawful action. He advises that, 'Muslims must be legitimate in their intentions when it comes to their goals, thoughts, and actions, for only a straight and allowed way can lead them to their exalted object' (Gülen, 2006c). Without legitimacy, neither action nor intention is acceptable even if Muslims should gain that for which they aimed.

We have discussed the secondary role of ideology or religion in communication and recruitment to terrorism. Gülen echoes the findings of researchers who point out the diverse conditions that provide a breeding-ground for terrorist groups. The recent history of colonialism; the tyranny of non-democratic, authoritarian leaders; the presence of various forms of suffering and injustice; and the lack of authoritative scholars provide opportunities for misleading individuals toward violent reactions that serve other interests (Gülen, 2006c).

We have above highlighted frustration as a leading cause of the tendencies to terrorism. This frustration serves as the turning point toward political violence. According to Gülen, in order to eliminate the tendency toward violence, the main focus should be on the individual who lives under these conditions that produce frustration. In some cases, moral support alone is enough for many people who are suffering under those conditions. Often, however, a systematic approach centred around education is the only lasting solution. Gülen believes that humanity is looking forward to the days where individuals endowed with high human values overcome those who favour hostility:

I have been looking forward to a better world resembling Paradise, where humanity can live in peace and tranquillity. Our world is tired of war and clashes. It direly needs mercy, affection, spiritual well-being, and peace more than air and water. I believe that people in every country are ready for such a world (Gülen, 2007d).

Conclusion

We began by examining origins and root causes of violence, especially political violence. Economic, political, social and cultural factors each play a role in individuals slipping onto the perilous slope of terrorism. Both governments as well as civic organizations have an obligation in responding to this modern phenomenon which has far reaching consequences for humanity. Recently religion, and in particular the name of Islam, has been juxtaposed with terrorist actions and individuals. Among opinion leaders who respond to terrorism, Gülen is distinguished by three factors.

First, Gülen has clearly voiced his unconditional condemnation of acts of violence against civilians and stated that involvement in terrorism cannot coincide with commitment to faith. Second, Gülen argued both as a human and as a Muslim scholar in systematic and convincing ways to distance his audience from having sympathy with the perpetrators of such actions.

Third, lasting solutions to the problem of terrorism have been generated by civil society organizations inspired and encouraged by Gülen, in the form of educational institutions inculcating a culture of tolerance and respect and in opportunities for upward mobility,

In other words, Gülen's ideas and vision have not remained in audio-tapes and books, but instead they have been realized in concrete projects in volatile regions of the world. From the beginning of his career, Gülen has been involved in the establishment of educational institutions and personally tutored some of their first teachers. He has personally experienced whether his proposals to humanity were workable or not. The results have so far been positive and there are tangible indicators of decreased tensions in communities with Gülen-inspired educational institutions in many regions of the world (Saritoprak, 2005). A review of Gülen's rhetoric and action reveals that he has understood the root causes of violence and political violence (terrorism), paving the way for him to pioneer sustainable ways to combat and prevent them.

We have pointed out the political and economic roots of terrorism and the role that ideology, or religion cast into an ideological form, plays in communicating with the community in order to recruit more support, rather than being itself the root cause of terrorism. Richardson comments that 'broad social, economic and cultural factors may be the underlying causes or rather the risk factors that make a society more or less susceptible to the appeal of terrorist groups' (Richardson, 2006: 93). Economic and other grievances only lead to terrorism if people feel that those grievances are a product of the political system, and that they are excluded from that system. Consequently, the response to the complex phenomenon of terrorism involves participation by political institutions, such as governmental agencies, as well as civil society organizations.

13

The work of Fethullah Gülen and the role of non-violence in a time of terror

STEVE WRIGHT

Peace by peace

The notion of peace by peace has a rich Western tradition from Tolstoy to Martin Luther King. In the East, the non-violent tradition is much more ancient. Emperor Asoka, presiding over India in the third century BCE slaughtered more than a hundred thousand before experiencing a Buddhist conversion which led him to proselytizing for non-violence, from a distinctly spiritual and pragmatic perspective (Seneviratana, 1994).

Middle Eastern spiritual leaders teaching non-violence have had an enormous significance in the West, but it is a truism that there has been much less of a 'connect' between spiritual theory and earthly praxis. Two thousand years of Christianity has not led to a reduction of violence – far from it since Christians have slaughtered each other for much of that period and most other faiths as well. And yet the diversity and complexity of the Christian community cannot be so easily dismissed in terms of their differing dimensions of tradition, time and space.

We know that many Christian communities, inspired by their faith, have successfully attempted to translate their spiritual ethics and a belief in non-violence into a practical set of transformative actions. For example,

Pax Christi and the Quakers teach peace through service at community, national and international levels. It is not an exaggeration to say, for example in the UK, that nearly all the most significant groupings for social change and peace have benefited from the funding of Quaker groups like the Joseph Rowntree Charitable Trust, without which a tremendous set of changes for the good would simply not have happened.

However, at a state level, despite the non-violent message of Christianity's founding figure, the practical messages have been much more mixed. Indeed within living memory we have witnessed military chaplains blessing nuclear missiles and a genocide against Jewish people being rationalized on ideological and utilitarian grounds by a self-defined Christian Hitler (Steigmann-Gall, 2003). During the Second World War, the head of the Catholic Church, Pope Pius XII, refused to speak out in opposition to Nazi crimes against the Jewish peoples and, while the Vatican has since apologized for this silence, it is a permanent stain on its ethics.

What is of most significance in these debates is the integrity of spiritual teaching about peace and non-violence and the processes by which such beliefs are made manifest in practice. An absence of integrity in such processes suggests either impotence or hypocrisy. But it could also be read as confusion. Just because the Nazis said they were Christians did not mean they were and there is much other evidence that Nazism as a movement was strongly anti-Christian, and strongly influenced by pagan, occultist and similar beliefs (Pauwels and Bergier, 2007; and Powe, 2006). Nevertheless, despite the content of Christianity's teaching, the so-called 'German Christian Movement' tried to enlist them into the service of National Socialist approaches to the Volk.

And this is my point: believability is the extent to which teaching and practice are one. This is what is so attractive about the Gülen movement to external observers since, even to an outsider, the motivation is to unify outward behaviour with spiritual credo. Peace is, of course, central to Islamic teaching. The Qur'an (59:23) refers to it being one of God's names. Islamic scholars have cogently argued that the Sunnah or Prophet's way, can be understood as a deliberate choosing of the path of non-violence – a distinctly Islamic approach to non-violence based on *dawah* or peaceful struggle for the propagation of Islam.

It is in this sense that Fethullah Gülen's contribution might best be understood through the lens of Western practices of non-violent action for social change. This remains a slow process of recognition since it is only in recent years that the larger peace research networks have begun to recognize and assimilate the thoughts of Islamic scholars on non-violence and that this form of non-violence is active and transformative (Paige, Satha-Anand and Gilliat, 2001). Of course within Islam, Arab elders have used such principles for centuries to resolve family and community disputes and there is a continuum of practice for scholars willing to research it as such (Abu-Nimer, 2003).

Historically, the East has provided us with some of our most inspirational teachers, translating their spiritual beliefs into a philosophy of both peace cultures and peace through non-violent direct action. All of us active in peace movements today will acknowledge our debt to Mahatma Gandhi. His quest was seen as a process of transformation, of tackling the violent injustices of the largest empire ever assembled. He rejected violence as a tactic because in the long term it was counter-productive. 'I object to violence because when it appears to do good, the good is only temporary; the evil it does is permanent' (Gandhi, 1925: 178). For Gandhi, 'Victory attained by violence is tantamount to a defeat, for it is momentary' (Gandhi, 1919: Leaflet 13).

There are certain similarities between Gandhi's deeply practical spiritual teaching and sayings and those of Fethullah Gülen – for example, Gandhi's persistent concern with the world of inner spiritual responsibility, crystallized in his often-quoted remark: 'As human beings our greatness lies not so much in being able to remake the world ... as in being able to remake ourselves' (cited by Easwaran, n.d.). Yet for Western peace activists, the power of Gandhi's contribution is that it incorporates dimensions of technique which can be replicated elsewhere. This is the framework that pioneer peace researcher Theodore Lentz once called a 'Science and Technology of Peace' (Lentz, 1972, see also Eckhart, 1971).

Both Gandhi and Gülen stress the importance of truthfulness and this is an important test for any movement towards peaceful change: does it work in practice? The quest for 'testing truth' occupied not only the earliest philosophers but also the earliest scientists. The seventeenth-century English natural philosopher, Francis Bacon, once said, 'Truth is so hard to tell, it sometimes needs fiction to make it plausible.' But he went on to conceptualize a founding notion of scientific practice, namely that of falsifiability. Bacon also said that: 'Truth emerges more readily from error than from confusion' (in Spedding et al., 1968: 210). In other words, all notions of truth should be open to question and testability.

This was an approach which put Copernicus and Galileo into conflict with the Church of Rome, because their astronomical observations and resultant hypotheses contradicted the then dominant doctrinal explanation of biblical doctrine. The result was a classic story of paradigm challenge and shift (Kuhn, 1962). Bacon himself was aware of the dangers of telling truth to power: 'Truth is a good dog; but always beware of barking too close to the heels of an error, lest you get your brains kicked out.' And yet Francis Bacon's abiding conclusion was that 'Truth is the daughter of time, not of authority' (in Spedding et al., 1968). Why is this relevant to any comparative discussion of modern notions of 'non-violence' especially in regard to Turkey?

Gülen's approach to non-violence is rooted in Anatolian Islamic belief systems which, to an outsider, are based on the timeless wisdom of the Qur'an which is viewed as immutable holy writ. However, a closer reading reveals that Gülen sees the inspiration of his faith as a work in progress rather than being 'set in concrete'. He values inter-faith dialogue and ongoing cultural exchange as evidenced by his role as Honorary President of the Journalists and Writers Foundation.

By contrast, alternative approaches to non-violence theory – such as Gene Sharp's tactics and theories of civil disobedience (Sharp, 1973), or Brian Martin's work on 'backfire techniques' – are essentially heuristic (Martin, 2007). They are about learning by doing. Sharp lists one hundred and ninety-eight methods of what are essentially techniques used as part of a political rather than a spiritual process of non-violent direct action. These include protest and persuasion; social, economic and political non-cooperation; and non-violent intervention.

Similarly, Brian Martin's work is a study of the dynamics of state power in facing down resistance and how certain tactics of non-violence can use Gene Sharp's techniques as a form of political jui-jitsu which has the power to make the weak stronger by making repressive policies of the authorities 'backfire'. Does that mean Gülen's work on non-violence is ossified by comparison? No, on the contrary, he is open to the scientific process and sees science and religion as complementary as long as there is a social responsibility among the scientists.

What it does mean is that there may be limits on the extent to which the different processes of nonviolence in action can cross-fertilize. Is such a conclusion deterministic? Again the answer is no, since at the core of Gülen's teachings, is the importance of education. His perspectives on technological innovation are instructive since Gülen emphasizes the importance of society understanding what else is innovated when new technologies are constructed.

In coming to any conclusions about the relevance of such differing paradigms of non-violence in practice and in faith, it is worth being humble. Most authors in this field have to admit to some level of ignorance of one path, or the other or both. The current author is no exception. I am sure that I have only a crude grasp of the writings of Fethullah Gülen; neither may I do justice to key non-violence theorists such as Gandhi or Sharp. Nevertheless, I think the exercise of comparison is worthwhile.

Western voices have stereotyped Islam to a dangerous extent as a violent, backward system of beliefs which breed a medieval approach to justice and a terrorist approach to world politics. Gülen is aware of these stereotypes which he has addressed in his typically thoughtful way. In the sense that he offers a powerful approach to spiritual change in Turkey and the wider world which is based on a non-violent understanding of core Islamic values, the non-Islamic world should listen.

Gülen has written widely on the Sufi notion of *Safa'* (purity) and the challenge of ridding the human heart of the things that contaminate it: jealousy, hatred, feelings of vengeance and suspicion. His antidote from the Qur'an is mercy, tolerance and forgiveness. Gülen's philosophy is beginning to be understood by non-Islamic scholars as offering a bridge between worlds. It is an inspirational philosophy whose essence is education in action, teaching love, tolerance and mutual cultural respect.

In many senses the Gülen movement is a practical global effort for peace and understanding. And yet paradoxically it is in Turkey is where its essence has been most widely understood and misunderstood. On the one hand by all accounts the moral teaching in Gülen schools offer an exemplary moral and practical training for young people. And yet there are sectors in the military that distrust any pro-Islamic movement of whatever description because of the threat they perceive to Turkey's avowed secular identity. Fethullah Gülen himself has made it clear that the movement has no interest in seizing economic, political or cultural power either inside or outside of the country. In an interview with Turkish newspaper *Zaman*, he has reiterated his spiritual credo of serving humankind by self-sacrifice:

> As in the past, I am currently maintaining the same distance to all political parties. Even if power, not only in Turkey, but that of the entire world, were to be presented to me as a gift, I have been long determined to reject it with contempt (Gülen, 2002).

Although we might take this at face value, perceptions are often just or even more important than realities. And this is possibly the missing link between our different cultural perspectives on non-violence. It is not enough simply to withdraw from future political challenges to a spiritual movement towards peace. Even though that might be necessary, it is not sufficient.

Gülen's expressed philosophy does not falter when it comes to characterizing the unacceptability of terrorism. For him, terrorism is against the very fabric of Islam. On the basis of his erudite understanding of the Qur'an: no Muslim can be a terrorist and no terrorist a Muslim. Western commentators lack the scholarly authority within Muslim communities that Gülen brings when he concludes that suicide bombing, whatever, wherever, whenever is absolutely forbidden in Islam and for those that commit such crimes, the logical prospect is eternal banishment. It is important that such debates over interpretation are had within the Muslim community and that powerful voices are heard that can, with full knowledge, declare and make an extremely articulate attack on those who would attempt to use religious justification to commit atrocities: 'Islam never approves of any kind of terrorism' (Gülen, 2007e).

There is no ambiguity there. And yet there is a need for caution. It is possible that a willingness clearly to define a position according to faith, while absolutely necessary, may still be insufficient. Those building new communities in turbulent times also need to better understand the dynamics of non-violent action in order to preserve their integrity, even in the face of those who seek to either undermine or destroy it. Other key figures have subsequently reinforced these messages, including Dr Muhammad Tahir-ul-Qadri's (2010) *fatwa* announcing that 'suicide bombings and attacks against civilian targets are not only condemned by Islam but render the perpetrators totally out of the fold of Islam, in other words to be unbelievers'.

Equally important in avoiding further polarization is the Western response. It is of historic significance that the then newly elected US President, Barack Obama, chose (in April 2009) Istanbul to make a pivotal speech addressing the Arab world with the bridging message: 'The United States is not and will never be at war with Islam.'

Cultures of peace

Under the auspices of the International Peace Research Association (IPRA), considerable analytical work has been done on what constitutes a true culture of peace. It is worth reflecting on these elements before moving to the specific question of comparative approaches to non-violence. One of the foremost minds conceptualizing the nature of cultures of peace is former IPRA Director, Professor Paul Smoker who, together with his wife Dr Linda Groff, articulated the necessary steps for creating such cultures (Smoker and Groff, 1995).

The approach of Smoker and Groff towards cultures of peace is unusual, comprehensive and apt since they are explicitly identifying dimensions that Gülen's teaching identifies as important: namely relationships with others, relationships with nature and relationships with God. Their view is holistic and assumes an inner-outer world relationship towards peace. They explore different levels of the evolution of the peace concept in the West. First of all, there is *peace as an absence of war* – in other words, peace as a precursor for making progress on the other dimensions of non-violent pace building.

Then there is peace as '*negative peace*' (in other words no war) and peace as '*positive peace*' (in other words, no structural violence). This summarizes the position of the Norwegian Peace Researcher, Professor Johan Galtung (1969). That is, even when there is an absence of overt conflict the system is still structurally violent if people starve when there is food available; if people do not receive medical treatment when the society has hospitals to treat them; if women and men of equal rank do not enjoy promotion because of gender or ethnic prejudices; and so on. 'Negative peace' is when there is still structural violence: positive peace is the absence of both overt and structural violence. Such notions may have particular bearing within an Islamic context if matters of faith preclude equal opportunities. There is also '*feminist peace*' (referring to the macro and micro levels of peace). To quote Smoker and Groff (1995):

During the 1970s and 80s, a fourth perspective was ushered in by feminist peace researchers, who extended both negative peace and positive peace to include violence and structural violence down to the individual level. The new definition of peace then included not only the abolition of macro level organized violence, such as war, but also doing away with micro level unorganized violence, such as rape in war or in the home. In addition, the concept of structural violence was similarly expanded to include personal, micro and macro-level structures that harm or discriminate against particular individuals or groups.

Such an approach is also related to what might be called 'Gaia-peace' (peace with the environment) and finally, also, 'holistic peace' (inner and outer peace). Smoker and Groff (1995) emphasize the importance of this last dimension, arguing that both outer peace-making (more emphasized in the West) has to be complemented by holistic inner peace (more practiced in the East). For them 'the achievement of either inner or outer peace helps create the conditions necessary for the creation of the other type of peace'. This is a crucial part of Gülen's teaching. Smoker and Groff suggest that multicultural visions of peace are required and formally made such an analysis to the UN over a decade ago (Smoker and Groff, 1995).

Sharp's tactics and politics of non-violence

Vision is one aspect; transformation is another. This author's concern is about how different approaches to non-violence can be operationalized at a rate that can make a difference and in a way that is self-reflexive so that new, more effective, ways of non-violent change can evolve. Gandhi's work on civil disobedience has been a magisterial influence on what has so far emerged in the West and probably the key exponent of tactics of non-violent action is the American Gene Sharp. In his first volume on non- violent action Sharp (1973) questions why there is such an inertia among populations who put up with cultures of violence and repression when they could enjoy a vastly different system if only they could collectively engage? He identifies habit behaviour; fear of sanctions; the inner constraining power of moral obligation; self-interest; psychological identification with the ruler; zones of indifference and an absence of self-confidence as key factors (Sharp, 1973).

Some of these lessons are pertinent to the Gülen movement as are the lessons Sharp elaborated about why a non-violent approach has not been recognized in the mainstream as a legitimate means of struggle for justice and a better world. Sharp concluded that there is, in fact, an invisible history and there are a number of reasons why such non-violent philosophies have failed to enter the national psyche. They include an absence of romanticized non-violent heroes given that historians have accepted the dominant culture's view that violence is the only legitimate form of combat. Sharp criticizes Western historians for their bias towards violence, viewing this as a conspiracy of the ruling class to keep the people ignorant of their own power. For him (Sharp, 1973: 73), non-violence requires a 'new way of viewing the world'. It is a paradigm whose time has not yet come. Non-violence has never been seen as a coherent conceptual system. Consequently, historical examples of nonviolent action are viewed as isolated events rather than as different aspects of the same technique of struggle.

For Sharp, 'Non-violence is unfairly compared to violence. Nonviolence is often used when violence has no chance of success. When nonviolence fails, the method is condemned. But when violence fails, the strategies or tactics are blamed – not violence itself as a method. Nonviolence successes are written off as flukes. Partial successes are seen as total failures' (Sharp, 1973: 16–20).

Brian Martin and the dynamics of backfire

In the third volume of Sharp's first book, he examines the dynamics of non-violent action as a means of understanding what works and why. Such analyses are crucial if non-violent processes are to become living heuristic realities rather than dry scholastic or monastic theories. Sharp teaches how the power imbalance between groups can be used to the advantage of the weak by a process of political jiu-jitsu and how these tactics can succeed even in the face of quite brutal repression. This was one of the first efforts to understand how non-violence can disperse power through communities, bringing increased self-esteem and personal development – phenomena that are also being reported in the emergent Gülen-inspired communities. Such healing and empowering processes lie in sharp distinction to the use of violence, which creates feelings of callousness and dehumanization which affect victims and victors alike.

The Australian researcher Professor Brian Martin has taken some of these analyses and techniques further in a theory which he calls 'backfire' (Martin, 2007). Typically, non-violent activists exposing injustices by the authorities against a weaker group, can precipitate righteous indignation or outrage. Martin examines the dynamics of these processes in order to empower those who would use non-violent action but then face official retribution. He concludes that perpetrators typically use five main methods to inhibit outrage and prevent backfires – namely, covering up the event; devaluing the target; reinterpreting what happened; using official channels to give the appearance of justice; and intimidating and bribing the people involved (Martin, 2007: 118–43).

Martin also examines the propaganda and 'black' or 'grey' media operations which typically accompany any official cover-up. These have the aim of creating public outrage against the target of the operation, and can be analysed using the same framework. To be effective, a 'black' operation uses deception to foster an interpretation that the victim was actually responsible. The ('black') attack is not covered up – it has to be open in order to backfire – but responsibility for it is hidden.

He provides invaluable information for countering such attacks, including exposing those really responsibility for the event; validating the target of the operation (the falsely alleged perpetrator); interpreting the official operation as unfair and underhanded; avoiding or discrediting official investigations, at least when they seem likely to dampen public outrage; and resisting intimidation and bribery. Such behaviour has spontaneously been evolved by many non-violent groups wishing to sustain behaviour consistent with their beliefs. In fact I would argue that the behaviour of Bediuzzaman Said Nursi is a case in point. Nursi used his spiritual insights to follow similar tactics albeit at a substantial personal cost to his health. (Markham and Ozdemir, 2005). These responses and counter responses can become quite complex. According to Martin and Gray (2007: 16):

> In a conflict between a powerful and a weak side – for example between a group of police and a single suspect, or between a government and a small group of opponents – the powerful side holds many advantages. If the weak side mounts an attack, this can provide the pretext for the powerful group to use its superior resources. The exception is when the powerful side is exposed in a gross abuse, for example when police seriously assault a suspect or troops gun down protesters and this abuse is exposed to a wide audience, leading to a change in public opinion.

Despite the fact that Fethullah Gülen has adopted an inspirational spiritual, rather than a politically instrumental, approach towards implementing non-violent pathways to peace, many of these negative techniques have been used against both him and his followers. This has been so much so that Gülen now lives in exile in the United States of America. In the sections that follow, the question is put about the extent to which the non-violent philosophies of Gülen resonate with the more 'Western' implementation and instrumentalist strategies outlined earlier and whether useful bridges can be built between these two worlds.

Gülen's non-violent spiritual paths and practices

Attempting any reasoned comparison of Gülen's non-violent philosophy with those of more Western practitioners is fraught with difficulties, not least because of the way that Gülen's life and work has been moulded by the very specific cultural roots of Anatolian Islam and the specific writings of Said Nursi, though it would be a mistake to think that Gülen's approach is merely a next generation of Nursi's approaches. A more accurate description of the relationship would be that of mentor (see Leaman, 2007). And yet there are some interesting overlaps. Nursi used the tactic of silent withdrawal and non-cooperation in many of his struggles towards resolving conflict without bloodshed. In many ways the maltreatment and imprisonment of Nursi is a classic case of backfire, since his repeated representation of the evidence to different tribunals and his unjust punishment actually served as a recruitment engine for his movement and brought about the exactly the opposite outcome of that desired by the authorities.

From an outsider's perspective, the Gülen movement can be considered to have an explicit ambition of eroding structural violence – for example, through providing education and shelter to youngsters. But any Western non-violence theorist, taking a purist approach, would find elements within the movement's organizations that do not square with classic non-hierarchic theories of peaceful cultures. Such criticisms could be seen as invalid by the Gülen community. Yet from a Western point of view, the centralization of power via the *buyuk abiler* (literally 'elder brothers') might be seen as evidence of hierarchy and an unequal distribution of power.

These 'elder brothers' are former students of Gülen who can talk informally about the movement and about their activities and how they are implementing its teachings on social responsibility. But insiders would say this is simply not true, and that it is merely an accusation without any evidence, since the movement is decentralized and only loosely connected, with *Abiler* acting only in an advisory capacity.

Many of these confusions will be influenced by cultural differences especially in regard to the traditional role of women in Turkish society and the central and unquestionable bedrock of the Qur'an which cannot be questioned in any way, without attracting counter-criticism. Western peace movements adopting non-violent strategies regard them all as a work in progress and not very much is so sacrosanct that it is beyond review. And yet this would be to miss or misinterpret another vital cultural ingredient – the remarkable generosity of Turkish people which in this author's experience is unfettered.

There are also difficulties in wedding all the prescriptions of the Sharia to a philosophy of complete non-violence. This is a contradiction which is not unique to Islam – Christian and Jewish views on punishment – turn the other cheek versus an eye for an eye – are cases in point, but again such a black and white interpretation can miss the core point, which is that justice should be proportional to the crime. Even the great Emperor Asoka, whose life's work became the promulgation of Buddhist scripture, refused to revoke the death penalty for reason of public order, despite this view being an outright contradiction of Buddhist teachings (Seneviratana, 1994).

In many senses, Gülen is following the holistic, spiritual and cultural approaches to peace identified earlier by Smoker and Groff. The movement inspired by him is now a global faith-based movement with schools in more than 100 countries, including Kazakhstan, Kenya, Bangladesh, Pakistan, Indonesia, Brazil and Bosnia.

Why should this matter? Gülen's teaching gives effect to the teaching of the Qur'an realizing it by performing daily acts of service based on peaceful social change. Such an approach in a time of terror can make a difference through inter-faith dialogue. To my mind, the Gülen-inspired Abant platform for dialogue is akin to the Pugwash movement when it first began its work to prevent nuclear war in the 1950s. Pugwash allowed a backchannel for diplomats and scientists to keep talking even during the difficult days of the Cold War and led to the processes which not only ended the Vietnam War but also the Cold War too.

Such inter-faith dialogue is more important now than ever. The simplistic negative Western stereotypes of Islam need to be constructively challenged by Muslims as well as academics, media and politicians in the West. Gülen's active compassion for peaceful change based on a precise reading of the Qur'an, can act as a powerful antidote to those who would smear Islam with the label of terrorism. Such work can only be achieved through creating a critical mass of thinkers and doers who will engage in peace in the wider world and that characterizes the movement today.

Conclusions

It is wise to be cautious given the turbulent political changes occurring both within Turkey and on its borders with Kurdistan, Iran, Bulgaria, Georgia, Greece, Armenia,; Azerbaijan, Iraq and Syria, and now, through a series of contagious spasm wars, the whole of the Middle East. It could be argued that the Gülen approach to peaceful change from a truly enlightened Islamic perspective is necessary, but not yet truly sufficient. It continues to be a work in progress.

During this time of rapid change and potential instability the very success of the Gülen movement could be misinterpreted by those with alternative agendas and alliances in the Middle East. In some senses the conference at which the paper was first given on which this chapter is based was an act of wisdom by the Gülen community in taking the initiative to broaden the worldwide base of those who are sympathetic to the credos of the movement and wish its work well. The challenge to us all is to find ways of future collaboration that do not undermine our strengths and differences but complement projects and processes with which we are broadly in tune.

As in previous times, wise authorities make provision for famine and flood when there are no signs that these are inevitable. So in this time, it is wise to think through future peaceful responses to challenges that may or may not come. For example, the extent to which the 'dialogue movement' can once again respond to state repression using non-violent means may become the test of the integrity of the movement. Many techniques evolved by non-violent activists elsewhere in the world could then come to be of use and significance for the Gülen movement. This is especially important given the current *zeitgeist* across the Middle East: the only way these new societies can grow free and survive the peace is through mutual tolerance, education and the eradication of overt and structural violence.

In all his writings, Gülen's answer to human conflict is love, mutual understanding, tolerance, dialogue and education. Again and again, Gülen draws these themes to the fore. For him they are fundamental and he says 'other things are accidental' (Gülen, 2004e). Of particular significance is Gülen's adherence to a philosophical position of non-violence when confronted with opposition, both tactical and moral. In his book, *Towards a Global Civilization of Love and Tolerance*, he cautions that we must be

> as if without hands against those who strike us and without speech against those who curse us. If they try to fracture us into pieces even fifty times, we still will remain unbroken and embrace everyone with love and compassion. And with love toward one another, we will walk toward tomorrow (Gülen, 2004e: 50).

Many commentators on Gülen's teachings also underline his emphasis on tolerance as a precursor for peaceful co-existence. Yilmaz (2007: 25) stresses Gülen's role in 'social-cultural activism' because of his exemplary role of establishing dialogue and building peace between Muslims and non-Muslims. For Yilmaz, here we have peace being built up at a micro-level. Gülen, like Rumi before him, both made inter-cultural dialogue 'their main tool of social innovation and conflict resolution for social inclusion, coherence and peaceful co-existence' (Yilmaz, 2007: 25). But Yilmaz (2007: 38–9) also recognizes that such an approach does not receive universal recognition with, for example, many Muslim opponents seeing Gülen's rapprochement with the Catholic Church as traitorous. Handling such wilful misinterpretations of Gülen's thought will be a future challenge for the movement both within and without Turkey.

Writers such as Richard Penaskovic (2010: 147) see Gülen as a bridge between Islam and the West, while others such as Klas Grinell (2010: 85) see him as transcending such divisions; for him, Gülen goes beyond boundaries and is a 'border transgressor'. For Karina Korostelina (2010: 123), Gülen takes this further by using dialogue as a source for peaceful co-existence between Muslims and Christians in a secular state. Here Gülen's approach is about heuristic process. Even though there are differences between East and West, dialogue can create the capacity to find 'relatedness' in people who are vastly different from us.

Others such as Robert Hunt have highlighted the need to more fully explore Gülen's contribution to the dialogue of religion and science, while recognizing key issues about relative legitimacy, 'Closely related to this must be an exploration of Gülen's teachings to post-modernity' (Hunt and Aslandoğan, 2006: 6). Hunt goes to the nub of the problem when he discusses the challenges of placing the movement in context, especially given the proven commitment of movement participants to engage with the multi-religious dimension of globalization through inter-faith dialogue. Hunt cogently argues the problem of competing meta-narratives and identifies the pitfall in the face of such meta-narrative claims, that all dialogue can cease because 'from within a meta-narrative there is no need to listen to the other' (Hunt and Aslandoğan, 2006: 9). The paradox for Hunt is that:

[A]t the same time, globalization is rapidly making dialogue between holders of meta-narrative claims a near existential necessity. Western scholars have been working diligently on this problem for some decades. A distinctly Islamic contribution would be of great value in understanding how Muslims can fruitfully relate to globalization (Hunt and Aslandoğan, 2006: 6).

The truth 'that is' and the truth 'that should be' are two very different worlds. Gülen's favoured approach has involved reform through education. If, as Victoria Levinskaya (2007: 333) tells us, the acquisition of modern knowledge is mandated by Islam itself, then holistic education has been Gülen's way.

Is there any evidence of success? The short answers is yes; the evidence is both magnificent in its level of individual achievement by both pupils and teachers in Gülen inspired schools, but also filled with promise for the potential it holds for transforming civil societies. But it has to be said that potential will remain only as a potential without a very clear set of policy initiatives to use such education and its positive effects. However, that education has a remarkable potential to unleash the social changes that will lead societies in transition away from division and the Janus-faced threats of terrorism and authoritarianism, to truly sustainable peaceful futures.

UNIVERSITY OF WINCHESTER LIBRARY

UNIVERSITY OF ILLINOIS

14

Combating terrorism in Britain: choice for policy makers

ASAF HUSSAIN AND IHSAN YILMAZ

Introduction

Terrorism is particularly targeting the Western world in which the USA, Britain and other parts of Europe have suffered terrorist attacks. When any country is attacked, in principle it has the right to defend itself. The question is: how should one engage in counter-attack? If one begins to think seriously about this then one needs to have additional information about whom one should attack and the nature of the attack? If one were fighting a conventional war on a battlefield, it would be a fight between one army against another. But if terrorist attacks have taken place within the country, it is beyond the pale of conventional attack for they are not in a battlefield. One not only has to identify the attackers but to think how they emerged in the first place and whether they will emerge again in the future or if it was more or a 'one-off' attack? In other words, terrorist attacks in various Western countries have become a very complex subject and often the response may not be effective.

In Britain the terrorist attacks on London Transport on 7 July 2005 (7/7) shocked the nation and have raised serious questions. The nation was shocked because the bombers were mainly British-born young men of Muslim background. After the 9/11 attacks on the USA (11 September 2001), the British government was aware that Britain would be targeted. But the assumption was that they would come from abroad and they could then possibly be detected and caught. This assumption was proved wrong for they were British-born Muslims (BBMs) or raised from early childhood in Britain by their migrant parents.

For the British government, the question was no longer if more attacks would follow – given that extremist and pro-violence ideology had appeared to permeate the British Muslim communities – but when, where and how. The BBMs factor had certainly complicated matters. The most important task in hand was to devise a workable and useful strategy of engagement and approach. Needless to say, a flawed strategy would only work to the terrorists' advantage, providing them with room and time to continue spreading their ideology.

The contention of this paper is that terrorism has to be combated by Islam as an instrument of counter-terrorism because terrorists are using it for legitimizing their actions. Pro-violence Muslims with their interpretations have equated Islam with terrorism, making it a religion which has no moral or ethical codes and allows one to kill innocent people including Muslims (bombing them inside and outside mosques and other places) and non-Muslims (killing them in trains, buses and other places). Since Islam has been reduced to the ideology of terrorism in the future every Muslim who believes in Islam is, or will be perceived as being, a potential terrorist. Islam therefore then has to be re-understood but the question then is: which Islam or whose interpretation of Islam? This chapter attempts to provide an answer to that question.

Britain has a large Muslim population and that is the reason that the authorities have seriously to consider this strategy. Pro-violence views circulating in Britain have to be discredited. If they are not, then the prevention of terrorism will be the only strategy for the British government. The answer that will be provided in this paper will reduce the potential dangers of terrorism – it will be an essential supplement and only then will prevention strategies result in success.

The British government engaged in dealing with Islam by: thinking of changing the nature of Islamic Studies in the universities (Siddiqui, 2007); initiating a Commission for Integration and Cohesion (Commission on Integration and Cohesion, 2007); and even by supporting some new Muslim organizations such as the British Muslim Forum. None of these policies have so far succeeded. Therefore it is essential first to survey the preventive strategies.

The preventive approach

The preventive approach is the most spontaneous one by any country in which a terrorist attack has taken place. The 'Prevent' programme was the main Labour government framework at the time of the conference where the original paper was given on which this chapter is based. The UK now has a new Conservative–Liberal government that was originally going to announce a new strategy in February 2011, but then the conference around that was cancelled. There seem to have been some internal differences in the Coalition about what the new approach should be. At an international security conference in February 2011, while the Conservative Prime Minister David Cameron linked his analysis of security approaches with what he called a failed 'state multiculturalism', the Conservative Party Chair, Baroness Warsi, has spoken of Islamophobia having now passed the 'coffee table test' in Britain. Clearly there have been some tensions to resolve in terms of a new government position.

Britain's preventive approach post-7/7 had many important aspects. First, it had to make all kinds of laws to prevent terrorism. Second, it had to increase detection measures. Third, it had to devise measures to contain attacks by terrorists with force. All this operated under the umbrella of Counter-Terrorism strategies. Since 2003, one of the key aims of British government's strategy (known as CONTEST) was to 'reduce the risk from international terrorism so that people can go about their business freely and with confidence' (Home Office, 2011a). The counter-terrorism strategy had four principal strands which were: Prevent, Pursue, Protect and Prepare. This was the major strategy of operations to safeguard the lives of the people. Another very important tactic was surveillance, for it was an indispensable way of gathering intelligence against terrorists. Surveillance tactics therefore meant that legislation was another strategy for preventing terrorism. The 'legislative framework' was for 'preventing and pursuing terrorist and those who support terrorist organizations' (Home Office, 2011a).

Responding to terrorist incidents was done at both national and regional levels. In terrorism decisions, the Home Secretary was involved since he was responsible for counter-terrorism across England, Wales and Scotland. On the regional level, the local authorities and the local governments were involved. The Regional Resilience Teams supported the Formation of Regional Resilience Forums which are made up of central government agencies, the armed forces, the emergency services and local authorities and provide a multi-agency strategic direction to civil protection planning at regional level (Home Office, 2011a).

In addition to these processes, a number of important bodies were established by the government and its agencies. The Prime Minister's office had its Cabinet Office Contingencies Secretariat (COBRA) which was the emergency co-ordinating committee comprising the Ministerial Committees on Defence and Overseas Policy, the Ministerial Committee on Intelligence Services, the Joint Intelligence Committee, Secret Intelligence Service (MI6), Government Communications Headquarters (GCHQ), Security Service (MI5), New Scotland Yard and many other elements (Gregory and Wilkinson, 2005).

It seemed that most of these counter-terrorism strategies were based on the past experience of the authorities with the Provisional Irish Republican Army (PIRA), which had haunted Britain for many years. But pro-violence Islamist ideology was a very different kind of terrorism for it had religious and not nationalist legitimation. Even the tactic of terrorism used was different from the PIRA, which had not produced suicide bombers. More recently, in the Good Friday Agreement, understandings were reached between the British and Irish governments and the main paramilitary and political groupings, but such an approach may not be straightforward with the Muslim pro-violence groups.

Dealing with this new kind of terrorism by force would be ineffective. For example, after 9/11, the USA declared its 'War on Terrorism' on Afghanistan. It succeeded in its regime change policy as Mullah Omar was removed. This approach of the US 'War on Terrorism', if evaluated from 9/11 until 2011, has still not demolished al-Qaeda. While President Bush and Prime Minister Blair have left office, and Osama Bin-Laden is now dead, al-Qaeda remains active. In fact, the so-called terrorism experts seem to be ignorant of the fact that the more sophisticated the preventive measures become, the more 'sophisticated' terrorists' tactics are becoming to cope with, and to bypass, these measures.

When the authorities finally became aware of the need to engage with the Muslim community in Britain the then Prime Minister of Britain, Tony Blair, identified 12 points to combat radicalism. An assessment of the 12-point strategy was that 'little has come out of it' (Gadher, 2007: 14). Blair also set up a Muslim Task Force. But a Labour Party peer, Lord Ahmed, commented that it had achieved 'virtually nothing' (Gadher, 2007: 14). While all of Blair's policies to combat terrorism failed, the subsequent British government under Prime Minister Gordon Brown seemed to be putting more emphasis on winning the battle of ideas ('hearts and minds') while also being tough on security. Gordon Brown believed that this was an ideological war akin to the Cold War. He directed ministers to come up with ideas by which minority groups could better be engaged and by which they might feel more a part of the UK. A senior government source said '[W]e can't win the battle of hearts and minds from Whitehall: it can be won only in local community but we can provide more support and strategic leadership' (in Gadher, 2007: 14).

The Brown government's thinking was in principle correct provided that its approach effectively engaged in the ideological war that has been going on. What will succeed is the ideological and not the electronic war. That will be the eradicative strategy for combating terrorism because it has to be a battle for the hearts and minds of Muslims in Britain.

The eradicative approach

The eradicative approach has to engage with the Muslim community. The Blair government was engaged with the Muslim community but its policies failed because it lacked insights into the Muslim community. According to Sayeda Warsi (now in the cabinet of the new Conservative–Liberal Coalition government but at the time she articulated this, Shadow Community Minister), 'the government failed' because 'it didn't engage wider and deeper to develop a true understanding of the Muslim community choosing instead to listen to self-appointed leaders' (Gadher, 2007: 14). Furthermore, according to Hassan Butt, a former member of a pro-violence group, 'most Muslim institutions in Britain just don't want to talk about theology. They refuse to broach the difficult and often complex truth that Islam can be interpreted as condoning violence against the unbeliever ... scholars must go back to the books and come forward with a refreshed set of rules and revised understanding of the rights and responsibilities of Muslims' (Gadher, 2007: 14). These observations are insightful and have to be taken seriously.

In their locations in various parts of the Muslim world, pro-violence Muslims started their struggle with the contextual factors of politics which they did not accept and developed sub-sectarian versions of Islam which emerged as pro-violence Islamism. Their struggle was to convert the nation-states into Islamist states and the use of violence became a tactic for eliminating their enemies. One may be confused as to what the sub-sectarian interpretations were. These sub-sectarian interpretations manipulated Islam to fulfil the ambitions of pro-violence leaders and their movements to obtain power. In order to achieve power, they were engaged in extremist tactics of terror.

Three names can be given as examples of those who distorted their sects through their sub-sectarian interpretations. These include Bin-Laden, a Wahhabi who distorted his sect's concepts; Ayman Zawahiri, who did the same from his sect of Salafism; and Mullah Omar who also did the same from his sect of Deobandism – all of them creating a base (al-Qaeda) for declaring war on the West and killing innocent people, including Muslims, anywhere in the world through terrorist tactics. All this falls under the category of pro-violence 'Islam', which emerged from extremist Muslims. The Muslim community in Britain comprises people belonging to both mainstream and extremist Muslims, and understanding this sectarian politics is important if the authorities want to combat terrorism in Britain. What needs to be made clear is that combating terrorism is not combating any sect but their sub-sectarian distortions which have produced illusionary and delusionary interpretations to attract recruits for terrorism.

Extremist pro-violence Muslims consider the West as the land of the *kuffar* (infidels) and the whole country to be *dar al-harb* (land of war). An important point to be understood here again is that not all the people belonging to the 'radical' and extremist groups are terrorist but only those who have turned towards pro-violence ideologies could then become potential terrorists and vulnerable to blindly accepting the sub-sectarian persuasions and recruitment approaches from al-Qaeda or other groups.

How these kind of conversions take place is beyond the purview of this chapter but suffice it to say that most of the terrorists produced in Britain have all come from pro-violence groups irrespective of to whatever sect they belonged. This is where the British government faces the problem of detecting terrorism, for it is an internal problem among the Muslim community. The intelligence agencies cannot be blamed for failure in detecting terrorists because such detection is difficult even for Muslims from within their own communities.

When the sub-sectarian versions of their sects from abroad enter into the minds of the BBMs and make them think of taking terrorist actions, then these versions will have to be discredited, which is not being done. This process of discreditation has to start to prevent such sub-sectarian ideas entering the minds of the BBMs. To be effective, the whole Muslim community will have to be made aware of how to combat terrorism by discovering sources from within the communities settled in various cities of Britain. This is a battle of ideas and such sub-sectarian groups are circulating in the world and are building their bridges to penetrate British society to fulfil their objective of global terrorism. It is the contention of this chapter that mainstream Muslims will help reduce the potential dangers of terrorism through winning the minds and hearts of ordinary Muslims.

An Islamic solution

The pro-violence Muslims cannot convince mainstream Muslims that terrorism is the right strategy for it is considered correctly to be beyond the pale of Islam itself. So the authorities have to think of how best to engage with Islam so it can project its authentic worldview. The worldview of Islam can best be projected through Muslim faith-based leaders, scholars and opinion-makers, such as Fethullah Gülen.

Gülen is from Turkey but his nationality does not matter, for his worldview of Islam is a mainstream Islamic interpretation to discredit and combat terrorism. The pro-violence Muslims have begun to regard Islam only as a political instrument and not as spiritual. Many studies about Islam label it as 'Political Islam' as if nothing else emerges from the faith. For Gülen this is a false assumption because Islam is not a political project to be implemented from the top. Islam is both a discourse and practice for the realization of a just and ethical society (Yilmaz, 2003: 225).

Gülen reiterates that Islam as a religion should not be reduced to being a party political identity. He is very critical of the 'instrumentalization' of religion in politics and engaging in politics on behalf of religion. Gülen's views have little to do with seeking political power. His discourse includes a critical rejection of the world while simultaneously calling for involvement in the world through rationally structured activities for the pleasure of God. These activities include the building of schools instead of mosques; investing in secular education instead of religious instruction; encouraging economic enterprises and requiring them to invest in education;

encouraging educational and economic enterprises to support each other; promoting individual and collective self-criticism; and supporting critically minded planning for future projects (see in detail Özdalga, 2000: 84–104).

For Gülen Islam, is 'the "middle way" of absolute balance – balance between materialism and spiritualism, between rationalism and mysticism, between worldliness and excessive asceticism, between the world and the next – and inclusive ways of all the previous prophets makes a choice according to the situation' (Kuru, 2003: 117). Gülen's understanding of Islam is not based on a fixed abstract model that excludes reinterpretation but it is open to both interpretations and 'experiences – to the cultural accumulation of this world. Gülen believes that there is a need for *ijtihad* (independent reasoning) in our age. He says that he respects the scholars of the past but also believes that *ijtihad* is a necessity because to freeze *ijtihad* means to imprison Islam in a given time and space' (Yilmaz, 2003: 221). Muslims have lost their civilization because there is not *ijtihad* but reliance on *taqlid* (imitation).

For Gülen, 'Ummah is more of a transnational socio-cultural entity, not a politico-legal one. He hopes that this socio-cultural entity will be instrumental in bringing general universal peace. He formulates a project of cooperation between Islam and the West to reach this desired, almost utopian, universal peace' (Yilmaz, 2003: 234–5).

Gülen believes that Islam is a religion of peace and wherever there were conflicts in countries like Albania, Kosovo, Macedonia, the Philippines, Banda Aceh, Northern Iraq, the Gülen movement schools addressed the problems of ethnic and religious conflicts (Saritoprak, 2005: 8). Gülen strongly emphasizes that acts of violence against innocent civilians including women and children are inhumane and he categorically, and without any reservation, condemns killing of innocent civilians, elderly, women and children. Gülen's thinking then poses this challenge to the Muslims to develop their selves within their faith and to become a powerful innovator of Islamic civilization. It is not surprising then why some Western scholars regard Gülen as 'one of the major figures in defining the contemporary global Islamic experience... his work helps to redefine the nature of Islamic discourse in the contemporary world' (Voll, 2003: 238).

It is this kind of vision from the Islamic worldview that has to be internalized by Muslims living in the West. Muslims who hate the Western countries in which they live are vulnerable to extremist and pro-violence interpretations. It is therefore important to change such Muslims' extremist and pro-violence world vision to the Gülenic world vision.

One of the most important ways of being the ambassador of Islam in the public arena is the self-development of Muslims with honour and dignity and, above all, credibility. This kind of development of their Islamic self-identities has to emerge from their spirituality. Gülen's understanding of what kind of Islamic identities Muslims should develop is very important for every Muslim. It means that: 'True Muslims are people of safety and trust, so much so that other Muslims can turn their backs on them without doubt or suspicion' (Saritoprak, 2005: 8–9).

Muslims have to develop these kinds of identities since extremist and pro-violence groups have demonized Islam with their terrorist actions. Living in Britain with this worldview of Islam, not only the image of Islam will redefine itself in the minds of non-Muslims, but Muslims themselves will be considered as assets – as 'golden' people who once belonged to the 'Golden age' of the Prophet. If Gülen's understanding of what it means to be a Muslim is promoted, then 'Islam' may be saved from the clutches of terrorist ideologies and rhetoric and constructive citizenship among Muslim communities in Britain will be facilitated.

Conclusion

This chapter has provided a brief exposition of the Islamic thinking of Fethullah Gülen. Clearly his views and school of thought need to be read and made accessible in Britain. Muslims will not react to or reject Gülen's teachings and views since they are not from outside the fold of Islam but from within.

From what has been discussed in this chapter some facts which specialists on terrorism or policy makers may not be aware of should be clearly understood. First, preventive measures of terrorism will never be effective when eradicative measures are not given sufficient attention. Eradicative measures reinforce preventive measures and will make them effective in achieving their ends. Second, engagement with preventative measures is complex and if corrective approaches are not taken, then it will fail. The pro-violence sub-sectarian interpretations of Islam cause terrorism. They have to be detected and measures have to be taken to reduce their potential danger.

Third, if one embarks on the path to terrorism which is emerging from various sects then engagement with Islam becomes necessary. But any engagement with Islam has to make clear which perspective of Islam one is supporting.

Finally, to discover Gülen's views is one thing but to reduce the danger of terrorism these views have to be implemented. In order to do this, some steps have to be taken which are suggested in the specific recommendations. For translating Gülen's views into action in Britain has to be done in a sophisticated manner, in relation to which the authors make the following four recommendations.

First of all, there is a need for the British government to come out openly in its support for Islam as one of the great faiths of the world. Misinformation and disinformation has spread, equating Islam with terrorism and this has to be rebutted by all politicians including the Prime Minister and other policy makers. Since the war on terrorism is being fought every day, and since it focuses on the Muslim terrorists, it is not surprising that the Global War on Terrorism (GWOT) has been interpreted by terrorist organizations as being war on Islam.

The British government has realized this and advised that the term GWOT should not be used. This was a good step but what is being recommended here is that all governments and authorities involved should make it clearer that they do not consider Islam to be responsible in any shape or form for the terrorism of some extremist groups. Since GWOT is ongoing, so should the frequency of this message be until ordinary Muslims are convinced that this is not a war against Muslims and that they are as much the victims of this plague as everyone else. It is this kind of projection that has not sufficiently come out from government. And this is necessary is because government cannot combat terrorism with preventive measures unless it joins hands with the Muslim community. But the Muslim community will not join hands with the British government if it suspects it of being anti-Islamic.

Thus the second point is that the credibility of the government has been at stake, for its GWOT has been considered as being a war on Islam. The past history of Britain from the Crusades to Colonialism has not been positive in relation to Islam. Its award of knighthood to Salman Rushdie reinforced the view of it being anti-Islamic. Although the award was given for his contribution to South Asian literature, it would appear that those who recommended it did not think what its political repercussions would be in the Muslim world. Their ignorance produced consequences that not only affected the national security of Britain (because a threat was made against Britain and the Queen by al-Qaeda) but Ayatollah Khomeini's *fatwa* again became activated, monetary awards were raised for beheading Rushdie and some even gave an award of SaifAllah (Sword of Allah) to Bin Laden! If such a knighthood was worth awarding when balanced with the security of the British public then such policies have to be rethought because they affect the credibility of the British government.

Third, terrorism cannot be combated only in Britain so it has to engage the Muslim world as well. The British government should know about its poor image in the Muslim world, along with that of the USA. This has to be improved and this can only be done officially through media policies of public diplomacy to raise the British image in the Muslim world in order to win the hearts and minds of Muslims. In order to do this it has openly to be one of the defenders of Islam as a great world religion.

Fourth and finally, there is no doubt that there is a struggle going one within the Muslim world, between the 'radical' and pro-violence and mainstream Muslims. Whatever labels are being used, the real struggle is between authentic and inauthentic Islam. The Western world clearly has to decide whom it supports, and it has to support mainstream Muslims through strong economic and political support both in the Muslim world and in Britain.

Although many more detailed recommendations can be made, for the purposes of this chapter, these four set the general tone and direction the British authorities need to follow to tackle extremist elements in society. This will help bring the Muslim community on board and pave the way towards a collective struggle against terrorist ideology.

Additional note

Just as this book was being prepared to go to press the UK Government Home Office announced the outcome of the review of Prevent. Because of the timing of this, it is only possible to insert a note about it here rather than specifically and directly to discuss it. However, the chapter does discuss issues of relevance to the main outlines of the revised strategy. According to the Home Office (2011b):

> The Prevent strategy has been re-focused following a review. The strategy now contains three objectives: to respond to the ideological challenge of terrorism and the threat from those who promote it; to prevent people from being drawn into terrorism and ensure that they are given appropriate advice and support; and to work with sectors and institutions where there are risks of radicalization that we need to address.

CONCLUSION FETHULLAH GÜLEN AND THE HIZMET: TOWARDS AN EVALUATION

PAUL WELLER AND IHSAN YILMAZ

Description and evaluation

In contrast to those who have perpetrated terror in Europe in the name of Islam, Fethullah Gülen and the Hizmet movement inspired by his teaching are phenomena that are only now coming more prominently to the attention of the wider public and institutions of European societies. This is therefore both an appropriate temporal juncture and place within this book to attempt to offer what can at this stage only be – by virtue of both the stage of development of the movement in Europe, and the space constraints of this concluding chapter – some notes *towards* a preliminary evaluation.

At the same time, however hesitantly this might be approached, it is important to make some attempt to do this. This is because the critical nature of the issues facing both Muslims themselves in Europe as well as the wider European societies of which European Muslims are a part means that simply to seek to observe and to describe the phenomena concerned, but without risking some evaluation, could be tantamount to an abrogation of responsibility.

Of course, careful description – rooted in study of the teaching of Fethullah Gülen relative to the broader Islamic and Muslim tradition, both historically and in the contemporary world, and in field research into the organizational initiative and forms taken by the movement in various European contexts – is of foundational importance to any possibility of making such an evaluation. And it has been towards such a textured description that the authors of this volume have contributed, while also themselves offering some evaluation based on the specificity of their particular chapters. But it is the task of the editors to try to stand back a little from the individual contributions – including the chapters to which they the editors have themselves contributed – in order to try to offer at least a preliminary evaluative overview.

Fethullah Gülen and the Hizmet in Turkey

In contrast to the situation in the wider Europe, both Fethullah Gülen and the Hizmet movement are very much more widely known in Turkey. There, they are part of the warp and woof of contemporary Turkish society.

Fethullah Gülen himself plays an important role in the devotional and personal approach to spirituality of very large numbers of individuals as evidenced by the honorific title of *hocaefendi* (or 'respected teacher') accorded to him by those who follow his teachings. But as is made clear in a number of this book's chapters, the Hizmet is also visible through the educational institutions and relief agency run by the movement, as well as via an interest-free Islamic bank, television stations, newspapers, hospitals, business and civil society organizations and other groups that are related to it.

In their engagement with these initiatives, many individuals and groups of a variety of religious, secular and political perspectives work on common goals either within, or in collaboration with, the various bodies that are related to the movement – as illustrated, for example, by the case of the Journalists and Writers Foundation, referred to by a number of the authors and chapters in this volume. At the same time, as has also been noted in various places throughout this volume, in a society that has been impacted by the radical secularist revolution of Mustafa Kemal Ataturk and even more so by the inheritance of those who understand themselves as Kemalists, there are sectors of Turkish society which view not only Fethullah Gülen and the Hizmet movement but almost all practising Muslim groups with suspicion as potentially posing an Islamic threat to the secular constitutional order of the Turkish state. As evidently could be seen in the headscarf ban at universities, with an aggressive secularist understanding, the Kemalist establishment has always perceived public manifestations of Islam as inimical and a threat to the secular regime, arguing that religion should be imprisoned in the individual conscience alone.

Thus during the period of Turkish military rule which began in 1971 Gülen spent some months in prison after being arrested for organizing summer camps for the dissemination of Islamic ideas which, at that time, was something that was viewed by the Turkish military as clandestine religious activity. In the early 1980s, following another military coup, another case was prepared against Gülen by the police, but in the end he was not arrested since the direct military rule had ended by 1983.

By the time Turgut Özal was prime minister (1983–9) and then president (1989–93), Gülen was able to live and work in relative freedom. Following another military intervention known as the 28 February postmodern coup process, and that directly targeted socially active Islamic groups, Gülen left Turkey for the United States on 22 March 1999 for health reasons. While he was in the USA, on 18 June 1999 controversy erupted around him when a private nationwide television (ATV) broadcast videotapes in which he appeared to be preaching for the need to overthrow the secular Turkish Republic in order to replace it with an Islamic state.

In relation to such charges, he flatly rejected all accusations and strongly stated that these videotapes were doctored in a sophisticated way, being created from a montage of images and recordings in order to denigrate and attack him. Prosecution charges were brought against him in 2000 while he was still in the USA where he continues to lives in Pennsylvania. Meanwhile, in Turkey, in 2003 his trial was 'postponed', subject to the possibility of it being reactivated if he were to be indicted with a similar crime in the following five years even though his lawyers objected to 'postponement' and asked for a clear verdict.

In 2006 Gülen was acquitted (see Harrington, 2011) of all charges at the Supreme Court of Appeals, known as one of the castles of the Kemalist establishment. Today, it is widely accepted that the 'images and recordings' were sent to the ATV television channel by the Military Chief of Staff. Indeed, this was on 2 June 2011 most recently and publicly repeated by renowned journalist and Kanal D news anchorman Mehmet Ali Birand on the secularist Dogan Media Group's news station CNN Turk.

The focus of the current volume is not on Turkey. Therefore the issues involved for Gülen himself and for the movement there cannot be fully explored in this conclusion. At the same time, in moving towards a preliminary evaluation in relation to Europe, it is important to be both aware and acknowledging of the dynamic around these matters that exists within the movement and also its detractors as between Turkey itself, the Turkish diaspora (in all its diversity) and the wider Europe, not forgetting also the connections forged and maintained through the influence of the media.

Evaluating Gülen's teaching

In relation both to the Turkish context and to the wider Europe that is the focus of this book, there are a number of ways in which one can go about beginning to evaluate the phenomena with which this book is concerned. It would be possible to attempt a theological evaluation. And this would, in many ways, reflect the dynamics that themselves inform the movement. However, a theological evaluation would not connect with all readers. Therefore, in this concluding chapter something more inclusive, limited and modest must be attempted.

In the first instance, there is the teaching of Gülen himself. While a full evaluation of Gülen's life and work is likely to need to await a longer historical perspective, what is possible is to engage with is the content of Gülen's publicly accessible thinking and teaching. Of course, focusing upon this does not replace the important and challenging issue that faces *all* religious leaders and groups in terms of the consistency or otherwise between their teaching and its actualization by their followers in historical practice. And so, after looking at Gülen's teaching, this conclusion will also go on to look at the movement itself.

In Gülen's view, Muslims can reside comfortably in secular environments as long as their religious freedoms are protected. He argues that within the boundaries of Anglo-Saxon understanding of a kind 'passive secularism' that is not hostile to public expressions of religion, Islam and the secular state could be compatible. He also explains that Islam does not have a problem with secular and human-made law:

> In Islam, the legislative and executive institutions have always been allowed to make laws. These are based on the needs and betterment of society and within the frame of general norms of law. On domestic issues in the Islamic community and its relationship with other nations, including economic, political and cultural relations, Muslims have always developed laws. The community members are required to obey the laws that one can identify as 'higher principles' as well as laws made by humans. Islam has no objection to undertaking *ijtihad* (independent reasoning), *istinbat* (deductive reasoning), and *istikhraj* (derivation) in the interpretation of Shari'ah principles (Gülen, 2005a: 450).

Gülen underlines that 'Islam does not propose a certain unchangeable form of government or attempt to shape it. Instead, Islam establishes fundamental principles that orient a government's general character, leaving it to the people to choose the type and form of government according to time and circumstances' (Gülen, 2006a: 14). According to him, the fundamental principles that Islam prescribes are those of a social contact and the election of a group of people to debate common issues (Gülen, 2006a: 17). However, he also argues that Islam considers that people are responsible for their own fate and thus governance:

> Islam considers a society to be composed of conscious individuals equipped with free will and having responsibility toward both themselves and others. Islam goes a step further by adding a cosmic dimension. It sees humanity as the 'motor' of history, contrary to fatalistic approaches of some of the nineteenth-century Western philosophies of history such as dialectical materialism and historicism. Just as every individual's will and behavior determine the outcome of his or her life in this world and in the hereafter, a society's progress or decline is determined by the

will, worldview, and lifestyle of its inhabitants. The Koran (13:11) says: 'God will not change the state of a people unless they change themselves [with respect to their beliefs, worldview, and lifestyle].' In other words, each society holds the reins of its fate in its own hands. The prophetic tradition emphasizes this idea: 'You will be ruled according to how you are'. This is the basic character and spirit of democracy, which does not conflict with any Islamic principle (Gülen, 2006a: 16).

In summary, Gülen (2006a: 19) argues that, 'As Islam holds individuals and societies responsible for their own fate, people must be responsible for governing themselves.' To a certain extent, the era of the Rightly Guided Caliphs of Islam illustrates the application of this norm of democracy. For Gülen, cosmologically speaking there is no doubt that God is the sovereign of everything in the universe. The thoughts and plans of human beings are always under the control of the power of the Omnipotent. However, this does not mean that humans have no will, inclination or choice. Humans are free to make choices in their personal lives. They are also free to make choices with regard to their social and political actions (Gülen, 2005a: 453). Gülen's understanding of majority rule does not involve a tyranny of the majority because, as he says:

> members of minority communities should be allowed to live according to their beliefs. If these sorts of legislations are made within the norms of international law and international agreements, Islam will have no objection to any of these. No one can ignore the universal values that the Qur'an and the Sunnah have presented with regard to the rights mentioned above (Gülen, 2005a: 451).

Whenever speaking on the issue of democracy, Gülen underlines that Islam is a religion and thus is more than a political method, system or ideology:

> On the issue of Islam and democracy, one should remember that the former is a divine and heavenly religion, while the latter is a form of government developed by humans. The main purposes of religion are faith (*iman*), servanthood to God (*'ubudiyyah*), knowledge of God (*ma'rifah*), and beautiful actions (*ihsan*). The Qur'an, in its hundreds of verses, invites people to the faith and worship of the True (*al-Haqq*). It also asks people to deepen their servanthood to God in a way that they may gain the consciousness of *ihsan*. 'To believe and do good deeds' is among the subjects that Qur'an emphatically stresses. It also frequently reminds people that they must develop a conscious relationship with God and act as if they see God, or as if they are seen by God (Gülen, 2005a: 451– 2).

Gülen also has sometimes been defined and criticized as a Turkish nationalist (Yavuz, 2003a: 24). But when analyzed in detail it will be seen that, for various reasons, this could not be an accurate description. First of all, as an observant Muslim he can be a patriot and love his people but this cannot be to the exclusion of others. On this issue, Gülen's thought is under the influence of the Islamic message that ennobles the status of human beings, irrespective of race, colour and gender and Gülen's primary and vital source in this regard is the word of God as revealed in *al-Qur'an* (Hussari, 2009: 71):

> O mankind, We have created you male and female, and appointed you races and tribes, that you may know one another; surely the noblest among you in the sight of God is the most God-fearing of you; God is All-knowing, All-aware (*Al-Hojorat*, XLIX: 13).

Second, Gülen has sympathizers all over the world, including many Kurds in Turkey. A nationalist stance would deter all these people. Third, one of his intellectual predecessors, Said Nursi, was a Kurd and Gülen has Kurdish friends in his close circle. In addition, an overwhelming majority of Gülen's close friends are from Western Anatolia, a region of Turkey that, unlike several inner Anatolian cities, has not been known for strongly conservative Turkish nationalist sentiments. Last but not the least, whenever Gülen talks positively about Turks, he makes clear that the main reason for his respect is his evaluation of the heroic service of Turks in the cause of Islam. But any nation that fares better will be appreciated by Gülen as he appreciates and admires past successful eras of several non-Turkish Muslim individuals and nations such as Abbasids and so on (Yilmaz, 2011: 260–1).

In his life and work, Fethullah Gülen has steered a course away from the tendency to ideologize and instrumentalize religion in politics. In his understanding, Islam is not reduced to an ideology. This is in contrast to 'Islamists' who have conceived of Islam as an identity, ideology and politics in a reductionist way and focused on religion instead of on religiosity. Gülen also flatly rejects the totalizing ideology of Islamism:

> This vision of Islam as a totalising ideology is totally against the spirit of Islam, which promotes the rule of law and openly rejects oppression against any segment of society. This spirit also promotes actions for the betterment of society in accordance with the view of the majority. Those who follow a more moderate pattern also believe that it would be much better to introduce Islam as a complement to democracy instead of presenting it as an ideology. Such an introduction of Islam may play an important role in the Muslim world through enriching local forms of democracy and extending it in such a way that helps humans develop and understanding of the relationship between the spiritual and material worlds. I believe that Islam also would enrich democracy in answering the deep needs of humans,

such as spiritual satisfaction, which cannot be fulfilled except through the remembrance of the Eternal One (Gülen, 2005a: 452).

Recently, Gülen has been arguing that in this age Islam does not need state support, which is a new *ijtihad*. He does not oppose the idea of the mutual autonomy of the state and Islam. Rather, he argues that if a state 'gives the opportunity to its citizens to practice their religion and supports them in their thinking, learning, and practice, this system is not considered to be against the teaching of the Qur'an. In the presence of such a state there is no need to seek an alternative state' (Gülen, 2005a: 451). He also told the well-known Turkish Islamist intellectual and *Zaman* daily columnist Ali Bulac (2005) that establishing and Islamic state is not a religious duty for Muslim individuals and that in this age civil society can independently maintain Islam even where Muslims are not in the majority.

Gülen's 'ultimate concern' (Tillich, 1951: 211) differs from many 'Islamists' – at least in the sense of what they do in temporal practice. While 'Islamists' focus on political acts, a socially active Gülen reiterates that the hereafter is much more important and worship is vitally important. He does not see the Qur'an as a political book or project:

> The Qur'an is a translation of the book of the universe, which comes from the divine commands of creation, an interpretation of the world of the unseen, of the visible and invisible. It is an explanation of the reflections of the divine names on earth and in the heavens. It is a prescription for the various problems of the Islamic world. It is a guide for bliss in this life and in the life to come. It is a great guide for the travellers in this world moving towards the hereafter. It is an inexhaustible source of wisdom. Such a book should not be reduced to the level of political discourse, nor should it be considered a book about political theories or forms of state. To consider the Qur'an as an instrument of political discourse is a great disrespect for the Holy Book and is an obstacle that prevents people from benefiting from this deep source of divine grace (Gülen, 2005a: 456).

Unlike Islamists, Gülen does not pursue an identity politics and does not define himself by the social, cultural or political Other. In other words, he does not have a constitutive other. To put it differently, as Gurbuz argues (2007: 104), 'unlike the confrontational New Social Movements, the Gülen movement has engaged in "moral opposition", in which the movement's actors seek to empathize with the adversary by creating (what Bakhtin calls) "dialogic relationships".' In Gülen's understanding, *umma* is not a utopian politico-legal entity, but a transnational socio-cultural one (Yilmaz, 2003: 235). Gülen makes it clear that:

> there is no such world as the Islamic world. There are places where Muslims live. They are many in some places and few in others. That is

Islamic culture ... No such world exists. There is individual Islam. There are some Muslims in different places around the world. Piece by piece, broken. I personally do not see the prosperous existence of Muslims. If Muslims, who will be in contact with the others and constitute a union, solve common problems, interpret the universe, read it really well, consider the universe carefully with the Koran, read the future very well, generate projects for the future, determine its place for the future, do not exist, I do not call it Islamic World. Since there is no such Islamic World, everyone does something according to him/her self. It could even be said that there are Muslims with their own truth on behalf of Islam ... (Gülen, 2004a).

As Kösebalaban (2003: 175) explains it, Gülen 'subscribes to a remarkably different interpretation of the Muslim world and realistically draws the boundaries where Turkey can play a leadership role'. Thus Gülen did not regard with much optimism the D-8 group of developing countries with large Muslim populations (Bangladesh, Egypt, Indonesia, Iran, Malaysia, Nigeria, Pakistan and Turkey) that have formed an alliance. In addition, unlike many Islamists, Gülen is not an essentialist:

Throughout time, civilizations have passed through a vaccination, that the elderly call '*telakkuh*' ... This vaccination occurred in the Ottoman period, too. So, today we have a great cultural accumulation varying from cultures of Byzantine, Helen, Hun, and Hittite civilizations, to the faith, moral and the living styles of Seljuks, Ottomans ... From this point of view, although the architects of thought, the intellectual workers, who want to build a new world in the future, may make use of our proper dynamics as their own sources, they will come across many residuals both from the ancient civilizations and of the actual events. In fact, Islam is not against such an interaction. Since, due to the fact that Islam is a universal religion that embraces everybody, wherever it reaches, it either leaves the principles that are not totally in contradiction with Islam as they have been, or it absorbs them (in Camcı and Ünal, 1999: 143, quoted in Altunoğlu, 1999: 77).

Evaluating the Hizmet

As a result of Gülen's teaching, as Turam (2011: 145) puts it, the movement 'does not confront the secular state. To the contrary, it has engaged and cooperated more efficiently with the secular state than many other secular(ist) groups'. Or as Kurtz (2005: 375) argues, the movement that Gülen has inspired is 'notable in that it was highly religious in a secularized context as well as apolitical in a highly politicized environment'. At the same time, according Mandaville (2011: 17) Gülen seeks 'to reconfigure the relationship between religion and public life in the modern Turkish republic – and it is this dimension of Gülen's work that has raised suspicions among some of the country's secular elites'.

Despite the clarity of Gülen's teaching on these matters, the suspicions and concerns that have been found in Turkey have, on occasion, also appeared in wider European settings. For example, in the Netherlands in 2009 the Dutch government commissioned an inquiry into the movement. The process was informed by information from the Dutch Intelligence Service. Its results showed that the movement did not obstruct integration in the Netherlands. Indeed, in responding to questions by commission members, the Integration Minister at the time, Eberhard van der Laan, highlighted that although opponents and sceptics argue that members of the movement hide their real intentions, in Holland, their work facilitates integration. Nevertheless, by 17 December 2010, the Dutch Parliament was still debating the movement on the basis of a motion put forward by Saadet Karabulut of the Socialist Party. During the debate, citing the general excellence of the schools supported by the movement, the Dutch Interior Minister, Piet Hein Donner said that the Gülen movement stands as a very successful group among Turks living in the Netherlands with regard to integration and that it did not pose any threat to the Dutch state. (*Today's Zamon*, 18. 12. 2010)

One aspect of the movement highlighted by Piet Hein Donner was that, in relation to the Hizmet, one might better talk of an alliance of loosely affiliated independent organizations rather than a movement, let alone an organization. Since it has no bureaucratic central authority structure that imposes doctrines or activities, the local institutions of the movement are formally independent and each developing project remains within the Islamic discourse of Gülen but responsive to local conditions (Yükleyen and Yurdakul, 2011: 75). As Mandaville (2011: 17) puts it:

> The various facets of the movement rely on personal ties and coordination among a vast network of members and activists who have passed through institutions affiliated with the group and then moved on in life, all the while retaining a sense of communion within Gülen's worldview and ethics. Gülen himself certainly assigns tasks and missions to his most senior and trusted followers, but does not possess centralised control over the activities of the movement in aggregate.

The organic and dynamic nature of the Hizmet means that there are different emphases to be found in different organizations and countries and one of these is the question of how far the Hizmet should either emphasize or de-emphasize its Turkish and Islamic roots. The chapters in this volume by Demir (Chapter 8) and Tetik (Chapter 9) clearly illustrate the issue with regard to 'Turkishness', while in relation to Islam, as Kurtz

(2005: 373) explains it, there is a paradoxical fusion by 'Gülen of intense faith commitment with tolerance' and which 'results in a paradigm of Islamic dialogue. As a movement founded to foster spiritual commitment to a faith tradition, it now reaches out to non-Muslim believers and even non-believers.' Thus, while the most participants of the movement are pious Muslims in their private lives and voluntarily strict about worship issues, in the public sphere of *dar al-hizmet* they are open to everyone regardless of their faith, creed, nationality, race and so on. Their motto is to accept everyone as they are. Kurtz (2005: 377) explains this paradox:

> Islam is seen as having various spheres – the institutional, the political, the personal, the spiritual, etc. The spiritual is viewed as the most important and equated with the widespread mystical tradition of Sufism. Because of these spheres, the Muslim path leads to a kind of openness to others that the institutional aspect of the faith cannot embrace. Whereas it is an institution's task to set up boundaries and emphasize difference, it is a spiritual tradition's task to open up the heart to a force that obliterates difference. From the height of spiritual experience the boundaries disappear in the same manner that national boundaries on earth become invisible when the planet is viewed from the moon.

In the words of Walton (2009: 41), the Gülen Community represents a kind of 'liberal piety in the context of the civil sphere: the inculcation of pious probity as cultural capital and the means to a global network of businesses, schools, and non-governmental organizations'. As a result, as Wanda Krause explains in the fourth chapter of this volume, the movement becomes a powerful civil society force because it forms a loose entity that, over several countries, transcends cultures, ethnicities and sometimes even religion itself. The movement, therefore, has the capacity to be more effective in its ambitions for greater world peace and individual and societal development.

For Europe and the European Union

Overall, Gülen himself sees the European and Islamic as complementary rather than contradictory and he encourages Turkish foreign-policy decision makers to remain fully on track with European Union membership (Kösebalaban, 2003: 182). In a 2006 piece entitled 'With Accession, Europe Would Know us Better', Gülen says, 'I have been in favour of EU membership for a long time' and that, 'In my opinion, the EU is something that the Turkish people long for' (2006: 40).

In his capacity as Honorary President of the Journalists and Writers Foundation, Gülen (2004a) sent a message to the Abant Platform meeting held on 3–4 December 2004 at the European Parliament in Brussels. In his message, Gülen made three key points about the developing relationships between Turkey and the EU. These included the idea that Turkish entry into the EU would be a fulfilment of the so-called 'contemporary civilisation' objective of Ataturk; that the historic role of the Turkish armed forces in this should not be forgotten, even though this is sometimes seen as one of the biggest obstacles for Turkey's full membership; and that Turkish membership of the EU would 'reinforce its role as the island of peace in the heart of the Eurasia' since 'a Turkey in the EU will more successfully realize its function to establish a bridge between the Islamic world and the West'.

Gülen's now clear position in favour of EU membership is especially significant given the more traditionalist historical background from which he came. This is because, following the Kemalist revolution, Turkish society was broadly split between those who understood themselves as Westernizers, and traditionalists who opposed this and for whom the decline of Turkey's role in the world was seen as linked with a failure of religiosity and the importation of alien cultural and religious values. Thus it had previously been the Kemalists who had understood themselves to be both modern and Western.

At the same time, significant numbers of religious Turks are concerned that Europe is 'a Christian club'. However, while coming from a religious background, instead of identifying external 'enemy images', Gülen increasingly began to argue that the problems of Turkish society were rooted in an internal societal ignorance that he compared to a blood cancer, the cure for which he identified as education. As Gülen (in Gundem, 2005) put it: 'Some Muslims have recently published and distributed books on such grounds: "if they (Europeans) come, they will influence us and steal our youth from us, with the way they look, their mentality, their conception of religion, their notion of God."'

But in a piece on 'Tolerance in the Life of the Individual and Society', Gülen (2004: 43) points out with regard to the already very large Turkish Muslim presence in the current member states of the EU that, 'our citizens in European countries can only live in harmony in those countries by means of a vast atmosphere of tolerance'. Therefore, to the argument that Europe is 'a Christian club' which because of this is alien to Turks and to Islam, Gülen speaks of 'some who have their doubts about their own religiosity' whereas, for himself, he says, 'I could be on familiar terms with Europe. Through membership I could perhaps better explain my culture and myself to them. Perhaps they would be touched and would know us better.'

Against terror

Finally, given the contextual starting point of this volume in the impact of the actions of those who have used terror in Europe in the name of Islam and as analysed in detail in this by book by Cinar and Asladoğan (Chapter 12); Wright (Chapter 13); and Hussain and Yilmaz (Chapter 14), as Hussari (2009: 69) very simply states the case, "Among the various responses issued by global Islamic movements that repudiated and denounced terrorism, Gülen's response has been the most articulate.'

BIBLIOGRAPHY

Abbas, T. ed. (2007), *Islamic Political Radicalism: A European Perspective*.
  Edinburgh: Edinburgh University Press.
Abu-Nimer, M. (2003), *Non-Violence and Peace Building in Islam: Theory and
  Practice*. Gainsville: University Press of Florida.
Afsaruddin, A. (2001), 'The philosophy of religious education: classical
  views and Fethullah Gulen's perspectives'. Online at: http://en.fgulen.com/
  conference-papers/the-fethullah-gulen-movement-i/2131-the-philosophy-of-
  islamic-education-classical-views-and-m-fethullah-gulens-perspectives.html
  (accessed 22.3.2011).
Agai, B. (2002), 'Fethullah Gülen and his movement's Islamic ethic of education'.
  Critique: Critical Middle Eastern Studies, 11, 1, 27–47.
—(2003), 'The Gülen movement's Islamic ethic of education' in M. H. Yavuz and
  J. L. Esposito (eds) *Turkish Islam and the Secular State: The Gülen Movement*.
  Syracuse, New York: Syracuse University Press, pp. 48–68.
Akman, N. (1995), 'Hoca'nın hedefi Amerika ve Almanya' [Hodja targets USA
  and Germany]. *Sabah*. 28.01.1995. Online at: http://tr.fgulen.com/content/
  view/7853/74/ (accessed 12.6.2011).
—(2004), *Zaman Daily*. 22.3.2004.
Akşin, S. (1999), 'The nature of the Kemalist revolution' in D. Shankland, *The
  Turkish Republic at 75 Years*. Huntington/Cambridgeshire: The Eothen Press,
  pp. 14–28.
Alan, Y. (2005), *Lisan ve Insan* [Language and Human]. Istanbul: Kaynak.
Allen, C. and Nielsen, J. (2002), *Summary Report on Islamophobia in the EU
  after 11 September 2001*. Vienna: European Monitoring Centre on Racism and
  Xenophobia.
Allievi, S. (2003), 'Sociology of a newcomer: Muslim migration to Italy – religious
  visibility, cultural and political reactions'. *Immigrants and Minorities*, 22, 2 and
  3, 141–54.
Alpay, S. (1995), 'Respect for Hodjaefendi'. *Milliyet*, 29.7.1995.
Al-Qushayri (2007), *Al-Qushayri's Epistle on Sufism* (Al-Risala al-qushayriyya fi
  'ilm al-tasawwuf) trans. Alexander Knysh, Lebanon: Garnet Publishing.
Altunoğlu, E. (1999), *Fethullah Gülen's Perception of State and Society*.
  Thesis submitted to the Institute of Social Sciences in partial fulfilment of
  the requirements for the degree of Master of Arts in Political Science and
  International Relations, Istanbul: Boğaziçi University.
American Institute for Contemporary German Studies, The (AICGS) (2007),
  *Transatlantic Dialogue on Religion, Values, and Politics an AICGS workshop in
  collaboration with the Program on Religion and Politics*, Theologische Fakultät,
  Humboldt Universität, 20.4.2007, Berlin, Germany.

Andeweg, R. (2000), 'Consociational democracy'. *Annual Review of Political Science*, 3, 509–36.

Andrews, A. (1994), 'The concept of sect and denomination in Islam'. *Religion Today*, 9, 6–10.

Annual Ramadan Friendship Dinner, The (2006, 4 October). Online at: http://www.turkishculturalcenter.org/ny-events/461-turkish-coffee-night-with-iftar-dinner.html (accessed 15.6.2011) (electronic publication only).

Antes, P. (1994), 'Islam in Europe' in S. Gill, G. D'Costa and U. King (eds) *Religion in Europe: Contemporary Perspectives*. Kampen: Kok Pharos, pp. 46–67.

Anwar, M., Blaschke, J. and Sander, A. (2004), *State Policies Towards Muslim Minorities: Sweden, Great Britain and Germany*. Berlin: Verlagsabteilung im Europäischen Migrationszentrum (EMZ).

Ateş, T., Karakaş, E. and Ortaylı, I. (2005), (eds) *Barış Köprüleri. Dünyaya Acilan Türk Okulları–I* [Bridges for peace: Turkish schools opening Turkish schools—I]. Istanbul, Turkey: Ufuk Books, Da Publishing.

Balcı, B. (2003), *Missionnaires de l'Islam en Asie centrale : Les écoles turques de Fethullah Gülen*. Paris: Maisonneuve and Larose.

Ballard, R. (1998), *Desh Pardesh: The South Asian Presence in Britain*. Hurst and Company.

Baskan, F. (2005), 'The Fethullah Gulen community: contribution or barrier to the consolidation of democracy in Turkey?'. *Middle Eastern Studies*, 41, 6, 849–61.

Bastenier, A. (1998), 'L'incidence du facteur religieux dans la conscience ethnique des immigres marocains en Belgique'. *Social Compass*, 45, 2, 195–218.

Başyurt, E. (2004), *Gerçekleşmesi zor bir hayal: Euro–Islam*. Aksiyon, Istanbul: Feza Gazetecilik.

Bayat, A. (2002), 'Piety, privilege and Egyptian youths', *ISIM Newsletter*, 10/2, 23.

—(2007), *Making Islam Democratic: Social Movements and the post-Islamist Turn*. Stanford, CA: Stanford University Press.

BBC News Channel (2003), 'UK Muslims shocked by "bombers"'. *BBC News Channel*. 1.5.2003. Online at: http://news.bbc.co.uk/1/hi/uk/2990841.stm (accessed 3.5.2010).

—(2005), 'London bomber: text in full'. *BBC News Channel*. 1.10.2005. Online at: http://news.bbc.co.uk/1/hi/uk/4206800.stm (accessed 3.5.2010).

—(2006), '7/7 pair 'Visited al-Qaeda camp'. *BBC News Channel*. 8.7.2006. Online at: http://news.bbc.co.uk/1/hi/uk/5161526.stm (accessed 3.5.2010).

—(2007), 'Blazing car crashes into airport'. *BBC News Channel*. 30.6.2007. Online at: http://news.bbc.co.uk/1/hi/scotland/6257194.stm (accessed 3.5.2010).

Beaugrande, R. de and Dressler, W. (1981), *Introduction to Text Linguistics*. London: Longman.

Beeson, T. (1974), *Discretion and Valour*. London: Collins.

Benford, R. and Snow, D. (2000), 'Framing processes and social movements: an overview and assessment'. *Annual Review of Sociology*, 26, 611–39.

Benjamin, W. (2011), *The Storyteller, Reflections on the Work of Nikolai Leskov*. Online at: http://slought.org/files/downloads/events/SF_1331-Benjamin.pdf (accessed 17.3.2011).

Bernstein, M. (1997), 'Celebration and suppression: the strategic use of identity by the lesbian and gay movement'. *The American Journal of Sociology*, 103, 3, 531–65.

Bhabha, H. (1994), *The Location of Culture*. London: Routledge.

Blei, K. (2002), *Freedom of Religion and Belief: Europe's Story*. Assen: Royal Van Gorcum.

Bilici, A. ed. (2006), *Neden Türkiye? Why Turkey?* Istanbul: Zaman Books.

Bilir, Ü. (2004), 'Turkey-Islam': recipe for success or hindrance to the integration of the Turkish diaspora community in Germany'. *Journal of Muslim Minority Affairs*, 24, 259–83.

Blair, T. (2007), 'Speech to the Los Angeles World Affairs Council'. 1.8.2006. Online at: http://www.number-10.gov.uk/output/Page9948.asp (accessed 3.5.2010).

Boix, C. (2004), 'Political Violence', *Yale Conference on: Order, Conflict and Violence*, 30 April–1 May.

Bourdieu, P. (2003), *Les Meditations Pascaliennes*. Paris: Folio Editions.

Bourdieu, P. and Passeron, J. C. (1970), *La Reproduction: Elements pour une théorie du systeme d'enseignement*. Paris: Editions de Minuit.

Bouzar, D. (2003), 'L'islam entre mythe et religion : le nouveau discours religieux dans les associations socio-culturelles musulmanes'. *Les Cahiers de la sécurité intérieure*, 54, 173–89 and at www.islamlaicite.org/article235.html (accessed 12.6.2011).

Bradley, H. (2005), 'İlgisizlik ve Dışlanma'. *Londra Gazete*, 17.2.2005.

BTYahoo News (2007), 'Tackling terror will take 15 years'. 8.7.2007. Online at: http://news.yahoo.com/itn/20070708/tuk-tackling-terror-will-take-15-years-dba1618.html (accessed 3.5.2010).

Buchanan, C. (1994), *Cut the Connection: Disestablishment and the Church of England*. London: Darton, Longman and Todd.

Bulac, A. (2005), 'Hocaefendi'ye Sorular' (Questions to Fethullah Gulen). *Zaman Daily*. 23.11.2005. Online at: http://www.zaman.com.tr/yazar. do?yazino=231669 (accessed 25.6.2011).

Bulut, F. (1998), *Kim Bu Fethullah Gülen: Dünü, Bugünü, Hedefi* [Who is this Fethullah Gülen? His Past, Today and Target]. Istanbul: Ozan Yayıncılık.

Bunting, M. (2007), 'Hearts and minds of young Muslims will be won or lost in the mosques'. *The Guardian*, 9.7.2007.

Camcı, S. and Ünal, K. (1999), *Fethullah Gülen in Konuşma ve Yazılarında Hoşgörü ve Diyalog İklimi*, İzmir: Merkür Yayıncılık.

Can, E. (1997), *Fethullah Gülen Hocaefendi ile Ufuk Turu* [The Tour d'Horizon with Fethullah Gülen Hocaefendi]. Istanbul: AD Publishing.

Çapan, E. ed. (2004), *Terror and Suicide Attacks: An Islamic Perspective*. Somerset, NJ: The Light Publishers.

Carothers, T. (1999), 'Civil society: think again'. *Foreign Policy*, 117, Winter, 18–29.

Carrell, P. (1982), 'Cohesion is not coherence'. *TESOL Quarterly*, 16, 4, 479.

Castles, S. and Miller, M. J. (2003), *The Age of Migration: International Population Movements in the Modern World*. Basingstoke: Palgrave MacMillan

Castles, S., Booth, H. and Wallace, T. (1984), *Here for Good: Western Europe's New Ethnic Minorities*. London: Pluto Press.

Çelik, G. (2010), *The Gülen Movement. Building Social Cohesion Through Dialogue and Education*. Delft, the Netherlands: Eburon.

—(2011), 'Peacebuilding through dialogue and education: lessons from the Gülen movement'. *Journal of Peacebuilding and Development*, 6, 1, 86–90.

Çelik, G. and Valkenberg, P. (2007). 'Gülen's approach to dialogue and peace'.

International Journal of Diversity in Organisations, Communities and Nations, 7, 1, 29–37.

Cesari, J. (1997), *Etre musulman en France aujourd'hui*. Paris: Hachette.

—(2002), 'Islam in France: the shaping of a religious minority' in Y. Haddad ed. *Muslims in the West: From Sojourners to Citizens*. New York: Oxford University Press, pp. 36–51.

—(2004), *L'Islam à l'épreuve de l'Occident*. Paris: La Découverte.

Çetinkaya, H. (2004), *Fethullah Gülen in Kırk Yıllık Serüveni* [The 40 Years Adventure of Fethullah Gülen]. Istanbul: Günizi Yayıncılık.

Chittick, W. (1989), *The Sufi Path of Knowledge: Ibn al-'Arabi's Metaphysics of Imagination*. New York: SUNY Press.

Chwe, M. S. Y. (2001), 'Is communal violence generally susceptible to contagion effects?' *Workshop on the Dynamics of Communal Violence*. New York University: The Brookings Institution.

Cinar, B. (1997), *Devlet Guvenligi, Istihbarat ve Terorizm* [State Security, Intelligence and Terrorism]. Ankara: Sam Yayinlari.

Clark, J. (1994), *Islamic Social-Welfare Organizations and the Legitimacy of the State in Egypt: Democratization or Islamization From Below?* unpublished PhD thesis. University of Toronto, Canada.

Clement, V. (2011), 'Faith-based schools in post-Soviet Turkmenistan'. *European Education*, 43, 1, 76–92.

Cochrane, F. and Dunn, S. (2002), *People Power?: The Role of the Voluntary and Community Sector in the Northern Ireland Conflict*. Cork: Cork University Press.

Commission on Integration and Cohesion (2007), *Our Shared Future*. London: Commission on Integration and Cohesion. Online at: http://collections. europarchive.org/tna/20080726153624/http://www.integrationandcohesion.org. uk/Our_final_report.aspx (accessed 3.5.2010).

Crisp, M. W. (1990), 'Introduction' in M. W. Crisp ed. *Terrorism, Protest and Power*. Aldershot and Brookfield: Edward Elgar, pp. 1–14.

Darsh, S. (1980), *Islam in Europe*. London: Ta-Ha Publishers.

Dassetto, F., Ferrari, S. and Marechal, B. (2007), *Islam in the European Union: What's at Stake in the Future?* Brussels: European Parliament.

Davie, G. (1994), *Religion in Britain Since 1945: Believing without Belonging*. Oxford: Wiley-Blackwell.

—(2000), *Religion in Modern Europe: A Memory Mutates*. Oxford: Oxford University Press.

Davis, G. (1999), *Repression, Rationality and Relative Deprivation: A Theoretical and Empirical Examination of Cross-National Variations in Political Violence*. Online at: http://economics.gmu.edu: http://economics.gmu.edu/working/ WPE_99/99_04.pdf (accessed 15.3.2007).

Demir, H. (2004), 'Hills like white eephants: analysis according to seven standards of text linguistics'. Online at: http://www.ingilish.com/hd7.htm (accessed 1.8.2007) (electronic publication only).

—(2007), 'New religious sociabilities in Euro-Islam: the organizational logics and recognition politics of Gülen movement in France and Germany' in Ihsan Yilmaz et al. *Peaceful Coexistence: Fethullah Gülen's Initiatives in the Contemporary World*, London: Leeds Metropolitian University Press, pp. 355–70.

Dialmy, A. (2007), 'Belonging and institution in Islam'. *Social Compass*, 54, 1, 63–75.

Easwaran, E. (n.d), 'The next Salt March – turning our backs on consumerism'. Online at: http://www.himalayaninstitute.org/yogaplus/article.aspx?id=3188 (accessed 24.6.2011).

Ebaugh, H. R. (2010), *The Gulen Movement: A Sociological Analysis of a Civic Movement Rooted in Moderate Islam*. Dordrecht, Netherlands: Springer.

Eckhardt, W. (1971), 'Symbiosis between peace research and peace action'. *Journal of Peace Research*, 8, 1, 67–70.

Eickelman, D. (1992), *Knowledge and Power in Morocco: The Education of a Twentieth Century Notable Princeton*. NJ: *Princeton University Press*.

Elsas, E. (1991), Turkish Islamic ideals of education: their possible function for Islamic identity and integration in Europe' in W. A. R. Shadid and P. S. van Koningsveld (eds) *The Integration of Islam and Hinduism in Western Europe*. Kampen: Kok Pharos Publishing House, pp. 174–87.

Erdoğan, L. (1997), *Fethullah Gülen Hocaefendi: Küçük Dünyam* [Fethullah Gülen Hocaefendi: My Small World]. Istanbul: AD Publishing.

—(2006), 'Kucuk Dunyam' [My Little World]. Istanbul: Ufuk Yayinlari.

Ergene, M. E. (2008), *Tradition Witnessing the Modern Age. An Analysis of the Gülen Movement*. Somerset, NJ: The Light Publishers.

Esposito, J. (2003), 'Modernising Islam and re-Islamisation in global perspective' in J. Esposito and F. Burgat (eds) *Modernising Islam: Religion in The Public Sphere in the Middle East and Europe*. London: Hurst and Company.

Esposito, J. and Voll, J. (2001), *Makers of Contemporary Islam*. New York: Oxford University Press.

Esposito, J. and Yilmaz, I. (eds) (2010), *Islam and Peacebuilding: Gülen Movement Initiatives*. New York: Blue Dome Press.

Favrot, L. (2004), *Tariq Ramadan dévoilé*. Lyon: Lyon Mag.

Fekete, L. (2004), 'Anti-Muslim racism and the European security state'. *Race and Class*, 46, 1, 3–29.

Filali-Ansari, A. (2003), *Réformer l'Islam?* Paris: La Découverte,

Finlay, A. (2004), 'Introduction' in A. Finlay ed. *Nationalism and Multiculturalism: Irish identity, Citizenship and the Peace Process*. London: Transaction Publishers, pp. 1–32.

Fourest, C. (2004), *Frère Tariq: discours stratégie et méthode de Tariq Ramadan*. Paris: Grasset.

Fraser, N. (1992), 'Rethinking the public sphere: a contribution to the critique of actually existing democracy' in C. Calhoun ed. *Habermas and the Public Sphere*. Cambridge, MA: MIT Press, pp. 109–42.

Gaborieau, M. and Zeghal, M. (2004), 'Autorités religieuses en islam'. *Archives de Sciences Sociales des Religions*, 125, 5–21.

Gadher, D. (2007), 'The battle for hearts and minds'. *The Sunday Times*. 8.7.2007, p. 14.

Galtung, J. (1969), 'Violence, peace and peace research'. *Journal of Peace Research*, 6, 3, 167–91.

Gandhi, M. (1919), *Satyagraha Leaflet 13*, 19.5.1919.

—(1925), YI, 21-5-1925, p. 178. Online at: http://www.mkgandhi.org/momgandhi/chap27.htm (accessed 24.6.2011).

Gause, F. G. (2005), 'Can democracy stop terrorism?'. *Foreign Affairs*, September–October, pp. 62–76.

Ghannouchi, R. (1999), *Muqarabat fi al-'ilmaniyya w'al-mujtam' al-madani* [Papers on Secularism and Civil Society]. London: Maghreb Center for Research and Translation.

Gill, R. (1975), *The Social Context of Theology: A Methodological Enquiry*. London: Blackwell.

Goffman, E. (1963), *Stigma: Notes on the Management of Spoiled Identity*. New York: Touchstone Books.

Göle, N. (1994), 'Towards an autonomization of politics and civil society in Turkey' in M. Heper and A. Evin (eds) *Politics in the Third Turkish Republic*, San Francisco and Oxford: Westview Press, pp. 213–22.

—(2005), *Interpénétrations. L'Islam et l'Europe*. Paris: Galaade Editions.

—(2006), 'Islamic visibilities and public sphere' in N. Göle and L. Ammann, *Islam in Public: Turkey, Iran and Europe*. Istanbul: Bilgi University Press, pp. 3–45.

Gözaydın, İ. B. (2009), 'The Fethullah Gülen movement and politics in Turkey: a chance for democratization or a trojan horse?'. *Democratization*, 16, 6, 1214–36.

Gregory, G. and Wilkinson, P. (2005), *Riding Pillion for Tackling Terrorism is a High Risk Policy*. London: Chatham House. ISP/NSC Briefing Paper 05/01.

Grinell, K. (2010), 'Border thinking: Fethullah Gülen and the East–West divide' in J. L. Esposito and I. Yilmaz (2010), *Islam and Peacebuilding: Gulen Movement Initiatives*. New York: Blue Dome Press, pp. 43–62.

Guelke, A. (2006), *Terrorism and Global Disorder: Political Violence in the Contemporary World*. London: IB Tauris.

Gulay, E. (2007), 'The Gulen phenomenon: a neo sufi challenge to Turkey's rival elite?'. *Critique: Critical Middle Eastern Studies*, 16, 1, 37–61.

Gülen, M. F. (1979), 'Bu Ağlamayı Dindirmek İçin Yavru [For Stopping This Crying of Baby]'. *Sızıntı*, 1, 1, 1–2.

—(1996), *Towards the Lost Paradise*. London: Truestar Ltd.

—(1997), *Fatiha Üzerine Mülahazalar* [Considerations on the Chapter Fatiha]. Izmir: Nil.

—(1998), Taha Akyol and Cengiz Çandar's interview with Fethullah Gülen, 27.2.1998 for NTV. Online at: http://tr.fGülen.com/content/view/1464/74/.

—(2000), 'The necessity of interfaith dialogue: a Muslim perspective'. *The Fountain*, 3, 31, 4–9.

—(2001a), 'Real Muslims cannot be terrorists'. *Turkish Daily News*. 19.9.2001.

—(2001b), Reha Muhtar's interview with Fethullah Gülen. 12.9.2001. Online at: http://tr.fGülen.com/content/view/222/5/ (accessed 6.3.2007).

—(2002), *Zaman*. 29.10.2002. Online at: http://tr.fgulen.com/content/view/13995/80/.

—(2003a), *Ruhumuzun heykelini dikerken* [The Statue of our Souls]. Istanbul: Gülen, M. F.

—(2003b), *Zamanın altın dilimi* [The golden period of time]. Istanbul: Nil.

—(2003c), 'Suicide attacks can not be reconciled with the universal call of Islam'. *Zaman Daily*. 16.11.2003. Online in Turkish at: http://tr.fGülen.com/content/view/3885/77/ (accessed 10.6.2011).

—(2004a), 'No Islamic world exists today'. Interview with N. Akman. *Zaman*. 22.3.2004. Online at: http://www.fethullahgulen.org/press-room/nuriye-akmans-interview/1726-no-islamic-world-exists-today.html (accessed 21.9.2008).

—(2004b), Interview with Fethullah Gülen. *Daily Nation*. 30.7.2004.

—(2004c), 'In true Islam, terror does not exist' in E. Çapan ed. *Terror and Suicide Attacks: An Islamic Perspective*. Somerset, NJ: The Light Publishers, pp. 1–8.

—(2004d), *Emerald Hills of the Heart: Key Concepts in the Practice of Sufism*. Volume 2. Somerset, NJ: The Light Publishers.

—(2004e), *Towards A Global Civilization of Love and Tolerance*. Somerset, NJ: The Light Publishers.

—(2005a), 'An interview with Fethullah Gülen' in *Islam in Contemporary Turkey: The Contributions of Fethullah Gülen*. *The Muslim World*. 95, 3, 447–67.

—(2005b), *Essentials of the Islamic Faith*. Somerset, NJ: The Light Publishers.

—(2005c), *Pearls of Wisdom*, second edition. Somerset, NJ: The Light Publishers.

—(2005d), *The Statue of Our Souls: Revival in Islamic Thought and Activism*. Somerset, NJ: The Light Publishers.

—(2006a), *Essays, Perspectives, Opinions*, second revised edition. Somerset, NJ: The Light Publishers.

—(2006b), (under pen-name Hikmet Isik) 'What does Islam say about killing an innocent person?'. *The Fountain*, 56. Online at: http://www.fountainmagazine. com/articles.php?SIN=7808256c10&k=792&840098454&show=part1 (accessed 10.6.2011).

—(2006c), 'Respect for humankind'. *The Fountain*, 53. Online at: http://www.fountainmagazine.com/articles.php?SIN=6e31958cbc&k=738& 593384988&show=part1 (accessed 13.8.2007). Also online at: http://www. fethullahgulen.org/recent-articles/2124-respect-for-humankind.html (accessed 5.6.2011).

—(2006d), 'Istighraq' [Immersion]. Online at: http://www.fethullahGülen.org/ sufism-2/2097-istighraq-immersion.html – original 1.5.2006, updated, 1.7.2007 (accessed 1.5.2010).

—(2006e), 'With accession, Europe would know us better' in A. Bilici ed. *Neden Türkiye? Why Turkey?* Istanbul: Zaman Books, pp. 39–40.

—(2007a), *Kirik Testi 1–5* [Broken Pitcher]. Istanbul: Journalists and Writers Foundation.

—(2007b), *Prizma 1–5 [Prism]*. Istanbul: Nil.

—(2007c), *Fasildan Fasila 1–5*. Istanbul. Nil.

—(2007d), 'Excerpts from F. Gülen's answers to questions on education and Turkish educational activities abroad'. Online at: http://en.fGülen.com/content/ view/779/2/ (accessed 14.8.2007).

—(2007e), 'Fethullah Gulen's response to September 11 attacks on US'. Newsletter, 20 June. Online at: http://www.cam.net.uk/home/aaa315/peace/islam.htm (accessed 20.6. 2011).

—(2009), '*Bir kere daha Aktif Sabir*' [One More Again Active Patience]. Online at: http://tr.fGülen.com/content/view/16551/17/ (accessed 12.1.2009).

—(2011a), *Lesser and Greater Jihad*. http://www.fethullahGülen.org/love-and-tolerance/272-jihadterrorismhuman-rights/1841-lesser-and-greater-jihad.html (accessed 7.4 2011).

—(2011b), Online at: http://www.fethullahGülen.org/Gülens-works/296-recent-articles/1878-three-groups-opposing-dialogue-kharijites-karmatis-anarchists. html (accessed 5.6.2011).

Gundem, M. (2005), 'Interview with Fethullah Gülen', 08–29 January 2005, Milliyet Daily, available at http://en.fgulen.com/press-room/mehmet-gundems-interview last visited on 26 August 2011.

Gurbuz, M. (2007), 'Performing moral opposition: musings on the strategy and identity in the Gülen Movement,' in I. Yilmaz et al., eds., *Muslim World in Transition: Contributions of the Gülen Movement*, London: Leeds Metropolitan University Press, pp. 104–17

Habermas, J. (1991), *The Structural Transformation of the Public Sphere: An Inquiry into a Category of Bourgeois Society*. Cambridge Massachusetts: MIT Press.

Hardy, P. (1972), *The Muslims of British India*. Cambridge: Cambridge University Press.

Harinck, G. (2006), 'Een leefbare oplossing, Katholieke en Protestantse tradities en de scheiding van kerk en staat' in M. ten Hooven en T. de Wit (eds) (2006) *Ongewenste Goden. De publieke rol van religie in Nederland*. Amsterdam: SUN, pp. 106–30.

Harrington, J. C. (2011), *Wrestling with Free Speech, Religious Freedom and Democracy in Turkey: The Political Times and Trials of Fethullah Gülen*. Lanham, Maryland: University Press of America.

Hendrick, J. D. (2009), 'Globalization, Islamic activism, and passive revolution in Turkey: the case of Fethullah Gülen'. *Journal of Power*, 2, 3, 343–68.

Henkel, H. (2004), 'Rethinking the dar al-harb: social change and changing perceptions of the West in Turkish Islam'. *Journal of Ethnic and Migration Studies*, 30, 5, 961–78.

Heper, M. et al. (1994), *Politics in the Third Turkish Republic*. Boulder, CO: Westview Press.

Hermansen, M. (2007), 'Understandings of "Community" within the Gülen Movement'. Online at: http://fethullahgulenconference.org/houston/index.php (accessed 12.8.2007).

Heywood, A. (2007), *Politics*, Third Edition. London: Palgrave Foundation.

Home Office (2011a), *Counter-Terrorism Strategy*. Online at: http://security. homeoffice.gov.uk/counterterrorism-strategy/about the strategy (accessed 29.3.2011).

Home Office (2011b), *Prevent Strategy 2011*, 7.6.2011. Online at: http://www. homeoffice.gov.uk/publications/counter-terrorism/prevent/prevent-strategy/ (accessed 4.7.2011).

Hooven, M. ten (2006), 'Religie verdeelt Nederland' in M. ten Hooven en T. de Wit (eds) (2006), *Ongewenste Goden. De publieke rol van religie in Nederland*, Amsterdam: Boon, pp. 13–37.

Hourani, A. (1961), 'Race, religion and the nation state' in *A Vision of History*. Beirut: Khayat.

House of Commons Communities and Local Government Committee (2010) *Preventing Violent Extremism*. London: The Stationery Office. Online at: http:// www.publications.parliament.uk/pa/cm200910/cmselect/cmcomloc/65/65.pdf (accessed 3.5.2010).

Hunt, R. and Aslandoğan, Y. (eds) (2006), *Muslim Citizens of the Globalized World: Contributions of the Gülen Movement*. Somerset, NJ: The Light Publishers.

Huntington, S. (1993), 'The clash of civilizations?'. *Foreign Affairs*, 72, 3, 22–49.

—(1996), *The Clash of Civilizations and the Remaking of World Order*. New York: Simon and Schuster.

Husain, E. (2007), *The Islamist: Why I Joined Radical Islam in Britain, What I Saw Inside and Why I Left*. London: Penguin.

Hussari, I. A. E. (2009), 'The Gulen movement: an Islamic response to terror as a global challenge'. *Central European Journal of International and Security Studies*, 3, 1, 64–78.

International Crisis Group (2007), *Islam and Identity in Germany*, International Crisis Group Report, No. 18, Berlin/Brussels, 14.3.2007.

Irvine, J. (2006), 'Gülen movement and Turkish integration' in R. Hunt and Y. Aslandoğan (eds) *Muslim Citizens of the Globalized World: Contributions of the Gülen Movement*. Somerset, NJ: The Light Publishers, pp. 57–72.

Islam is Peace. Online at: http://www.islamispeace.org.uk (accessed 3.5.2010).

Jarman, N. (2002), *Managing Disorder: Responding to Interface Violence in North Belfast*. Belfast: Office of the First Minister and Deputy First Minister.

Jenkins, R. (1967), *Essays and Speeches*. London: Collins.

—(1989), 'On race relations and the Rushdie affair'. *The Independent Magazine*. 18.3.89.

Joly, D. (1988), 'Making a place for Islam in British society: Muslims in Birmingham in T. Gerholm and Y. Lithman (eds) *The New Islamic Presence in Western Europe*. New York: Mansell, pp. 32–52.

Juergensmeyer, M. (2003), *Terror in the Mind of God*. Berkeley, CA: University of California Press.

—(2005), 'Religion' in *Addressing the Causes of Terrorism, The Club de Madrid Series on Democracy and Terrorism, Volume I*, Club de Madrid and online at: http://media.clubmadrid.org/docs/CdM-Series-on-Terrorism-Vol-1.pdf (accessed 14.6.2011).

Kandil, A. (1999), 'Women and civil society' in A. Kandil ed. *Civil Society at the Millennium*. Civicus, Connecticut: Kumarian Press, pp. 57–68.

Karlığa, B. (1998), *Kültürlerarası Diyalog Sempozyumu*. Istanbul: Erkâm Mat.

Kaya, A. (2007), *Euro-Turks: Dwelling in a Space of Their Own*. Online at: http://www.aicgs.org/analysis/c/kayaapr07.aspx (accessed 10.6.2011).

Kedourie, E. (1994), *Demoracy and Arabic Political Culture*. London: Frank Cass.

Kepel, G. (2003), *Jihad: The Trail of Political Islam*. Cambridge: Belknap Press of Harvard University Press.

Kepel, G. and Richard, Y. (1990), *Intellectuels et Militants de l'Islam Contemporain*. Paris: Edition du Seuil.

Kettani, M. (1979), *The Muslim Minorities*. Leicester: The Islamic Foundation.

Khan, M. A. (2009), 'A universal Islamic phenomenon in Turkish religious practice: the Gülen case'. *The Fountain*, 70, July–August. Online at: http://fountainmagazine.com/article.php?ARTICLEID=1040 (accessed 21.6.2011).

King, R. ed. (1993), *Mass Migration in Europe: Legacy and Future*. New York: John Wiley and Sons.

Kömeçoğlu, U. (1997), *A Sociologically Interpretative Approach to the Fethullah Gülen Movement*, Unpublished MA thesis. Istanbul: Bogazici University.

Koningsveld, van, P. and Shadid, W. (2002), 'The negative image of Islam and Muslims in the West: causes and solution' in W. Shadid and P. van Koningsveld (eds) *Religious Freedom and the Neutrality of the State: The Position of Islam in the European Union*. Leuven: Peeters, pp. 174–92.

Korostelina, K. (2010), 'Dialogue as a source for peaceful co-existence' in J.

Esposito and I. Yilmaz (eds) *Islam and Peacebuilding: Gülen Movement Initiatives*. New York: Blue Dome Press, pp. 103–21.

Kösebalaban, H. (2003), 'The making of enemy and friend: Fethullah Gulen's national-security identity' in H. Yavuz and J. Esposito (eds) *Turkish Islam and the Secular State The Gülen Movement*. New York: Syracuse University Press, pp. 170–84.

Koyuncu-Lorasdaği, B. (2010), 'The prospects and pitfalls of the religious nationalist movement in Turkey: the case of the Gülen movement'. *Middle Eastern Studies*, 46, 2, 221–34.

Kramer, G. (2010), *Hasan al-Banna (Makers of the Muslim World)*. Oxford: Oneworld Publications.

Kuhn, T. (1962), *The Structure of Scientific Revolutions*. Chicago: University of Chicago Press.

Kullberg, A. and Jokinen, C. (2004), *From Terror to Terrorism: the Logic on the Roots of Selective Political Violence*. University of Turku: Research Unit for Conflicts and Terrorism. Also online at: http://www.aheku.org/page-id-1082.html (accessed 14.6.2011).

Kumar, C. R. (2007), 'Terrorism and human security'. *The Hindu*, electronic edition of India's National Newspaper. 27.8.2007. Online at: http://www.hindu.com/2007/08/27/stories/2007082755951300.htm (accessed 14.6.2011).

Kundnani, A. (2007), 'Integrationism: the politics of anti-Muslim racism'. *Race and Class*, 48, 4, 26–44.

—(2009) *Spooked: How Not To Prevent Violent Extremism*. London: Institute of Race Relations.

Kurokawa, K. (1987), *Each One a Hero: Philosophy of Symbiosis*. Tokyo: Tokuma Publishing Co.

Kurtz, L. R. (2005), 'Gülen's paradox: combining commitment and tolerance'. *Muslim World*, 95, 3, 373–84.

Kuru, A. T. (2003), 'Fethullah Gülen's search for a middle way between modernity and Muslim tradition' in H. Yavuz and J. Esposito (eds) *Turkish Islam and the Secular State: The Gülen Movement*. Syracuse: Syracuse University Press, pp. 115–30.

—(2005), 'Globalization and diversification of Islamist movements: three Turkish cases'. *Political Science Quarterly*, 120, 2, 252–74.

Lægard, S. (2007), 'The cartoon controversy: offence, identity, oppression?'. *Political Studies*, 55, 3, 481–98.

Lamine, A. (2004), *La coexistence des Dieux, Pluralité religieuse et laïcité*. Paris: Puf.

Lave, J. and Wenger. E. (1991), *Situated Learning: Legitimate Peripheral Participation*. New York: Cambridge University Press.

Leaman, O. (2007), 'Towards an understanding of Gülen's methodology', in Yilmaz et al. (eds) *Muslim World in Transition: Contributions of the Gülen Movement*. London: Leeds Metropolitan University Press, pp. 503–10.

Lentin, R. and McVeigh, R. (2006), *After Optimism? Ireland, Racism and Globalisation*. Dublin: Metro Eireann Publications.

Lentz, T. F. (1972), *Towards A Technology Of Peace*. St Louis: Lentz Peace Research Laboratory.

Leveau, R. (1988), 'The Islamic presence in France' in T. Gerholm and Y.Lithman (eds) *New Islamic Presence in Western Europe*. London and New York: Mansell, pp. 107–22.

LeVine, M. (2003), '"Human nationalisms" versus "Inhuman globalisms": cultural economies of globalisation and the re-imagining of Muslim identities in Europe and the Middle East' in S. Allievi and J. Nielsen (eds) *Muslim Networks and Transnational Communities in and Across Europe*. Leiden and Boston: Brill, pp. 78–126.

Levinskaya, V. (2007), 'Resemblance of Fethullah Gülen's ideas and current political developments in Uzbekistan' in I. Yilmaz et al. (eds) *Peaceful Coexistence: Fethullah Gülen's Initiatives in the Contemporary World*. London: Leeds Metropolitan University Press, pp. 331–43.

Lewis, B. (2002), *What Went Wrong?: Western Impact and Middle Eastern Response*. Oxford: Oxford University Press.

Lijphart, A. (1977), *Democracy in Plural Societies*. London: Yale University Press.

Lorcerie, F. (2003), *L'Ecole et le défi ethnique: Education et intégration*. Paris: ESF and INRP.

McGarry, J. and O'Leary, B. (2004), *The Northern Ireland Conflict: Consociational Engagements*. Oxford: Oxford University Press.

McVeigh, R. and Rolston, B. (2007), 'From Good Friday to good relations: sectarianism, racism and the Northern Ircland state'. *Race and Class*, 48, 1, 1–23.

Ma'oz, A. (1978), 'Islamic-Arabism versus pluralism: the failure of intergroup accommodation the Middle East' in N. Rhoodie ed. *Intergroup Accommodation in Plural Societies*. London: Macmillan, pp. 115–42.

Madeley, J. and Enyedi, Z. (eds) (2003), *Church and State in Contemporary Europe: The Chimera of Neutrality*. London: Frank Cass.

Mandaville, P. (2001), *Transnational Muslim Politics: Reimagining the Umma*. London: Routledge.

—(2007), 'Globalization and the politics of religious knowledge: pluralizing authority in the Muslim world'. *Theory, Culture and Society*, 24, 2.

—(2011), 'Transnational Muslim solidarities and everyday life'. *Nations and Nationalism*, 17, 1, 7–24.

Mann-Kler, D. (2002), 'Identity and racism in Northern Ireland' in R. Lentin and R. McVeigh (eds) *Racism and Anti-Racism in Ireland*. Belfast: Beyond the Pale, pp. 63–72.

Markham, I. and Ozdemir, O. (2005), *Globalization, Ethics and Islam – the Case of Bediuzzaman Said Nursi*. Aldershot: Ashgate.

Marranci, G. (2005), 'Pakistanis in Northern Ireland in the aftermath of September 11' in T. Abbas ed. *Muslim Britain: Communities under Pressure*. London: Zed Books, pp. 222–33.

Martin, B. (2007), *Justice Ignited: The Dynamics of Backfire*. Lanham, MD: Rowman and Littlefield.

Martin, B. and Gray, T. (2007), 'Backfires: white, black and grey'. *Journal of Information Warfare*, 7, 1, 7–16.

Michel, T. (2001), 'Fethullah Gulen and the Gulen Schools', unpublished paper presented at the Conference on *Islamic Modernism: Fethullah Gülen and Contemporary Islam*, at Georgetown University, 26–27 April.

—(2003), 'Fethullah Gülen as educator' in J. Esposito and H. Yavuz (eds) *Turkish Islam and The Secular State, The Gülen Movement*. New York, Syracuse University Press, pp. 69–84.

Modood, T. (2007), *Multiculturalism*. Cambridge: Polity Press.

Mollov, B. (2005), *Religion and Religious Extremism*. Madrid: International Summit on Democracy, Terrorism and Security.

Murray, S. (2004), *Post-Christendom*. Milton Keynes: Paternoster Press.

Nasreddine, D. (2004), *Turkish Communities in Europe: Societies Within Societies*. Online at: http://www.islamonline.net/English/artculture/2004/11/article05. shtml (accessed 10.6.2011).

National Commission on Terrorist Attacks Upon the United States (2004), *The 9/11 Commission Report: The Full Final Report of the National Commission on Terrorist Attacks Upon the United States*. Washington, DC: National Commission on Terrorist Attacks Upon the United States.

National Intelligence Council (2008), *Global Trends 2025: A Transformed World*. (pdf). Washington, DC: US Government Printing Office. Online at: http://www.dni.gov/nic/NIC_2025_project.html (accessed 4.5.2008).

Neubert, A. and G. M. Shreve (1992), *Translation as Text*. Kent, Ohio: Kent State University Press.

Nielsen, J. (1991), 'Muslim organisations in Europe: integration or isolation?' in W. Shadid and P. van Koningsveld (eds) *The Integration of Islam and Hinduism in Western Europe*. Kampen: Kok Pharos Publishing House.

—(1995), 'State, religion and laïcité: the Western European experience' in T. Mitri ed. *Religion, Law and Society: A Christian–Muslim Discussion*. Geneva: World Council of Churches, pp. 100–10.

—(2004), *Muslims in Western Europe*. Edinburgh: Edinburgh University Press.

O'Brien, R. (2004), 'Situational factors contributing to the expression of aggression on the roads'. *IATSS Research*, 28, 101–7.

Özdalga, E. (1999), 'Entrepreneurs with a mission: Turkish Islamists building schools along the Silk Road'. Washington, DC: Paper delivered at the Annual Conference of the North American Middle East Studies Association, 19–22.11.1999.

—(2000), 'Worldly ascetism in Islamic casting: Fethullah Gulen's inspired piety and activisms'. *Critique: Journal for Critical Studies of the Middle East*, 17, 84–104.

—(2005), 'Redeemer or outsider? The Gülen community in the civilizing process'. *The Muslim World*, 95, 3, 429–46.

—(2007), *İslamcılığın Türkiye Seyri*. İstanbul: İletişim Yayınları.

Paige, G., Satha-Anand, C. and Gilliat, S. (2001), *Islam and Non-Violence*. Honolulu, Hawai'i: Centre For Global Non-Violence.

Pape, R. (2005), *Dying to Win: The Strategic Logic of Suicide Terrorism*. New York: Random House.

Pauly, R. (2004), *Islam in Europe: Integration or Marginalisation?* Aldershot: Ashgate

Pauwels, L. and Bergier, J. (2007), *The Morning of the Magicians*. London: Souvenir Press.

Pedersen, L. (1999), *Newer Islamic Movements in Western Europe*. Aldershot: Ashgate.

Penaskovic, R. (2010), 'Gülen on healing the rift between Islam and the West' in J. L. Esposito and I. Yilmaz (eds) *Islam and Peacebuilding: Gulen Movement Initiatives*. New York: Blue Dome Press, pp. 101–21.

Perrier, G. (2009), 'Une confrérie turque ouvre un collège républicain en France' [A Turkish fraternity inaugurated a republican school in France]. *Le Monde*. 29.12.2009. Online at: http://www.lemonde.fr/societe/article/2009/12/29/

les-eclaireurs-de-l-islam-suscitent-la-controverse_1285751_3224.html (accessed 12.6.2011).

Phillips, T. (2005), 'After 7/7: sleepwalking to segregation'. *Commission for Racial Equality*, 22.9.2005.

Post, H. (1989), *Pillarization: An Analysis of Dutch and Belgian Society*. Aldershot: Avebury.

Powe, K. (2006), *New Religions and the Nazis*. Abingdon: Routledge.

Ramadan, T. (1997), 'The Islam we need' ('L'islam dont on a besoin'). Le Bourget: Paper presented at the annual conference JMF Centre, 30.6.1997.

—(1999), *To Be a European Muslim*. Leicester: The Islamic Foundation.

—(2003), *Western Muslims and the Future of Islam*. New York: Oxford University Press USA.

—(2004), *Western Muslims and the Future of Islam*. Oxford: Oxford University Press.

Ramadan, T. and A. Gresh (2000), *L'Islam en questions*. Actes-Sud: Sindbad.

Rand Report (2007), at http://www.rand.org/pubs/monographs/MG483/ (accessed 4.6.2011).

Richardson, L. (2006). *What Terrorists Want: Understanding the Terrorist Threat*. London: John Murray.

Robbers, G. ed. (1996), *State and Church in the European Union*. Baden-Baden: Nomos Verlagsgesellschaft.

Robertson, R. (1997), 'Glocalization: time-space and homogeneity-heterogeneity' in M. Featherstone, S. Lash and R. Robertson (eds) *Global Modernities*. London: Sage Publications, pp. 25–44.

Robinson, F. (1988), *Varieties of South Asian Islam*. Coventry: Centre for Research in Ethnic Relations, University of Warwick.

Rotberg, R. I. (2002), 'The new nature of nation-state failure'. *The Washington Quarterly*, 25, 3, 85–96.

Roussillon, A. (2005), *La Pensée islamique contemporaine*, Paris, Téraèdre.

Roy, O. (1996), *The Failure of Political Islam*. Cambridge: Mass., Harvard University Press.

– (2004a), *Globalised Islam: The Search for a New Ummah*, London: Hurst.

– ed. (2004b), *La Turquie aujourd'hui, un pays européen ?*, Paris: Universalis.

Roy, O. and P. Haenni (eds) (1999), *Le post-islamisme*, numéro spécial de *la Revue des mondes musulmans et de la Méditerranée*, 85, 85–6.

Runnymede Trust, The (1997), *Islamophobia: A Challenge for Us All*. London: Runnymede Trust.

Rushdie, S. (1988), *The Satanic Verses*. London: Viking Penguin.

Ryan, M. (1996), *Another Ireland: An Introduction to Ireland's Ethnic-Religious Minority Communities*. Belfast: Stranmillis College.

Said, E. (1995), *Orientalism*, reprint cum 'Afterword'. London: Penguin Books.

Sander, A. (1991), 'The road from musalla to mosque: the process of integration and institutionalisation of Islam in Sweden' in W. Shadid and P. van Koningsveld (eds) *The Integration of Islam and Hinduism in Western Europe*. Kampen: Kok Pharos Publishing House, pp. 62–88.

Saritoprak, Z. (2003), 'Fethullah Gülen: a sufi in his own way' in H. Yavuz. and J. Esposito (eds) *Turkish Islam and the Secular State: The Gülen Movement*. New York: Syracuse University Press, pp. 156–69.

—(2005), 'An Islamic approach to peace and nonviolence: a Turkish experience'. *The Muslim World*, 95, 3, 413–27.

Saritoprak, Z. and Griffith, S. (2005), 'Fethullah Gülen and the "People of the Book": a voice from Turkey for interfaith dialogue'. *The Muslim World*, 95, 3, 329–40.

Schwedler, J. (1995), 'Introduction' in J. Schwedler ed. *Toward Civil Society in the Middle East? A Primer*. Boulder, CO: Lynne Rienner, pp. 1–32.

Seneviratana, A. ed.. (1994), *King Asoka and Buddhism – Historical and Literary Studies*. Kandy, Sri Lanka: Buddhist Publication Society and online at: http://urbandharma.org/pdf/king_asoka.pdf (accessed 24.6.2011).

Sevindi, N. (2002), *Fethullah Gülen ile New York Sohbetleri* [New York Conversations with Fethullah Gülen and Global Tolerance]. Istanbul: Timas Yayinlari.

Shadid, A. (2002), *Legacy of the Prophet: Despots, Democrats, and the New Politics of Islam*. Boulder, CO: Westview Press.

Shadid, W. and van Koningsveld, P. (1991), 'Institutionalisation and integration of Islam in the Netherlands' in W. Shadid and P. van Koningsveld (eds) *The Integration of Islam and Hinduism in Western Europe*. Kampen: Kok Pharos Publishing House, pp. 89–122.

Shain, Y. (1995), 'Multicultural foreign policy'. *Foreign Policy*, 25th anniversary issue (autumn) 100, 69–87.

Sharansky, N. (2002), *Democracy for Peace*. Washington, DC: American Enterprise Institute.

Sharansky, N. and Dermer, R. (2006), *The Case for Democracy: The Power of Freedom to Overcome Tyranny and Terror*. New York: Public Affairs.

Sharp, G. (1973), *The Politics of Non-Violent Action*. Boston, MA: Sargent.

—(2005), *Waging Non-Violent Struggle: 20th Century Practice and 21st Century Potential*. Boston, MA: Extending Horizons Books.

Siddiqui, A. (2007), *Islam At Universities in England: Meeting the Needs and Investing in the Future. Report Submitted to Bill Rammell MP* [Minister of State for Lifelong Learning, Further and Higher Education].

Silke, A. (2001), 'Terrorism: an action plan'. *The Psychologist*, 14, 11, 580–1.

Smoker, P. and Groff, L. (1995), 'Spirituality, religion, and peace: exploring the foundations for inner-outer peace in the 21st century' in *Conference Proceedings, Second UNESCO Conference on 'Contributions of Religions to a Culture of Peace'*. Barcelona, December found in (1995) *Creating Global-Local Cultures of Peace*. Online at: http://www.gmu.edu/academic/pcs/smoker.htm (accessed 24.6.2011, and reprinted online at: http://www.rosecroixjournal.org/issues/2007/articles/vol4_21_44_groff.pdf).

Spedding, J., Ellis, R., Ellis, L. and Heath, D. (1968), *The Works of Francis Bacon*. New York: Garrett Press.

Stake, R. E. (1995), *The Art of Case Study Research*. Thousand Oaks, CA: Sage.

Starr, K. (1998). *The Role of Civil Disobedience in Democracy*. Online at: http://www.civilliberties.org/sum98role.html (accessed 22.3.2011).

Steigmann-Gall, R. (2003), *The Holy Reich: Nazi Conceptions of Christianity, 1919–1945*. Cambridge: Cambridge University Press.

Stuart, M. (2004), *Post-Christendom*. Milton Keynes: Paternoster Press.

Sypnowich, C. (2010), 'Law and ideology' in *The Stanford Encyclopedia of Philosophy* (Fall Edition). Online at: http://plato.stanford.edu/entries/law-ideology/

Tahir-ul-Qadri, M. (2010), 'Fatwa'. Online at: http://www.tahir-ul-qadri.com/ fatwa-suicide-bombing-and-terrorism.html (accessed 8.4.2011).

Tas, N. (2004), 'Analysis of a text from a newspaper', at http://www.ingilish.com/ ned3.htm (accessed 1.8.2007) (electronic publication only).

Taylor, C. (1994), 'The politics of recognition' in C. Taylor et al. (eds) *Multiculturalism: Examining the Politics of Recognition*. Princeton: Princeton University Press, pp. 25–74.

Thomä-Venske, H. (1988), 'The religious life of Muslims in Berlin' in T. Gerholm and Y. Lithman (eds) *The New Islamic Presence in Western Europe*. New York: Mansell, pp. 78–87.

Tietze, N. (2004), 'The forms of Muslim religiosity in France and in Germany, in poly-ethnic societies: problems of cultural distinctions' (Russian) in S.V. Prodjogina, M. Wieviorka, L.A.Birchanskaya (eds) *Polyethnic Societies: The Problems of Cultural Diversities*. Moscow: Institute of Oriental Studies NAR and Center for Sociological Analysis and Intervention, pp. 143–51.

Tillich, P. (1951), *Systematic Theology: Volume One*, Chicago: University of Chicago Press.

Today's Zaman, (2010), 'Dutch Minister gives Turkish Deputy a lesson on freedoms', 21.12.2010.

Tore, B., Carlsson, Y. and Haaland, T. (2004), *Hate Crime or Gang Conflict? Violence between Youth Groups in a Norwegian City*. Online at: http://www. ncjrs.gov/pdffiles1/nij/mesko/208021.pdf (accessed 21.6.2011).

Touraine, A. (1997), *Pourrons-nous vivre ensemble? Égaux et différents*. Paris: Fayard Editions.

Turam, B. (2003), 'National loyalties and international undertakings: the case of the Gülen community in Kazakhstan' in H. Yavuz and J. Esposito (eds) *Turkish Islam and the Secular State: The Gülen Movement*. New York: Syracuse University Press, pp. 184–207.

—(2004), 'The politics of engagement between Islam and the secular state: ambivalences of civil society'. *British Journal of Sociology*, 55, 2, 59–81.

—(2011), 'Ordinary Muslims: power and space in everyday life'. *International Journal of Middle East Studies*, 43, 1, 144–6.

Ünal, A. and Williams, A. (eds) (2000), *Advocate of Dialogue: Fethullah Gülen*. Fairfax, Virginia: The Fountain.

Van Dijk, T. (1998), *Ideology. A Multidisciplinary Study*. London: Sage.

Voll, J. (1983), 'Renewal and reform in Islamic history: Tajdid and Islah' in J. Esposito ed. *Voices of Resurgent Islam*. New York: Oxford University Press.

—(2003), 'Fethullah Gülen: transcending modernity in the new Islamic discourse' in H. Yavuz and J. L. Esposito (eds) *Turkish Islam and Secular State: The Güden Movement*. Syracuse, New York: Syracuse University Press, pp. 238–50.

Walton, J. F. (2009), *Horizons and Histories of Liberal Piety: Civil Islam and Secularism in Contemporary Turkey*. A Dissertation Submitted to the Faculty of the Division of The Social Sciences in Candidacy for the Degree of Doctor of Philosophy, Illinois, Chicago: The University Of Chicago.

Walzer, M. (2002), 'Five questions about terrorism'. *Dissent*, 49, 1, 5–9.

Watt, M. (1971), *Muslim Intellectual: A Study of al-Ghazali*. Edinburgh: Edinburgh University Press. Online at: www.muslimphilosophy.com/gz/articles/ watt-p1.htm (electronic publication only at) (accessed 12.11.2008).

Weber, B. (1995), 'Immigration and politics in Germany'. *The Journal of the International Institute*, 2, 3. Online at: http://quod.lib.umich.edu/cgi/t/text/text-idx?c=jii;cc=jii;q1=weber;rgn=main;view=text;idno=4750978.0002.306 (accessed 10.6.2011).

Weller, P. (2002a), 'Insiders or outsiders?: religions, state(s) and societies: propositions for Europe. Part I'. *The Baptist Quarterly*, 39, 5, 211–22.

—(2002b), 'Insiders or outsiders?: religions, state(s) and societies: propositions for Europe. Part II'. *The Baptist Quarterly*, 39, 6, 276–86.

—(2002c), 'Insiders or outsiders?: religions, state(s) and societies' in A. Race and I. Shafer (eds) *Religions in Dialogue: From Theocracy to Democracy*. Aldershot: Ashgate, pp. 93–208.

—(2005a), *Time for a Change: Reconfiguring Religion, State and Society*. London: T & T Clark.

—(2005b), 'Religions and social capital: theses on religion, state(s) and society(ies): with particular reference to the United Kingdom and the European Union'. *The Journal of International Migration and Integration*, 9, 2, 271–89.

—(2006a), 'Addressing religious discrimination and Islamophobia: Muslims and liberal democracies. The case of the United Kingdom'. *The Journal of Islamic Studies*, 17, 3, 295–325.

—(2006b), '"Human rights", "religion" and the "secular": variant configurations of religions, state(s) and society(ies)'. *Religion and Human Rights: An International Journal*, 1, 1, 17–39.

—(2006c), 'Fethullah Gülen, religions, globalisation and dialogue' in R. Hunt and Y. Aslandoğan (eds) *Muslim Citizens of the Globalized World: Contributions of the Gülen Movement*. Somerset, NJ: The Light Inc. and IID Press, pp. 75–88.

Weller, P. ed. (2007a), *Religion in the UK: Directory, 2007–10*. Derby: University of Derby and Multi-Faith Centre at the University of Derby.

—(2007b), ' 'Human rights', 'religion' and the 'secular': variant configurations religion, state(s) and society(ies)', in N. Ghanea, A. Stephen and R. Walden (eds) *Does God Believe in Human Rights: Essays on Religion and Human Rights*. Leiden: Martinus Nijhoff Publishers, pp. 147–79.

—(2008), *Religious Diversity in the UK: Contours and Issues*. London and New York: Continuum.

—(2009), *A Mirror for our Times: 'The Rushdie Affair' and the Future of Multiculturalism*. London: Continuum.

—(2010), 'Fethullah Gülen: an Islamic sign of hope for an inclusive Europe'. Online at: http://www.fethullahgulen.org/press-room / columns/3676-paul-weller-todays-zaman-fethullah-gulen-an-islamic-sign-of-hope-for-an-inclusive-europe.html (accessed 10.6.2011).

Weller, P., Feldman, A. and Purdam, K. (2004), 'Muslims and religious discrimination in England and Wales' in J. Malik ed. *Muslim Minority Societies in Europe: From the Margin to the Centre*. Münster: LIT Verlag, pp. 115–44.

Wilkinson, P. (1974), *Political Terrorism*. London: Macmillan.

– (1977), *Terrorism and the Liberal State*. London: Macmillan.

Williams, B. (2004), 'What is terrorism? Problems of legal definition'. *University of NSW Law Journal*, 27, 2, 270–95.

Wilson, R. and Wilford, R. (2003), 'Northern Ireland: a route to stability?'. *The Devolution Papers*, Birmingham: ESRC.

Windsor, J. (2003), 'Promoting democratization can combat terrorism'. *The Washington Quarterly*, 26, 3, 43–58.

Word Reference Com (2006), *World Dictionary*. Online at: http://www. wordreference.com/definition/tolerance (accessed 5.5.2006).

Yavuz, M. H. (2000), 'Being modern in the Nurcu way'. *ISIM Newsletter*, 6, 7–14.

—(2003a), 'The Gülen movement: Turkey's puritans' in M. H. Yavuz and J. L. Esposito (eds) *Turkish Islam and the Secular State: The Gülen Movement*. Syracuse, New York: Syracuse University Press, pp. 19–47.

—(2003b), *Islamic Political Identity in Turkey*. New York: Oxford University Press.

Yavuz, M. H. and Esposito, J. L. (2003a), 'Islam in Turkey: retreat from the secular path?' in M. H. Yavuz and J. L. Esposito (eds) *Turkish Islam and the Secular State: The Gulen Movement*. Syracuse, New York: Syracuse University Press, pp. xiii–xxiii.

Yavuz, M. H. and Esposito, J. L. (eds) (2003b), *Turkish Islam and the Secular State: The Gülen Movement*. Syracuse: Syracuse University Press.

Yilmaz, I. (2002), 'The challenge of post-modern legality and Muslim legal pluralism in England'. *Journal of Ethnic and Migration Studies*, 28, 2, 343–54.

—(2003), '*Ijtihad* and *Tajdid* by conduct: the Gülen movement' in M. H. Yavuz and J. L. Esposito (eds) *Turkish Islam and the Secular State: The Gülen Movement*. Syracuse, New York: Syracuse University Press, pp. 208–37.

—(2004), 'Marriage solemnization among Turks in Britain: the emergence of a hybrid Anglo-Muslim Turkish law'. *Journal of Muslim Affairs*, 24, 1, 57–66.

—(2005a), *Muslim Law, Politics and Society in Modern Nation States: Dynamic Legal Pluralisms in England, Turkey and Pakistan*. Aldershot: Ashgate Press.

—(2005b), 'State, law, civil society and Islam in contemporary Turkey'. *The Muslim World*, 95, 3, 385–411.

—(2007), 'Social innovation for peaceful co-existence' in I. Yilmaz et al. (eds) *Peaceful Coexistence: Fethullah Gülen's Initiatives in the Contemporary World*. London: Leeds Metropolitan University Press, pp. 25–41.

—(2011), 'Beyond post-Islamism: transformation of Turkish Islamism toward "civil Islam" and its potential influence in the Muslim world'. *European Journal of Economic and Political Studies*, 4, 1, 245–80.

Yilmaz, I. et al. (eds) (2007a), *Muslim World in Transition: Contributions of the Gülen Movement*. London: Leeds Metropolitan University Press.

—(2007b), *Peaceful Coexistence: Fethullah Gülen's Initiatives in the Contemporary World*. London: Leeds Metropolitan University Press.

Yin, K.R. (2002), *Case Study Research. Design and Methods*. Third edition. Applied social research method series. Volume 5. Thousand Oaks CA: Sage.

Young, J. C. (1995), *Colonial Desire: Hybridity in Culture, Theory and Race*. London: Routledge.

Yucel, S. (2010), 'Fethullah Gülen: spiritual leader in a global Islamic context'. *Journal of Religion and Society*, 12, 1–19.

Yükleyen, A. (2009), 'Localizing Islam in Europe: religious activism among Turkish Islamic organizations in the Netherlands'. *Journal of Muslim Minority Affairs*, 29, 3, 291– 309.

Yükleyen, A. and Yurdakul, G. (2011), 'Islamic activism and immigrant integration: Turkish organizations in Germany'. *Immigrants and Minorities*, 29, 1, 64–85.

Zaman, M. (2002), *The Ulama in Contemporary Islam: Custodians of Change*. Princeton: Princeton University Press.

Zebiri, K. (1998), 'Review of Maududi and the making of Islamic
    fundamentalism'. *Bulletin of the School of Oriental and African Studies*, 61, 1,
    167–8.
Zeghal, M. (1996). *Gardiens de l'islam. Les oulémas d'Al Azhar dans l'Egypte
    contemporaine*. Paris: Presses.

INDEX

The index does not cover the preliminary pages of the book and the introduction that are both paginated in small Roman numerals

Topic Index

The following entries reflect key topics referred to in the text of the book

Authors and Editors Index

Where quoted from their work and/or referred to by others in the text of the book, and specifically in these capacities

Named Individuals Index

Where identified in the text of the book by name or title, other than when quoted or referred to as authors. This includes when quoted in newspaper articles or in other publications of which they are not the named author or editor.

Organization Index

As referred to by name in the text of the book

Place Index

Of places referred to within the text of the book.